ANTINOMIES OF SOCIETY

ANTINOMIES OF SOCIETY

Essays on Ideologies and Institutions

André Béteille

Oxford University Press is a department of the University of Oxford. It furthers the University's objective of excellence in research, scholarship, and education by publishing worldwide. Oxford is a registered trademark of Oxford University Press in the UK and in certain other countries

Published in India by
Oxford University Press
2/11 Ground Floor, Ansari Road, Daryaganj, New Delhi 110 002, India

First Edition published in 2000
Oxford India Paperbacks 2002

ISBN-13: 978-0-19-566318-1
ISBN-10: 0-19-566318-7

Printed in India by Repro Knowledgecast Limited, Thane

For

DHARMA KUMAR

Do not go gentle into that good night,
Old age should burn and rave at close of day;
Rage, rage against the dying of the light

Acknowledgements

Acknowledgement has been made at the bottom of the first page of each essay to the place of its original publication. Some of the essays have been recast in order to reduce repetition.

I have incurred debts to many individuals and institutions in the preparation of these essays. These are too numerous to be acknowledged or even listed in full. Apart from my own colleagues and students in the department of sociology, I have received help from many persons in the department of economics at the Delhi School of Economics, and I have gained much from my long association with the Institute of Economic Growth.

I owe a special debt of gratitude to Professor Vinay Kumar Srivastava of the department of anthropology for preparing the Index and to Dr Gopa Sabharwal of Lady Sri Ram College for helping with the proofs. I would also like to thank Anindita Chakrabarti, Nayanika Mathur and Sirisha Indukuri for their help in the final stages of the preparation of the book.

ANDRÉ BÉTEILLE

Contents

Introduction

This collection deals with certain aspects of contemporary life in a sociological perspective. Although contemporary Indian society figures prominently in most if not all of the essays, they also have a more general purpose in applying and developing the concepts, methods and theories of sociology. Whatever may be the judgement on the merits of the present collection, I am convinced that the work of sociology has advanced sufficiently in this country for it to be able to make some contribution to the discipline at large. It is with this conviction that I plan to put forward before long a second collection of papers devoted to approach and method in sociology.

While the individual essays deal with a range of substantive issues, the underlying concern of the collection as a whole is with antinomies, and it is that underlying concern that gives to the book such unity as it has. By 'antinomies' I mean the contradictions, oppositions and tensions inherent in the norms and values through which societies regulate or seek to regulate themselves and continue their existence. Anyone who is engaged in the study of a complex and changing society must turn his attention, sooner or later, to these antinomies. This should not be taken to mean that an account of the norms and values of a society, no matter how detailed or exhaustive, can lead to a complete understanding of its operation; for that we need to know a great many things in addition, including the demographic, economic and other features of its morphology. But the focus of this collection is on the former and not the latter.

The antinomies of which I speak are social facts in the sense that they have social causes and social consequences, taking a variety of forms in different societies in different phases of their development. Such antinomies take their most acute forms in large and complex societies undergoing major transformations, as in India, but they are present in one form or another in all human societies. In any event, no society in the contemporary world can be correctly described as simple or stable or unchanging. The idea that there are contradictions, oppositions and tensions among norms and values figures, sometimes prominently, throughout the book, irrespective of the substantive problem being addressed. Hence the choice of the title, although the phrase chosen is not widely employed in the sociological literature.

It is characteristic of societies marked by acute antinomies that the lines separating the normal and the pathological become blurred. What appears as normal to some appears pathological to others; or, a person might condemn as pathological a mode of conduct in some but excuse the same conduct in others by invoking the press of circumstance. This leads to endless moralizing, which I consider detrimental to objective and systematic analysis. These essays were written from the standpoint of the sociologist and not the moralist. The effort in each of them has been to examine a topic without bias and prejudice while keeping under restraint my own preferences to the maximum extent possible.

Several of the essays deal with ideologies such as Marxism, secularism and nationalism, whether directly or obliquely. Since I have tried to explain in the very first essay what I mean by ideology, I will not repeat that exercise here. At the same time, I do wish to stress that I do not regard sociology as an ideology, although it may be put to ideological uses. What is called the sociology of science misses its target when it seeks to represent science, including social science, as itself an ideology like any other. The historical evidence shows that ideologies such as Marxism and nationalism have been on the whole inimical to the development of sociology, at least as I understand the term.

The essays deal also with institutions, and sometimes in a very direct and central way. The study of institutions is of great importance to sociology, and may be said to give the discipline its distinctive orientation. It brings together the basic concerns of sociology: social morphology or the structure of roles and relationships on the one hand, and, on the other, the norms and values that give meaning and legitimacy to those roles and relationships. Emancipationist forms of Marxism and feminism have drawn attention to the constraints imposed by institutions on human action, and have paid little attention to the facilities they offer to their members. Defenders of institutions such as family, church and state have represented them as ends in themselves without which human action would be without object and without meaning.

The sociologist cannot neglect to study what an institution means to its own members even while analysing the uses to which it is put by themselves and by others.

Since the essays brought together in this volume look at society and its institutions from a particular point of view, it may be helpful to the reader if I recount very briefly the stages through which I arrived at that point of view. Nine of the twelve essays were published, fairly close to each other, in the decade of the nineties. The first three were published, also close to each other, a decade or more earlier. I have included them here because they foreshadow the themes of the later essays and also throw light on the connections among them.

My early interest as a sociologist was in the empirical study of social structure, with special emphasis on social stratification. The focus of attention was, firstly, on the enduring groups and the enduring relations among them, and, secondly, on the networks of interpersonal relations cutting across those groups and linking them together. In my first book, which was a monograph on a south Indian village, I described the caste structure, the class system and the distribution of power in the village, and the relations between the three (Béteille 1965). Each had for me a kind of objective existence, and I set out to examine the associations between the three dimensions of stratification, that is, caste, class and power, the changes in those associations, and the factors responsible for the changes. To employ a distinction we owe to Durkheim, my first work was a study in social morphology rather than in collective representations.

After publishing my monograph in 1965, I remained engaged for some time in the study of caste and class as aspects or dimensions of stratification or inequality. Each seemed to take a variety of forms in different places at different times. Like many other sociologists in the sixties and seventies, I set about recording and analysing the changing relations between caste and class in their different forms and at different levels of territorial organization (Béteille 1969, 1974). It may be said that I was much more concerned at that time with the existential structure than with the normative structure, or with what existed on the ground and could be observed from outside than with what the people themselves considered to be right, proper and desirable.

My interests began to expand gradually, partly as a result of my longstanding fascination for comparative studies. I became increasingly aware that societies differed not only in the nature and extent of inequalities and disparities as indicated by objective external criteria, but also in the significance they assigned to these inequalities and disparities. More and more of my attention began to be occupied by the normative structure of society, conceived broadly, and at first somewhat loosely, to include both norms and values. But I did not in any serious sense abandon my interest in social morphology, returning to it again and again in the course of my writing.

I was struck by the disharmony or discordance between the existential and the normative orders. It seemed that there was much greater concordance between the two in many past societies where inequalities and disparities not only existed in fact, but were also accepted by and large as right, proper and desirable. Law, morality and to some extent religion as well were changing in the direction of greater equality, but the social morphology continued to be marked by inequalities and disparities of many kinds. Jawaharlal Nehru (1961: 521) had written on the eve of independence, 'The spirit of the age is in favour of equality, though practice denies it almost everywhere'; but, being an optimist, had added, 'Yet, the spirit of the age will triumph.' My optimism has narrower limits, and I feel more at ease with the observation made by Raymond Aron more than two decades later. His view was that modern societies were both 'egalitarian in aspiration and hierarchical in organization' (Aron 1968: xv); that appealed to me because it pointed to a very deep-seated contradiction.

Although I was greatly impressed by the work of Louis Dumont, on which I have commented extensively, I was not wholly convinced by his stark opposition between hierarchical and egalitarian societies. For one thing, he had chosen the wrong time to represent the Indian social order as a consistent and complete hierarchy, for even as his work was taking shape, the hierarchy was being attacked from many sides, though by no means with complete success. I found his representation of modern western society as 'egalitarian' even more unsatisfactory, and his treatment of the stratification problem superficial. Dumont maintained that inequality or stratification in western societies was a matter merely of fact, unlike hierarchy in India which was at bottom a matter of value. I, on the other hand, had come to accept the view of Parsons that stratification in American society—or, for that matter, in any society—could not be meaningfully interpreted without taking into account the core values of that society.

From this it appeared that the contradiction existed not simply between the normative and the existential orders, but also within what I had at first taken to be a single and consistent normative order. I had started from the position that stratification or inequality had several dimensions that were mutually irreducible. I was resolutely opposed to the view that in the long run, class—or power, or status—determined the operation of all other forms of inequality. It took me a long time to recognize that the idea of equality, and not just the reality of inequality, was made up of more than one component, and that the idea itself was ambiguous because of the inescapable tensions among its various components. This accounts for some of the antinomies of society. In the days of the great Mandal agitation, the proponents and the opponents of reservation both appealed to the principle of equality, forcefully, passionately and often sincerely while putting forward their opposite demands.

There are tensions not only within equality, but also between equality and other cherished values, such as individual freedom. Nor is that all. There are new norms that are at odds with ancient and deep-seated values. Or again, there are disjunctions, and often serious ones, between law and custom. The laws have been changed very radically in India to establish both equality and individual freedom as fundamental rights; but the bias of custom tends to be in the opposite direction. These tensions, oppositions and contradictions become fully apparent only when we try to understand how a specific institution conducts its affairs.

The first three essays, written between 1978 and 1982, all engage with Marxism in one way or another. Marxism has had a creative influence on my work, I believe mainly because I never gave myself up wholly to its charms. Although I did not become a Marxist at any stage, in the sixties and seventies, I could hardly ignore the fact that Marxism had become the Latin of the times. It has now become a little difficult to appreciate the enormous appeal of Marxism for Indian intellectuals in the early decades of independence. It had a dominant influence in intellectual circles in Calcutta where I was a student in the fifties, and a considerable presence in the Delhi School of Economics in my early years as a teacher. I owe my own strong sense of the constraints imposed by social morphology on human action as much to Marx as to Durkheim. But I never shared the view of many of my younger colleagues and students that Marxism could be an alternative to sociology, and I have always been sceptical about the Marxist vision of the unity of theory and practice, or of the unity of science and politics. I was attracted by the way in which the Marxists I knew could point out the contradictions in American or British or even Indian society; but I was repelled by their refusal to see the contradictions in Soviet or Chinese society.

The essay on ideologies looks at what may be called the dialectics of power and values. It argues that the pursuit of power corrupts the very values in whose cause power is pursued. It examines the tensions between the two, but refuses to acknowledge that there is any final resolution of the tension. The essay on Marxism shows how difficult it is to combine a deep and unwavering commitment to a particular doctrine with equal respect for all doctrines, a theme that emerges again when we look at the predicament of secularism in a world of competing religious faiths. The essay on intellectuals was published originally as a companion to the one on ideologies. It questions, though obliquely, the idea of the organic intellectual. It also reviews the claims of different institutional settings for providing the best conditions for the pursuit of ideas.

The essay, 'Secularism and the Intellectuals' is written from the standpoint of a secular intellectual. It makes a distinction between secularization as a long-term social trend, and secularism as a conscious and consistent ideology. Some of the antinomies of contemporary India arise from the fact that it has a secular state with a secular constitutional and legal order in a society that is permeated by a multiplicity of religious beliefs and practices as well as deep social divisions based on religion. In these circumstances, the progress of secularization has been highly uneven, and secular institutions have had only a limited success in acquiring firm foundations.

The three essays that follow as chapters 5, 6 and 7 all deal with the modern university as a site for the creation and transmission of knowledge. Some of the issues discussed in them are foreshadowed in an earlier essay, published in *Minerva* in 1981, but not included in this collection (Béteille 1981; see also Béteille 1992). Chapter 5, also published earlier in *Minerva*, begins with the question of what it means to be a teacher in an Indian university today; it is based largely on my own experience, which I have also recounted elsewhere (Béteille 1993), as a university teacher in one of India's premier centres of learning. The account of an individual career is followed by an essay on universities as centres of learning which discusses the fluid and shifting expectations that people both within and outside the universities have of them.

The piece on universities as institutions was written as a companion to another piece, not published here, dealing with other institutions such as family and caste. It makes the point strongly that what sustains an institution is not simply its morphology or external characteristics but also the meaning and legitimacy it has for its own members. It tries to explain how the conflicting demands made on the university from both within and outside lead to a confusion of meaning and an erosion of legitimacy.

Chapter 8, 'Civil Society and Its Institutions', first published in 1996 and substantially revised for this collection, presents a specific view of civil society. That view centres around the three interrelated concepts of state, citizenship and mediating institutions. The institutions considered decisive for the health and well-being of civil society are what I call open and secular institutions of the kind described in the preceding chapter. But open and secular institutions do not constitute the whole of any society, least of all of Indian society. Their significance has to be understood in relation to religious institutions and to communities of birth with which they are sometimes, though by no means always, in opposition.

A brief piece on 'India's Heritage of Diversity' is followed by a longer and more detailed analysis, in chapter 10, of the conflict of norms and values in Indian society. The shorter piece explains that while a great deal of diversity was not only accommodated but also encouraged by law, morality and religion in the past, diversity was in that age organized hierarchically and in a manner that left very little room for the freedom of individual choice. The problem today is to retain the respect for diversity while ensuring greater equality and greater individual freedom. The longer essay analyses the conflict of norms and values with special reference to the problems of the backward classes and of religious minorities. It also reflects on the extent to which the conflict of norms and values might be resolved by a more effective legal system and a more meaningful educational system.

The last two essays, on 'Governance' and on 'Empowerment', are to some extent complementary to each other. The former focuses on authority, or what may more aptly be called the frailty in authority, with special reference to the administrative executive. It was written to provide a sociological overview for a symposium in which a group of mature civil servants reflected on their experiences of governance as members of the Indian Administrative Service. It discusses, among other things, the contrasting sources of legitimacy of the administrative and the political executives under a democratic system of governance. The essay on empowerment examines the limits to the redistribution of power, and the implications of that redistribution for the institutions of civil society and their structures of authority.

These essays represent a small part of the work, both published and unpublished, being done by a large number of sociologists in India. Indian sociologists like other Indians are much better with the spoken than with the written word, and that is certainly a handicap for the cumulative growth of a discipline. It is true that they work under adverse conditions but it cannot be denied that they are often self-indulgent in their adversity. Indian sociologists would contribute more to their discipline if they took a more responsible attitude towards what they have as well as what they lack. They lack many things, but what they have as a profession is not insubstantial.

While, as I have said, the focus of attention in this work is mainly on contemporary Indian society, I have sought to deepen the understanding of institutions and ideologies in it by drawing upon the experiences of other societies that I consider relevant to the discussion. There is little case-by-case comparison of one society with another, but comparison and contrast have been used throughout to draw attention to both common and distinctive features.

I have drawn freely on the general body of sociological arguments, concepts and methods, and adapted them to my use wherever it appeared appropriate. I believe that there is and ought to be only one general sociology, and that the idea of alternative sociologies is misconceived. It is true that what I regard as general sociology is a very loosely integrated body of concepts, methods and theories, biased strongly by the experiences of western societies. But its present biases need not be considered eternal and everlasting. Moreover, the very looseness of the discipline allows it to accommodate new elements without requiring those elements to begin on an independent career of their own. Sociology began with the study of western society by western sociologists; as other societies come to be studied with greater insight and imagination by sociologists from all parts of the world, their studies are bound to alter the present shape of general sociology.

The urge to develop an alternative sociology for India arises partly from resentment among Indian sociologists that their own work is neglected not only outside India but also by their fellow sociologists in

India. It is true that the work of Indian sociologists is neglected, sometimes unjustly, both within and outside India, but in matters of the mind, resentment leads only to obscurity and not clarity.

I believe that the antinomies of society which I have tried to explore provisionally and tentatively in the present collection of essays provide a large and challenging field for sociological enquiry and investigation. These antinomies are present not only in India, but in every large, complex and changing society in the contemporary world. They have not received from sociologists, whether in India or outside India, the serious scholarly attention they deserve. The study of Indian society offers many possibilities for the enrichment of general sociology as it exists today. But those possibilities will not be realized in a short time or by a single generation; and they will not be realized if Indian sociologists lose heart because their work is neglected by others.

The conflict of norms and values, which provides the focus for this collection of essays, is an important feature of all contemporary societies, but American sociologists studying their own society tend to pass lightly over it. In particular, the contrast, on the plane of norms and values, between western societies as egalitarian and other societies as hierarchical is shallow and misleading. The argument of Gunnar Myrdal (1944) that the American Creed affirming the equality of all human beings was contradicted by the conduct of Americans in matters relating to race, is true but it does not go far enough. For the contradiction is not simply between norm and conduct; it is lodged inside the very system of norms and values of American society.

The functional approach of Talcott Parsons, which has left a lasting impression on contemporary sociology, did well by focusing attention on norms and values, but it did not dwell sufficiently on the contradictions, oppositions and tensions among them. Marxism, which offered the strongest challenge to functional analysis in the sixties, seventies and eighties, dealt effectively with contradictions, but did not give to norms and values the attention they deserve as basic and irreducible components of the social order. Describing, interpreting and analysing the antinomies of society seems to me to offer fruitful possibilities for adding to our understanding not only of Indian society but also of human societies in general.

References

Aron, Raymond. 1968. *Progress and Disillusion*. London: Pall Mall.

Béteille, André. 1965. *Caste, Class and Power*. Berkeley: University of California Press.

—— 1969. *Castes: Old and New*. Bombay: Asia Publishing House.

—— 1974. *Studies in Agrarian Social Structure*. Delhi: Oxford University Press.

—— 1981. 'The Indian University', *Minerva*, vol. XIX, no. 2, pp. 282–310.

—— 1992. 'Comments', *Minerva*, vol. XXX, no. 2, pp. 206–10.

—— 1993. 'My Formative Years in the Delhi School of Economics' in Dharma Kumar and Dilip Mookherjee (eds), *D. School: Reflections on the Delhi School of Economics*. Delhi: Oxford University Press, pp. 53–67.

Myrdal, Gunnar. 1944. *An American Dilemma*. New York: Harper.

Nehru, Jawaharlal. 1961. *The Discovery of India*. Bombay: Asia Publishing House.

1

Ideologies*

The fundamental problem of sociology, as I see it, is the dialectic between systems of value and structures of power. I use the word dialectic hesitantly because it has been so overworked in recent years as to have become virtually a cliché. I also use it broadly without the presupposition that the system is carried through by it necessarily from lower to higher levels. What the sociologist sets out to understand is how in every society people single out certain things in life for special attention, things which they hold dear, which they cherish or value; how they try to protect these from distortion and corruption by the existing powers; how they strive for power themselves so as to achieve a fuller realization of their cherished values; and how, having attained power, they distort and corrupt these very values or seek to suppress the cherished values of others.

Thus, no matter what specific meaning we may decide in the end to give to it, the context for the discussion of ideology must be a broad one. An ideology cannot be understood simply on its own terms, in terms of either its argument or its vision, howsoever important these might be. Ideologies seek to connect the universe of values with the realm of power, and it is essential to see what is involved in this. Before doing so, it may be useful to try to place this problem of connecting the one with the other in its modern setting.

A characteristic feature of the modern world is the preoccupation with ideologies, one's own as well as those of others. This remained true even while pronouncements were being made in the fifties and

* Originally published as 'Ideologies: Commitment and Partisanship' in *L'Homme: revue française d'anthropologie* XVIII (3–4) 47–67, 1978. Subsequently republished in *Ideologies and Intellectuals*, Delhi: Oxford University Press, 1980.

sixties in influential academic circles in America about the 'end of ideology'. As events soon afterwards were to show, ideology had by no means been banished from America, not to speak of Europe. As for the countries of Africa, Asia and Latin America—the so-called Third World—ideology, far from being dead, was gaining a new lease of life from the challenges of a post-colonial era. The argument about the end of ideology only confirmed the opinion of intellectuals from these countries about the pervasiveness of the ethnocentric bias in so much of what passes for sociology in the western world.

In saying that the preoccupation with ideologies is a characteristic feature of modern times, one must emphasize the extent to which this preoccupation is conscious and articulate. Every age and every society has had its own particular dialectic of ideas and interests, but in our age it has become part of a much larger consciousness than in the past. Even while saying this one must proceed with caution, for nothing is more easy—or more tempting—than to exaggerate the uniqueness of one's own age, particularly in the matter of consciousness.

Much has been said about the moral certitude that is believed to have prevailed in past societies, in contrast to the moral incertitude characteristic of present ones. Perhaps there was a measure of moral certitude in Christian and Islamic societies, at least so long as they were not seriously disturbed by sects and heresies that challenged or threatened the established order. It is difficult to say as much of traditional Indian society, where Hinduism tolerated—some would say encouraged—the co-existence of a diversity of sects and philosophical systems. Certainly, the degree of heterodoxy permitted in Hindu India was on the whole far larger than in Stalin's Russia or in Hitler's Germany, although nothing definite can be said about the political implications of this permissiveness.

The practical activity of the contemporary intellectual is directed in a large measure to the political order and in only a small measure to the religious order, using these two terms in their conventional sense. This is no less true today of intellectuals in so-called traditional societies than of their counterparts in so-called modern societies. The Indian example illustrates the point very well; professional intellectuals—academics, journalists and, to a lesser extent, creative writers—feel perfectly at ease in discussing politics, but almost embarrassed to speak or write about religion in a serious way.

The withdrawal of active intellectual interest from established religion does not necessarily imply the disappearance or even the decline of what may in a broad sense be described as the sacred. Indeed, a concern for the sacred is precisely what modern ideologies have in common with traditional religions, even though the manner in which this concern is articulated may be different in the two cases. A major area of concern for intellectuals in all societies of the past has been with problems of immortality and of life after death.[1] This is now barely an area of practical concern for the contemporary intellectual, whose attention is focused to a far greater extent on the political order here and now. The distinctively modern attitude towards the sacred seems to be that what is sacred has to be realized in this world, for there is no other world in which to realize it.

The concern with the political order here and now is accompanied by what Mannheim described as the 'intellectual restiveness' characteristic of our times (Mannheim 1960). First of all, there has been a phenomenal increase in the number of intellectuals, and a corresponding diversification in their roles. Secondly, there have been massive movements of intellectuals across classes, across regions and across the countries of the world. All this has created unprecedented possibilities for direct communication between intellectuals and the people for and about whom they write.

Students of western society and culture have commented widely on the increasing diversity of class backgrounds from which intellectuals are recruited, and on the implications of this for the development of a reciprocity of perspectives. Again, in the Soviet Union and other socialist countries, the 'intelligentsia' are described as a stratum and not a class, for the very reason that they come from various sections of society and presumably do not represent the interests of any one particular section. There can be no denying the extent to which intellectuals have become mobile in the modern world, but whether this has led to a true reciprocity of perspectives or merely to 'intellectual restiveness' is not an easy question to answer.

Even more than in the case of persons who move from one class to another, the exposure to a variety of intellectual perspectives has a marked effect on those who move from one civilizational context to a different one. This can be seen quite clearly in the situation of western educated intellectuals in the countries of Asia, Africa, and also Latin America. This situation itself differs from one country to another, depending, firstly, on the scale of the exposure to the intellectual culture of the west, and, secondly, on the richness and vigour of the indigenous intellectual tradition in the country concerned.

The ambiguities in the situation of the western-educated intellectual in the Third World are seen very well in the case of India which has, on the one hand, the largest number of such intellectuals outside the west, and on the other, one of the oldest and most elaborate intellectual traditions of the world. From the end of the nineteenth century onwards Indians began to travel to England and later America in order to study in the centres of higher learning, and some of them stayed there long enough to become closely involved in western society and culture. The volume of this traffic has, if anything, increased since Independence, and there must now be many thousand Indian intellectuals—scientists, scholars and writers—who have had professional employment in both India and the west.

What are the ideals of a universal intellectual community? Whatever they may be, the faith of Third World intellectuals in these ideals grows increasingly thin as they confront the realities of the distribution of power among nations and reflect on the implications of academic colonialism. Nor can they easily turn back and create a new and satisfying set of ideals out of the tribal or hierarchical worlds that they have inherited from the past. And so, the restiveness grows.

It would be a mistake to regard this restiveness as being simply a problem of the distribution of power. It is above all a reflection of the failure to find any satisfying intellectual solution to this problem. No intellectual solution can be found satisfying today if it addresses itself, as it often did in the past, to a world beyond the earthly one or even to a remote future. It has to relate itself to the present world of day-to-day realities, to this generation or at most the next. Hence the immediacy of the link between ideas and the realm of power.

The intellectual has thus come to define his responsibilities in a new way. There is today, particularly in the Third World but also elsewhere, a kind of phrenetic urgency to make intellectual activity 'socially relevant'. Again, it is not as if intellectual activity anywhere at any time could remain wholly detached from its social context. But either the 'ivory-tower intellectual' actually existed in the past, or else he is a figure of fiction created by the present-day intellectual to offset the new role that he would like to assign to himself.

No matter what might have been the case in other times, a considerable amount of intellectual activity is today directed explicitly, openly and self-consciously towards the existing order of society and in particular the existing distribution of power. Intellectuals have been seized with the idea that the world can and must be changed, and that they must create the climate for this change despite the resistance of those in power. This is the broad context in which the problem of ideology has to be considered.

In working towards a reasonable discussion of ideology I find it essential to start from the position that an ideology, like a religion, is not necessarily bad even when one does not have an ideology (or a religion) of one's own. Clifford Geertz was right in pointing out that to describe ideology as distortion is like describing religion as superstition (Geertz 1964), and in both cases the description obstructs discussion instead of facilitating it. But that perhaps is not the point: the point is whether those who would object, with good reason, to ideology being described as distortion might not also object to its being compared with religion.

However, it is not true that people have in general a negative view of ideology. This might have been so in the United States at the time when the collection of essays entitled *Ideology and Discontent* was being put together; it certainly is not so today in the countries of the Third World, in west Europe and perhaps even in the United States. Indeed, the pendulum seems to have swung to the opposite extreme; in India at least it is the intellectual who disclaims any ideological attachment who may be required to account for his peculiar insufficiency.

A newspaper headline on 8 June 1977 in *The Statesman*, one of India's leading dailies, read: 'Janata Has No Ideology, Says Chavan'. Mr Y.B. Chavan, leader of the Congress party, then in opposition in the Indian parliament, was attacking the ruling Janata party in an idiom whose meaning would be at once understood by any Indian intellectual and indeed by any intelligent reader of *The Statesman*. For a government or a party or a leader to have no ideology is to betray the lack of a coherent vision of the future and an articulated plan of action—in short, a lack of principle. For the intellectual no less than for the politician, to admit to a lack of ideology is to come dangerously close to drawing on oneself the charge of opportunism.

In India and perhaps also elsewhere, whether one has a positive or a negative attitude to ideology depends in some measure on the role one sees it playing in the process of change. To criticize a person or a party for having no ideology is also to say that the party or the person has no clear vision of a better future, and hence neither the will nor the ability to construct a better society. In this kind of usage ideology is seen as a pledge, as it were, of this will and this ability. Without an ideology, change will lack direction, and, lacking direction, it will quickly run its course.

But this is not the only usage of ideology. For if it is seen as an engine of change, it is seen also as an instrument of the status quo. The resistance to change comes not only from established political authority and entrenched economic interests, but also from habits of mind that are set in the mould of particular ideas and beliefs. These ideas and beliefs, which support the existing order of society, have also their systematizers, but their role is seen as being somehow covert and subtle in contrast to the open and forthright positions adopted by those who propound ideologies of change.

Of all the distinctions that may be made among ideologies today, it would appear that the most important is the one between ideologies of change and of the status quo. The contrast is sharpest in the countries of Asia, Africa and Latin America, where the former are aggressive and the latter, at best, apologetic. When Mr Chavan says that the Janata Party has no ideology, what he means is that they are not 'progressive', that they are unable and unwilling to disturb the status quo; no doubt they also harness beliefs and ideas to achieve their purpose, but such an assortment of beliefs and ideas can hardly be dignified with the name of ideology.

The aggressive postures of the ideologies of change and the defensive ones of the ideologies of status quo make it extraordinarily difficult to bring them on to the same plane of analysis. Few would admit today, perhaps even to themselves, to being ideologists of the status quo, while on the other hand, it is difficult to restrain the enthusiasm of those who believe themselves to be ideologists of revolutionary change. All of this involves some evasiveness and much self-congratulation and it is thus that, despite Geertz's eminently reasonable admonitions, it is not always easy to resist the temptation to dismiss all ideology as mystification.

The meaning of the word 'ideology' has undergone strange transformations in its passage over the centuries and across the continents. Much has been said about Napoleon's dismissive attitude to ideologies and ideologists as being concerned with unreal, impractical and trivial matters. Today ideologies are not necessarily or even generally considered impractical: political leaders defer to the need for them, and some intellectuals at least are inclined to regard everything else as trivial, if not impractical. In the twentieth century both Lenin and Mao not only made their own revolutions but also wrote their own books.

(Gandhi was not a revolutionary in the same sense, but he wrote profusely as also did Nehru who was more self-consciously an intellectual.)

Today in the ex-colonial countries ideology is thought of—by both politicians and intellectuals—as an indispensable instrument of change, whereas a hundred years ago in Europe it was more typically considered to be an obstacle to change. For Marx ideology was above all 'bourgeois ideology', i.e. a form of false consciousness which obstructed the development of true or proletarian consciousness. The contrast was typically between bourgeois *ideology* and proletarian *consciousness*.

It was no doubt in deference to this usage that Mannheim, who was otherwise a critic of Marx, sought to introduce the distinction between ideologies and utopias, the former oriented to the status quo and the latter to change (Mannheim 1960). But history has overtaken the usage, and it would be specious to insist that there is no communist ideology but only a communist utopia, or that there is no capitalist utopia but only a capitalist ideology. When Mr Chavan says that the Janata party has no ideology, people understand at once what he means; they would be puzzled were he to say that the Janata party has no utopia.

Even fifty years ago Mannheim was able to note no more than a 'pseudo-unity' among the various meanings given to the word 'ideology' (Mannheim 1960). From what I have already said it should be evident that since Mannheim wrote, the range of meanings has expanded rather than contracted; new meanings have come into play without the old ones becoming wholly obsolete. It will serve little purpose to try to fix a single, unvarying meaning to the term and to hope thereby to banish other meanings out of court. A term such as ideology—like terms signifying other key concepts such as class, race or nation—must take into account a series of changing referents if it is to serve as a useful basis for discussion. When the reality itself is ambiguous, there is the risk of leaving out some important dimension of it in the zeal for giving it a tight and rigorous definition.

But, granted that there is no real unity among the various meanings attached to the term ideology, it is not necessary to take into account all its available meanings in discussing the subject here. To attempt to give a summary of these various meanings or even to make an inventory of them would be an enterprise in itself which I shall avoid. Instead, I shall try to elaborate one possible meaning of the term which seems to me to correspond fairly well with the concerns of at least a large number of those who speak or write about ideologies.

An ideology is that set of ideas and beliefs which seeks to articulate the basic values of a group of people—what they cherish for themselves and for others—to the distribution of power in society. An ideology is not a systematic theory, although it has systematic properties and it often strives to be a theory. An ideology may or may not succeed in articulating basic values to the distribution of power, but such articulation is part of its purpose and design. Also—*pace* Mannheim—an ideology may seek to strengthen the existing distribution of power (the status quo) in order to achieve a better and fuller realization of the values it espouses, or it may seek to subvert it with a similar end in view.

Ideologies have a range of concerns from the abstract to the concrete. In concrete terms their most important concerns are with the institutions of society. For it is these institutions that embody the values cherished by people and are at the same time objects of contention among them in their struggle for power. It is thus that the institutions of work and leisure, of family, caste and community come to occupy a central place in ideological debate and discourse.

An ideology, as I understand it, looks both ways: it looks to values on the one side and to power on the other. A scheme or plan, no matter how ingenious or coherent, which seeks merely to acquire or retain the instruments of power, can hardly be called an ideology if it has little or no concern for the values cherished by people. On the other hand, a set of ideas which seeks merely to give expression to the basic values of people with complete unconcern for power and politics can hardly be called an ideology in the proper sense of the term.

I believe that it is essential to distinguish ideology from what may be called Realpolitik. It is also important to distinguish it from religion in the specific sense. It is not easy to do this consistently in either case. And because ideology tries to be a bridge between two aspects of reality that are themselves disparate and heterogeneous, it does not lend itself to a neat and elegant definition.

In the modern world politics has greatly extended its scope: the struggle for power among princes can no longer be confined to the court, insulated from the day-to-day concerns and demands of ordinary people. In other words, politics has to strive continuously to relate itself to the fluid and amorphous values of a changing society; it is, as it were, constantly on trial in the arena of public life. The sheer struggle for power cannot be its own justification today; at the very least it has to be camouflaged by the promise of a better social order for the people. Nor is this promise merely a camouflage, for in the age of democracy politics can hardly hope to succeed unless it takes the concerns and the demands of the people seriously.

This is not to say that the sheer struggle for power could be its own justification in any age or any society. But 'participation' in politics has acquired a new significance today, if not in practice at least in principle. This gives a special urgency to the task of linking the political process to the values of the people, especially in the countries of the Third World where these values are often out of step with those of the leaders of opinion as well as political leaders. If democracy means bringing politics to the doorstep of the people, then democratic politics can hardly work except through conscious and continuous interaction with their values.

There was an undeniable link between religion and the struggle for power in earlier ages, but this link was in general more subtle, less direct, less evident, less conscious and certainly less explicit than is the link between modern ideologies and modern political systems. Sometimes the link between religion and the struggle for power is thrown into sharp relief as, for instance, in various phases of the development of Islam, or more generally, during the rise and fall of sectarian movements. Nevertheless, the proposition holds that religion in the ordinary sense has many concerns—major ones at that—which have little to do with the struggle for power although, of course, no religion can be wholly indifferent to this struggle.

Religions as generally understood have mystical and contemplative elements, and in some religions these elements are very strong. All are in one way or another concerned with the problems of personal salvation, and some explicitly recommend the renunciation of this world as an aid to salvation. Renunciation of the world is antithetical to the spirit of ideology, which is concerned with either a defence of the world here and now or its transformation through the struggle for power.

Thus it is important to keep in mind the overlap as well as the differences between religions as conventionally understood and ideologies as conceived here. Because of the differences, the analogy between religion and ideology, often made with the object of debunking the latter, is misleading; the analogy is misleading whether or not it is made with the object of debunking a particular ideology. At the same time, had there been no real or substantial overlap, the analogy could hardly be so effective in debunking. It is interesting that the proponents of some ideologies, such as nationalism, find the analogy far less offensive (or embarrassing) than do the proponents of other ideologies, such as communism.

An ideology as a set of connected beliefs and ideas has to be distinguished from the basic values it seeks to articulate. There is no reason to assume that the former accurately mirrors the latter. To do so might indeed be contrary to the design of some ideologies, if not of ideologies as such. This is obviously true of what may be called radical ideologies, particularly in the countries of Asia, Africa and Latin America (the so-called traditional societies), but it is also true, though less obviously, of liberal ideologies and perhaps of conservative ideologies as well.

In describing an ideology as a set of ideas and beliefs I have so far used the phrase 'ideas and beliefs' in a loose way, without trying to be very specific as to what ideas are and what beliefs are. While it may be necessary to distinguish between an ideology on the one hand and an outlook or a creed on the other (Shils 1972, see particularly the essay entitled 'Ideology'), one must recognize that ideologies differ a great deal among themselves, both in their mode of conceptualization and in their form of expression.

Without attempting to resolve them, Plamenatz has pointed to the ambiguities commonly encountered in the use of words such as 'ideas' and 'beliefs.' 'Sometimes we say "idea" when we might just as well say "belief" .... But by "idea" we sometimes mean "concept"; we mean not a belief but something used to express beliefs' (Plamenatz 1971: 16). Now, in the study of ideologies it is important to recognize that beliefs may be expressed not only by means of concepts but also through the use of symbols: one important way in which ideologies differ from theories is in the use they make of symbols.

In modern times Georges Sorel was among the first to clearly grasp the significance of symbols, as opposed to concepts, in the struggle for power. He sought to present his own ideology, that of syndicalism, not as a theory but as a myth. But there was something paradoxical about the very nature of Sorel's enterprise. He was a theoretician despite his profound lack of faith in theories; he analysed the nature and significance of symbols despite his plea for the subordination of analysis to intuition; and in the end his 'myth' was put to uses that were very different from the ones for which he had tried to create them. The real importance of Sorel's work would seem to lie in the way in which it reveals the tension between symbols and concepts, between a vision and a theory.[2]

Sorel saw very well that the world could be changed through a struggle for power only if this struggle engaged men's emotions and not just their reason. Men are not always easily moved by an appeal to their reason and large ideas are often but weakly expressed by concepts. Hence Sorel's attempt to construct a myth which would be charged with images, metaphors and symbols. Obviously, there can be an articulation of the basic values of people to the distribution of power in society through a system of symbols and not merely through a system of concepts. And, as Sorel's work shows, one might attempt to bring about this articulation in a conscious, open and systematic way.

Among contemporary social scientists, Clifford Geertz has argued forcefully for the due recognition of the symbolic elements contained in each and every ideology (Geertz 1964). Ideologies use symbols to express themselves and in the absence of an established science of 'symbolic action' one may easily misconstrue their significance. A symbolic statement has to be understood in the context of a particular idiom, and to translate it literally into a different idiom is to reduce it to absurdity. Those who dismiss ideological statements as distortions are themselves often guilty of distorting the true significance of such statements by a failure to relate them to their proper symbolic context.

The study of symbolism has now emerged as an important branch of anthropology. It has contributed richly to the understanding of religious beliefs and ideas, particularly in primitive societies. What was earlier considered to be either irrational or incoherent is now illuminated by being related to its particular context of symbols. So great has been the success of this kind of enterprise that some anthropologists, including perhaps Geertz himself, tend to view the whole of cultural anthropology as being essentially a study of symbols and their meanings.

Though fruitful and rewarding up to a point, the study of symbolism, at least in its present anthropological incarnation, is riddled with ambiguities. Obviously, if we are to understand statements made in a cultural idiom other than our own, we must have some grasp of the system of symbols and their meanings which together constitute that cultural idiom. The word 'yellow' or 'brother-in-law' might signify various things in various contexts, so that a literal, single-phrase translation is not only inadequate but often misleading. If we are to understand the significance of a particular political statement made by an

Indonesian nationalist, we must have some familiarity with the images, metaphors and symbols commonly in use among Indonesian nationalists.

While all of this is true and very illuminating in the study of, say, religion among the Nuer, it begins to appear a little trite when applied to the analysis of political debate in one's own society. This is not to say that we know everything that needs to be known in our own society of symbolism in general, or even political symbolism in particular. Rather, the method of apt illustration, which appears so convincing when applied to the study of symbolism in cultures other than our own, tends to be less than satisfying when applied to the study of it in our own. Also, the method of structuralism, which has cracked the code of primitive cosmologies with such apparent success, has not really told us very much that was not already known about symbolism in modern political ideologies.

It would appear that we lose as much by treating every political statement as a symbolic statement as we do by treating every such statement as a statement of scientific theory. Every modern ideology makes use of both concepts and symbols, and very little is gained by obscuring the distinction between the two. We have to recognize this even while admitting that it is difficult to keep the distinction between them clear and that the western ethnocentric bias has worked havoc with our understanding of non-western cultures by a literal and simple-minded translation of symbols in one system into concepts in another.

How do we distinguish between a symbol and a concept? The fact is that we recognize the distinction well enough even though we are not always able to formulate it in a precise or systematic way. We recognize that the same phrase or term such as 'class' or 'nation' or 'race' may be used as either a symbol or a concept and that their signification is not the same in the two cases. We say, for instance, that the phrase 'proletariat' has become a symbol; but is that to say that there cannot be a concept of the proletariat? Indeed, the same author might in the same text use the same phrase, for instance 'proletariat' or 'bourgeoisie', employing it now as a symbol for its dramatic force and again as a concept for its analytical edge.

A concept seeks to disclose its meaning whereas the full meaning of a symbol remains hidden; or to put it differently, the meaning of a concept is stated, i.e. made explicit, whereas the meaning of a symbol is unstated, i.e. left implicit. The conceptual elements in thought seek to control, to define and to limit the meanings of words; whereas, in

Whitehead's expressive language, 'the symbolic elements in life have a tendency to run wild, like the vegetation in a tropical forest' (Whitehead 1959: 61).

Ideologies deal in large ideas such as equality, liberty, humanity, solidarity and progress, and, in any case, it is not easy to tie such ideas down within the defined limits of a concept. It is doubtful whether we will ever be able to define terms such as these with the same precision with which we define terms such as household, stratum or population. We do no doubt have concepts of equality, liberty and progress; but these concepts need to be supplemented by symbols to express the full range of their meanings.

The inadequacy of concepts in expressing deep and powerful feelings has been particularly well appreciated by those concerned with the religious view of life. This is clearly seen in the exposition of the idea of the holy by the great Protestant theologian, Rudolf Otto. He drew attention to the peculiar nature of the numinous, and the difficulty of containing it within the bounds of a concept, but pressed all the same for a rigorous approach to its understanding and exposition. He called for 'a serious attempt to analyse all the more exactly the *feeling* which remains where the *concept* fails, and to introduce a terminology which is not any the more loose or indeterminate for having necessarily to make use of *symbols*' (Otto 1958: xxi, emphases in original).

Nor is this dependence on symbols confined to religion. Political leaders too freely make use of symbols when they feel the need to express the ineffable, as Sorel recognized very well. The very ambiguity of their meaning enables the ideologue to deploy symbols with skill and effect, and so to move people in a way in which perhaps no concept can move them. A symbol conveys not only an immediate meaning but also the promise of a richer meaning than that seen on the surface. To turn a symbol into a concept is to rob it of its magic; to turn a concept into a symbol is to open the mind to unlimited possibilities. Those who engage in ideological debate have sometimes a deeper and finer awareness of this than do cultural anthropologists trained in the methods of structural analysis.

If we are to understand what ideologies are and what they do, we must recognize not only the distinction between concepts and symbols but also the difference between being swayed by symbols and using them to sway others. Those who seek to articulate the basic values of people to the distribution of power in society harness both concepts and symbols to their task, and do so with varying degrees of self-awareness. This is far from saying that ideologues are people who manipulate symbols to achieve power for themselves. Rather, the true ideologue is swayed by his own symbols as much as he sways others by them; he is convinced by his own concepts as much as he convinces others by them.

Ideologies differ greatly not only in what they say but also in the ways in which they are presented. At one end there are statements which present themselves in the form of scientific theories; at the other, literary works such as novels, plays or poems which convey messages in a very different form. The same ideology is, characteristically, stated in all these various ways and, not infrequently, the same statement contains various and heterogeneous elements. Its tone of acrimony apart, Engels's description of the writings of earlier socialists as a 'mishmash of less strikingly critical statements, economic theories, pictures of future society' (Engels 1954: 32) makes a point that holds for many ideologies and not just the 'pre-scientific' ones of the early nineteenth century.

Engels's own pamphlet, *Socialism: Utopian and Scientific*, is, to my mind, one of the best examples of an ideological statement presented in the form of a scientific theory. It enjoyed enormous success on publication and, as the author pointed out in his Introduction to the English edition of 1892, it was more widely translated, if not more widely read, in its time than even *The Communist Manifesto* (Engels 1970). The two pamphlets are separated by about thirty years in time, and, although they discuss the realization of the same kind of values and of the same struggle for power, there are notable differences of expression. The *Manifesto* is heavy with imagery, metaphor and symbolism; *Socialism*, by contrast, relies much on concepts elaborated and refined by Marx during the years that stand between the two publications.

Socialism presents itself as a reasoned argument, showing that the realization of equality and justice through the conflict of classes will follow from the nature of the historical process. Both the values to be realized and the struggle for their realization are shown to be dependent on laws which can be discovered by the methods of science. The appeal is to the reader's reason, not to his passion or faith, and facts and arguments are presented in an ordered and systematic way. Engels writes in the belief that he is presenting his case in the manner of a scientist—hence the title of the pamphlet—although he does refer, perhaps inadvertently, to 'the revelation of the secret of capitalist production' by Marx (ibid.: 133).

The case for socialism is sought to be established through a more or less systematic use of concepts. Terms such as 'commodity', 'exchange', 'mode of production', 'productive forces', 'surplus value' and 'wage labour' are clearly used in the way in which one might use concepts for the purpose of scientific analysis. Moreover, for a fuller understanding of their meanings these concepts are referred back to Marx's *Capital*, one of the most important scientific treatises of the time.

Even the symbolism of the *Manifesto* is embedded in a conceptual scheme whose basic contours are made clear and explicit. It is not merely a call for action, but also an appeal to reason. That this appeal has successfully cut across the barriers of many cultures is evident from the popularity of translations of the *Manifesto* in a variety of languages.

As indicated earlier, ideological statements are presented in 'literary' as well as 'scientific' works, and the former of course make use of imagery, metaphor and symbolism in a much more obvious manner. A literary work may not be intended by its author to serve as an ideological statement, or mainly as one, but may in effect come to play that part. Much depends on the success with which it is able to relate the underlying values of a people to the existing structure of power, and the conviction with which it is able to show that these values can be more fully realized only with the replacement of the existing structure of power by a new one. In doing this it presents not so much a new theory as a new vision: new concepts perhaps, but, even more than these, new symbols.

Literary writers—novelists, playwrights and poets—have played a prominent part in giving shape to nationalist ideologies in the countries of Asia, Africa and Latin America. This is easy to understand. Nationalism, no matter what its economic and political doctrines, must after all be anchored in a specific culture. Even when it claims to articulate universal values, it has to invoke a particular historical tradition and a particular historical destiny. It cannot rely merely on general concepts but has to create or rejuvenate specific symbols. It is perhaps no accident that Mao Tse-tung, unlike Karl Marx, was also a poet.

Among those who have contributed to the development of nationalist ideologies in this way, many have been ambidextrous as writers. They have produced creative literature—novels, plays and poems—as well as essays, pamphlets and tracts. When similar concerns are expressed in different forms by the same writer, one can gain a better understanding of the interplay between concepts and symbols within a given framework of ideas and beliefs. A novelist or a playwright or a poet does not give up the use of symbols when he composes a tract; only, he has then to state his argument and make his reasoning explicit.

Bankimchandra Chatterji (1838–94), the first great novelist of modern India, was almost an exact contemporary of Engels. His writings in the Bengali language helped to create a particular kind of political consciousness among the leaders of the nationalist movement in Bengal and, to a lesser extent, in the rest of India. Bankimchandra was an extraordinarily versatile writer. His Bengali writings are divided almost equally between novels on the one hand, and essays, pamphlets and tracts on the other.[3] Although he is much more widely known for his novels—which have been translated into several Indian languages as well as English—his other writings display a remarkable intellect seeking to grapple with ideas flowing both from the Hindu literary tradition and western writers ranging from Rousseau to John Stuart Mill.

In 1882, at the height of his literary career, Bankimchandra published a novel called *Anandamath* which became at once a symbol and a weapon in the hands of Hindu nationalists.[4] As a twentieth-century editor of his works has written, 'At one time the patriotic activist held the Gita in one hand and *Anandamath* in the other' (Chatterji 1382: vol. I, p. 41). Bankimchandra's nationalism was of a particular kind; it was Hindu rather than Indian nationalism and, as such, it carried a discordant note into the next phase of the nationalist movement when Hindu–Muslim unity became a major concern under the leadership of men like Nehru. On the other hand, Bankim's Hindu nationalism did not demand a rejection of the west: rather, it called for an incorporation of the positive qualities of the contemporary western civilization.

The story of *Anandamath* is based on the Sannyasi rebellion of 1772. Its principal characters are a group of ascetics dedicated to the cause of their land. The land is personified as the mother and the ascetics refer to each other as her *santan* or children. They have renounced all personal material concerns until such time as their land is liberated and restored to peace and plenitude. They live together in an abandoned monastery, united into a brotherhood by the worship of the mother and the practice of arms. Moral and physical courage are the two qualities they value most and their primary objective is to free their motherland from the yoke of foreign rule.

The climax of the story is a battle in which the Sannyasis deal a crushing blow to the united British and Muslim forces. But their victory does not lead to the establishment of a new Hindu polity in place of the prevailing oppressive regime. The fruits of victory have to be renounced because Hindu society must first prepare itself for self-governance. The Hindus must rouse themselves from their age-long torpor: they must 'once more become great in knowledge, virtue and power'. Till then they must submit to British rule and learn from the British the ways of acquiring external knowledge which they once had but later lost.

Literary critics in Bengal have found fault with *Anandamath* for being too didactic and conveying its political message too openly and explicitly. In other words, they have found its symbolism to be lacking in subtlety. Judged by the standards of literary criticism today, the use of symbolism is indeed heavy-handed, for it leaves all too little to the imagination of even the ordinary reader, not to speak of the trained anthropologist.

Indeed, *Anandamath* is redolent of symbolism: the withdrawal into the forest, the practice of *brahmacharya* (celibacy), the saffron robes, and a hundred other images and metaphors reiterate the message of the author. The land, with its many splendours, is presented as the mother goddess, and the people as her devotees. The hymn 'Bande Mataram' (Hail Mother!), which later became a national song, is presented for the first time in *Anandamath*. The book is permeated by the symbolism of the mother cult. At the very end *pratistha* (institution) and *bisarjan* (renunciation) are shown hand in hand; *bisarjan* leads *pratistha* away, for the people are not yet ready to inherit the land.

The message that was so powerfully conveyed by *Anandamath* was in fact part of a larger system of beliefs and ideas which Bankimchandra explored in his other writings as well. Bankimchandra not only had his own theory about the relationship between Hindu culture and Indian polity, he was also a formidable polemicist.[5] In his polemic with contemporaries he used to great advantage his intimate knowledge of Sanskrit literature as well as his extensive reading in western philosophy and science. Bankimchandra must have been well aware of the difference between the symbolic presentation of ideas in a novel and their conceptual analysis in an essay.

Bankimchandra's essays covered a very wide range—from religion and science at one end to race and nationality at the other. He had been greatly influenced by both Auguste Comte and John Stuart Mill. In his tract on religion (*Dharmatattva* [Chatterji 1382: vol. II, pp. 584–679]), he argued that Hinduism ought to be capacious enough to accommodate what was good and true in modern civilization. Though a conservative—in the current phrase a 'revivalist'—he could see very well the evils in his own society: he compared the domination of one race by another in colonialism with the domination of one caste by another in Hinduism and found the latter to be sometimes more brutal than the former.[6] He recognized that in the nineteenth century western civilization was vibrant with life and Hindu civilization decaying and moribund, and argued that the encounter between the two ought to be used by the latter to its advantage.

Bankimchandra believed—and also argued—that politics cannot be independent of religion and culture. Before they could establish a healthy polity, Hindus would have to first revitalize their religion and culture. If British rule provided the opportunity for doing this then it should be welcomed as providential. He certainly was inspired by the vision of a 'national revolution' but did not think that in the second half of the nineteenth century the time for it was ripe.

It has been said that the basic question raised by Bankimchandra in *Anandamath* was whether the Hindus were justified in attempting to overthrow British rule by violent means. Because he answered the question in the negative, he has been described as an apologist for British rule, and, of course, people did not forget that for the best part of his working life he was a middle-level civil servant under the British. For all this, Bankimchandra's answer to the question he raised was not a simple one; it was complex in argument and rich in meaning.

Among other things, Bankimchandra had to deal with the problem of physical courage. After centuries of defeat and subjugation the Hindus had come to regard themselves as a race of weaklings. So he had to show them that their weakness was a matter of circumstance, not nature. (They could win battles not only against the Muslims but also against the British.) At the same time, winning victories in battle was only a small part of life. The British had come to stay not simply because they had won battles but because they had brought civilzation and good government. By the same token, if British rule turned into disorder it could and should be overthrown; at the same time, the Hindus must prepare themselves not only physically but also morally in order to earn the right of self-governance.

Bankimchandra's writings on nationalism—*Anandamath* in particular—are ideological in the true sense of the term for they deal with 'knowledge, virtue and power', the grand themes of ideological writings, and they deal with them in a critical and self-conscious manner.

Knowledge, virtue and power are large ideas, and it would be a wonder if Bankimchandra with his great literary gifts, did not make extensive use of images, metaphors and symbols to express them. But the symbolism gives us only one side of the picture; on the other side is Bankimchandra's argument—always clear, always forceful, even in his novels. His writings on nationalism are ideological not because of their symbolism but because of their argument. An ideology may conceivably do without symbolism; without an argument it could hardly be an ideology.

Clearly, an ideology may be used in the calculated pursuit of the interests of individuals and collectivities; but this is far from saying that such is their main purpose or function. While we all speak of individual interest and collective interest, it really is very difficult to give the term 'interest' a clear and unambiguous definition, particularly in so far as it relates to collectivities rather than individuals. In any study of ideologies it is important to recognize the various types of collectivities involved and to keep in mind the distinctions among them. Individual interests, we know, are fluid and changing, and perhaps we misjudge the nature of collective life in assigning fixed and unchanging interests to collectivities.

When we argue about the interests of a class, a nation, or a race we often argue by analogy with the interests we know various individuals have. In the context of ideologies the problem of defining interests is closely related to that of defining the collectivities to which these interests are ascribed. An ideology might promote the interests of a caucus, a party, a class, a nation or a race. When it claims to promote the interests of humanity, should we suspect its bona fides any more than when it claims to promote the interests of a class or a nation?

While it is obvious that ideologies play a part in the promotion of interests, it should be no less obvious that they also contribute to the realization of values. It is here that the ambiguity inherent in the concept of interest comes to the surface. For it can be argued that the protagonists of any ideology have at least an interest in promoting the values espoused by that ideology, even when those happen to be universal human values. In any case, it is not very illuminating to say that a proletarian ideology seeks to promote the interests of a class or that a nationalist ideology seeks to promote the interests of a nation. However, when people speak about an ideology as an instrument for the pursuit of interests, they have in mind interests not made explicit by the ideology.

Ideologies do not make explicit everything for which they strive, but surely there must be something perverse in beginning the analysis of an ideology by setting aside what it does make explicit. The view that ideology is false consciousness is no less simple-minded than the view that accepts an ideology at its face value. Indeed, the two views often co-exist in the mind of the same person: the ideology of the other person is false consciousness, hence it has to be explained in terms of interests; one's own ideology strives to realize what it says ought to be realized, hence it must be understood in terms of values.

It would be absurd to suggest that in writing *Socialism: Utopian and Scientific*, Engels was concerned mainly with the promotion of his private interests. Undoubtedly, it was meant to further the interests of the working class movement and some of its organizations; that was its stated purpose. But the movement itself set out to realize certain values, not simply for the working class in the strict sense but for humanity as a whole. Movements and organizations create their own interests with which the private interests of individuals get entangled, and these need to be studied, but their study can only be a supplement to the study of ideologies and not a substitute for it.

The historical significance of statements like *Socialism*—and, even more so, the *Manifesto*—lies in the extent to which they have helped people recognize, redefine and transform their basic values across countries, across civilizations. Equality and inequality, solidarity and conflict, freedom and servitude, communion and alienation—all these are given a new and enriched significance in the context of the dialectic between the real and the possible. An ideology addresses itself to the possibilities contained in the human condition and not merely to the existing conflict of interests.

In the case of Bankimchandra, personal involvement in any movement or organization associated with the ideology he helped to create was even more remote. It might of course be said that his argument that British rule in India was providential fitted well his own position as a civil servant under the British. But to say only this would be to ignore completely the range and richness of his argument and its effect on later generations of militant nationalists who were, in fact, inspired by it to attempt the overthrow of British rule by violent means.

An ideology has a life of its own but the nourishment on which it grows comes from diverse sources. There are, first of all, rival ideologies:

in discussing ideologies one thinks almost automatically of protagonists and adversaries. An ideology is, in some sense, an argument, and one argues not only with people but also against them. Sometimes one argues against hidden or even imaginary adversaries. Perhaps it is characteristic of the modern age that rival ideologies, rival theories regarding the relationship between human values and the instruments of power not only co-exist, but are allowed to do so in the full light of day.

To the extent that an ideology is an argument or a debate, it is concerned with truth and error. An ideology must try to demonstrate the truth of its position not only to those who are for it but at least also to those who are uncommitted, if not even to those who are against it. When Engels set out to demonstrate the truth of socialism, he was constrained by the logic of his own argument, and not simply by the calculus of material interests. Similarly, Bankimchandra's argument about Hindu society had its own logic which appealed to people even at a time when there was hardly any movement or organization to carry the argument into the political arena.

As an ideology develops, old arguments are restated, some are dropped, some change their course and new ones emerge: this is true, after all, for any system of ideas, including scientific theories. Ideologies by their very nature make use of concepts and symbols which are ambiguous and rich in implicit meaning. The process by which these implicit meanings are made explicit is both complex and uncertain in its course: it is a process in which both the proponents of an ideology and their adversaries participate.

There are other constraints which shape the development of ideologies over and above the constraints imposed by the rules of intellectual discourse. These are constraints which arise out of the struggle for power in which ideologies are intimately involved. They play a more direct and a more manifest part in the shaping of ideologies than in the shaping of other systems of ideas and beliefs, say in science or religion. This is to be expected, since ideologies are by their nature concerned with politics, with the struggle for power, unlike science and religion.

An ideology is something more than merely a theory about the relations between the values of a society and its distribution of power. It seeks not only to describe or to analyse, but also to intervene. It takes for granted neither the prevailing values nor the existing distribution of power. Marx spoke for all ideologues when he said: 'Philosophers have only interpreted the world in various ways; the problem is to change it'—or, for those with a different inclination, to prevent its being changed.

Ideologies seek to change the world not merely through the pursuit of ideas but also through the pursuit of power. The pursuit of power has its own demands, which sooner or later transform the concern for truth as such into concern for rectitude, for party reasons or for reasons of state. An ideology is not an outcome of a disinterested pursuit of ideas, a pursuit of ideas for their own sake; ideologues view such pursuits with hostility, which is often a disguise for fear.

If ideologies repudiate the disinterested pursuit of ideas for their own sake as a desirable or even possible goal, then what kind of involvement does an ideology entail? In principle this can be and often is believed to be commitment to a cause, but in practice it is also partisanship for a movement, an organization and a leader. An ideology might set a political movement on its course and give it direction, but it also becomes dependent for its authoritative interpretation on those actually conducting the struggle for power. For such persons, the correct interpretation of their ideology becomes too serious a matter to be left entirely to intellectuals to decide.

It may well be that there is no such thing as a wholly uncommitted intellectual, one who regards competing schemes of value with perfect neutrality. For one thing, it would be difficult to see the motive force behind such a person's intellectual activity. Even more than that, a student of society must feel impelled to pit his own values against those of the social universe he seeks to explore and understand. But does this necessarily require him to bind himself to a particular political project, the programme of a particular movement, a particular organization, a particular leader? Perhaps we will have to make a distinction between commitment, which is the lot of all intellectuals as of all human beings, and partisanship which is an adventure of a special kind.

Notes

1. The best statement of this problem, as far as I know, is in Dostoevsky's *The Brothers Karamazov*, Part I, Book II, chapters V and VI, in the dialogue between Father Zossima and Ivan Karamazov: Ivan says, 'There is no virtue if there is no immortality.'
2. See, in particular, Sorel 1915.
3. Bankimchandra Chatterji also wrote in English, but his English writing did

not get a wide readership. *Bankim Rachnabali* (1382; Bengali calendar) is a three-volume edition of his work of which vol. I consists of his novels (in Bengali), vol. II his other writings in Bengali, and vol. III his writings in English.

4. This novel is singled out for special mention in the article on Bankimchandra Chatterji in successive editions of *Encyclopaedia Britannica.*

5. There is a vast literature on Bankimchandra in Bengali. A useful English commentary on his work is M.K. Haldar 1977.

6. In an essay on self-rule and alien rule in Chatterji 1382, vol. II, pp. 241–5.

7. Mannheim, for instance, refers time and again to 'adversaries' and 'opponents' in his *Ideology and Utopia* (1960).

References

Apter, David (ed.). 1964. *Ideology and Discontent*. New York: The Free Press.

Chatterji, Bankimchandra. 1382 (Bengali calendar). *Bankim Rachnabali*. 3 vols. Calcutta: Sahitya Samsad.

Engels, Frederick. 1954. *Anti-Duhring*. Moscow: Foreign Languages Publishing House.

—— 1970. *Socialism: Utopian and Scientific*, in Karl Marx and Frederick Engels. *Selected Works in Three Volumes*. Moscow: Progress Publishers, vol. III, pp. 95–151.

Geertz, Clifford. 1964. 'Ideology as a Cultural System' in Apter (ed.), *Ideology and Discontent*, pp. 47–76.

Haldar, M.K. 1977. *Renaissance and Reaction in Nineteenth-Century Bengal*. Calcutta: Minerva Associates.

Mannheim, Karl. 1960. *Ideology and Utopia*. London: Routledge and Kegan Paul.

Otto, Rudolf. 1958. *The Idea of the Holy*. London: Oxford University Press.

Plamentaz, John. 1971. *Ideology*. London: Macmillan.

Shils, Edward. 1972. *The Intellectual and the Powers and Other Essays*. Chicago: The University of Chicago Press.

Sorel, Georges. 1915. *Reflections on Violence*. London: George Allen and Unwin.

Whitehead, A.N. 1959. *Symbolism, Its Meaning and Effect*. New York: Capricorn Books.

2

Marxism, Pluralism and Orthodoxy*

If we get a few more of these professors spinning out their theories, we shall be lost.

G.Y. Zinoviev at the Fifth World Congress of the Comintern

In the second half of the twentieth century it is no longer possible to speak of Marxism in the singular; one has to speak of it in the plural. This is true in an obvious sense of Marxist practice, but it is true also of Marxist theory which is my present concern. It will be hard to identify any single approach to the understanding of either man or society—or history, or culture, or nature—that will be accepted as authoritative by all Marxists today. It is said that what is distinctive about the Marxist approach is that it is dialectical. But to describe an approach to society as 'dialectical' is a little like describing it as 'scientific'; Marxists are no more agreed on what they understand by the dialectic than are social scientists on what they understand by science. Marxism has come to signify various things to various people, not only among its adversaries but also among its protagonists. Maxime Rodinson, the renowned Islamic scholar and for many years a member of the French Communist Party, has put it thus: 'For me there is not just *one* Marxism, but *several* Marxisms, all with a common core, it is true, but

* Originally published as the M.N. Roy Memorial Lecture in 1982, and subsequently republished in *Essays in Comparative Sociology*, Delhi: Oxford University Press, 1987.

also with many divergences, each version as legitimate as any other' (Rodinson 1980: 5).

Marxism has grown in depth and variety, not only with the passage of time but also by its diffusion across the different parts of the world. Marx's own thought was deeply rooted in the intellectual culture of mid-nineteenth-century Europe. His concern was primarily with the problems of European society, to the solution of which he applied concepts and categories derived from the resources of European science and European philosophy. In the hundred years since he died, Marx's ideas have found new homes with very different intellectual traditions and requirements. This acclimatization has called for a continuous process of adaptation, innovation and reinterpretation.

The variety of forms taken by Marxism may be seen as a sign of its vitality and capacity for growth. It is a central part of the Marxist doctrine that life and thought do not remain the same everywhere or for ever, and that changes in the material conditions of life demand changes in the forms of thought. It would be difficult to exaggerate the changes that have taken place in the conditions of life since the time of Marx. Some of them have resulted from ideas implanted by Marx himself and it is not surprising that these changes, by altering the context of his ideas, have given them a new significance.

The divergences in Marxism relate not merely to matters of detail or to points of application, but reach into fundamental questions of theory and method. In other words, not only are there different conceptions of 'mode of production' and 'social formation', or of the relationship between thought and action (or existence and consciousness, or technology and social structure) but these different, or even rival, conceptions are all advocated, forcefully and persuasively, in the name of Marxism.

The interpretation of authoritative texts is an important part of all scholarly disciplines, certainly those concerned with the human sciences. In the absence of some reliance on the authority of texts, intellectual discourse would lose all continuity with the past. Among Marxists, intellectual discourse has centred to an unusual degree on the correct interpretation of authoritative texts. Marx occupies a unique position among modern thinkers in the volume and range of interpretations which have taken his ideas as their subject. Marxists, anti-Marxists and ex-Marxists have contended for a hundred years over the true import of his words, and the question of what Marx really meant has been reopened again and again by philosophers, historians, economists, sociologists and others. A well-known contemporary critic has used the phrase 'equivocal and inexhaustible' to characterize his work.[1]

The stupendous volume of interpretive literature has perhaps made Marx's thought appear more equivocal and inexhaustible than it might by itself be. It has tended to act as a screen between the ordinary reader and what Marx himself wrote, obscuring and confusing even those passages and texts that are simple and easy to read. It is a sign of the greatness of Marx that more people learn his thoughts by what they hear than by what they read, and even among the highly educated, people can passionately attack and defend these thoughts without being acquainted with them at first hand.

It is not as if the understanding and interpretation of Marx's work present no genuine problems. While these problems should not be given too much importance, they cannot be ignored. Marx was both a scholar trained to the requirements of scholarly discipline and an activist alive to the advantages of quick, not to say instantaneous, response to important political events. He wrote a great deal on a large number of subjects. He also read a great deal and kept himself remarkably well informed on the events of the day. He reacted at once to concrete events and abstract ideas. He adopted more than one style of writing, just as he wrote for more than one kind of audience. In the event, his work does not have the kind of perfect unity which the uninformed too readily assume to be the hallmark of every great mind.

Although Marx wrote a great deal, much of this remained unpublished in his own lifetime. It is doubtful that all of what he left unpublished was intended to be published, although some clearly was. Many of Marx's unpublished writings began to appear in print from 1932 onwards, first in the original and then in various translations. The publication of these manuscripts—in particular the *Economic and Philosophic Manuscripts of 1844* and the *Grundrisse*—became major events in the intellectual history of Marxism. Some felt that they rendered obsolete much of the interpretation of Marx's thought till then considered authoritative. Others maintained that since they were in the main notes, drafts and sketches which Marx chose to leave unpublished, they did not have the same authority as what he himself published in his own lifetime.

Within Marx's varied intellectual output a unique position is occupied by *Capital*. In a sense his entire intellectual life after 1844 centred around the writing of this work, and the study and preparation required for its writing. Only the first of the three volumes of the work we know today as *Capital* was published by Marx in his own lifetime and, although he lived for more than fifteen years after its publication, he did not publish any further volumes. Volumes 2 and 3 were put together by Engels, from drafts and notes left behind by Marx, and published after his death. Not surprisingly, Engels was criticized at once—by some for editing the work too little and by others for editing it too much.[2]

The three volumes of *Capital* taken together constitute a monument of intellectual endeavour on a scale rarely attained in history. Nevertheless, the work abounds in gaps, repetitions and obscurities,[3] and one of the greatest economists of the present century was provoked into describing it as 'an obsolete economic textbook' (Keynes 1933: 300). Whatever may be the final verdict on Marx's theory and method, it is evident that he had rather less certitude about them than many of his followers would like him to have had.[4] Had he arrived at a position which in his own considered judgement appeared as definitive, he would hardly have left his notes and papers in the state in which he did after nearly forty years of concentrated reflection and research. The plain fact is that Marx hesitated between alternative formulations, not merely on points of detail but on fundamental matters, as will be evident from a comparison of the unpublished draft later published as *Grundrisse* and Volume 1 of *Capital*.

Throughout the nineteenth century and until World War I Marxism had its intellectual home in western Europe, particularly in Germany, France and England.[5] These are the countries in which Marx and Engels lived, and about which they primarily wrote. Although as a body of living ideas Marxism has continued to flourish more actively, more vigorously and more luxuriantly in western Europe than elsewhere, the success of the Revolution of 1917 deprived west European Marxism of the unique intellectual authority it had till then enjoyed throughout the world. Ironically, some of the most brilliant Marxists in western Europe themselves contributed to the devaluation of their own intellectual capital by submitting to the intellectual authority of Soviet Marxism.[6]

The triumph of Soviet Marxism owed a great deal to state power but it also owed something to the appeal of strong ideas directly and forcefully expressed. Much of what was presented as Marxism in the Soviet

Union at the height of Stalin's authority is today derided by the more acute and subtle interpreters of Marxism in the west and their followers elsewhere.[7] For all that, Soviet Marxism had in its day a real intellectual appeal for millions of people whose main, if not sole, exposure to Marxism was through the works of Lenin and Stalin.[8] It will be a mistake to think that that appeal has disappeared for ever or can never be quickened to new life again.

The outstanding feature of Soviet Marxism, in contrast with Occidental Marxism, is its unity and continuity as an intellectual system. A great deal of this has been due to the discipline of party and state, but it would be a mistake to ignore what it owes to the Russian intellectual tradition. The kind of materialist doctrine that became established as the official form of Marxism under Stalin in fact enjoyed great influence among Russian Marxists long before the Bolshevik Revolution. Soviet Marxism grew within a particular material and intellectual environment; and, while it is true that the Bolshevik Revolution changed much of the material culture of the old Russia, it is doubtful that it changed as much of the basic categories of its intellectual culture.[9] At any rate, one is struck by the uniformity of the categories used in social analysis from Plekhanov down to the most recent Soviet textbooks of sociology.

Soviet Marxism is characterized by a number of interrelated features. There is first of all, the adherence to materialism in its various forms: materialist philosophy, dialectical materialism, the materialist interpretation of history. Then there is the preoccupation with the scientific laws of social dynamics, including the preoccupation with causality and determinism as understood in the natural sciences. Finally, there is the characteristic analytical scheme dividing society into 'base' and 'superstructure', and assigning causal priority to the former over the latter. In all these regards Soviet Marxism has remained much closer to the spirit of the Second International, with its view of Marxism as the doctrine of 'scientific socialism', than many contemporary forms of Occidental Marxism.[10]

Was Marx himself a materialist? Is it possible to reject materialism—not just 'mechanical' materialism but materialism as such—and still remain a Marxist? Contemporary western Marxists are by no means in complete agreement on these questions. At any rate, Marx's own writings do not give evidence of the kind of intransigent materialism that has been attributed to him by some of his most authoritative interpreters.

In an essay published shortly after the October Revolution, Bertrand Russell drew attention to the tremendous emphasis on materialism in Bolshevik theory, after pointing to the lack of any necessary connection between 'philosophical materialism' and the 'materialistic conception of history' (Russell 1949: 59–60). The foundations of Russian Marxism were laid by Plekhanov whose theoretical works remained influential despite his later differences with Lenin. Pre- and post-Revolutionary Russian Marxists, Bolsheviks and Mensheviks, Stalinists and Trotskyists were all influenced by Plekhanov's philosophical writings about which Lenin said that nothing better had been written on Marxism anywhere in the world.

Plekhanov's influential point of view is set out in a work published in 1895 under the title of *The Development of the Monist View of History*. It had originally been entitled *In Defence of Materialism*, but that title had to be changed in order to evade censorship. The book sets out to establish the superiority, firstly, of materialism over all other philosophical systems; and, secondly, of dialectical materialism over all other forms of materialism. It is an attack not only on idealism but also on all forms of dualism which refuse to acknowledge the logical and historical priority of matter over mind. The book is written in a didactic style intended to settle once and for all the basic questions of theory and method.

Marxism was represented as materialism of an even more uncompromising kind in a work published fourteen years later by Lenin under the title of *Materialism and Empirio-criticism*. The importance of this work for the development of Soviet Marxism can hardly be overstated. In it Lenin pressed the case for partisanship in philosophy and social theory. There were two opposed camps in philosophy—materialism and idealism—between which one had to choose since there was no middle ground. Those who vacillated between the two in the name of 'empirio-criticism', or 'empiriomonism', or plain agnosticism were in fact idealists in disguise who needed to be exposed. In Lenin's words, 'Marx and Engels were partisans in philosophy from start to finish, they were able to detect the deviations from materialism and concessions to idealism and fideism in every one of the "recent" trends' (Lenin 1977: 318).

It is now a commonplace among European Marxists that Marx was by no means a partisan for philosophical materialism. Some writers have sought to attribute to Engels the elements of materialism that might have crept into the writings of Marx, inadvertently as it were.[11]

These are not new arguments. Lenin was perfectly familiar with them, and his work was in fact directed against those who sought to deny that Marx was a partisan for materialism and to suggest that there might be a basic difference of outlook between Engels and Marx.[12] Differences between Marx and Engels there no doubt were, but is would be strange indeed if Engels had so completely misunderstood Marx on such a fundamental point as some of the anti-materialist adherents of Marxism appear to suggest.[13]

Commitment to materialism meant for Plekhanov, Lenin and others assigning clear priority to the external order of nature over the internal order of spirit, mind or consciousness. These thinkers saw the social world as an external world, made up of definite relations between men that were indispensable and independent of their will.[14] This external order of society was, in their view, like the external order of nature, governed by immutable laws which could be discovered and formulated, if not with the same exactitude, at least with something of the exactitude, of the laws of nature. Marxism provided a method for the discovery and formulation of these laws which far surpassed in range and power the methods of bourgeois political economy and bourgeois sociology.

The case for causality and determinism was made forcefully by Bukharin in a popular manual entitled *Historical Materialism*. 'Society and its evolution are as much subject to natural law as is everything else in the universe,' wrote Bukharin; and, again, 'The only correct point of view is that of determinism' (Bukharin 1969: 46, 37). Bukharin's popular manual was attacked by more sophisticated Marxists,[15] partly because his formulations were crude and over-simple; but also because Bukharin became an easy target after his estrangement from Stalin. Bukharin's formulations were indeed oversimple; but, then, it was only by virtue of being presented in the form of simple aphorisms that Marxism could take a hold over the minds of millions of ordinary people.

Once again, the ideal of a natural science of society, with its presuppositions regarding causality and determinism were more consistently articulated by Engels than by Marx, but it would be disingenuous to pretend that Marx never found the idea appealing or that he ever renounced it clearly and categorically.[16] The idea that Marxism provides the correct scientific explanation of social reality appealed greatly to the best minds of the Second International.[17] It became codified in the Soviet Union and, under the name of 'diamat', it has provided the groundwork for the education of millions of students there and in other socialist countries. It is difficult to see what Marxism would be in the countries of the Third World without the belief in the efficacy of its scientific laws.

The scientific understanding of society requires, according to many Marxists of the present as well as the past, giving priority to the laws of economics. As Plekhanov put it, '*The psychology of society is always expedient in relation to its economy, always corresponds to it, is always determined by it*' (Plekhanov 1956: 165, italics in original). The distinction between 'economics' and 'psychology', needless to say, expresses the distinction between base and superstructure (or between social existence and social consciousness), regarded by many, if not most, people as the hallmark of Marxism considered as a scientific doctrine.

Here again, it was Lenin who formulated the distinction most clearly and reacted most sharply to attempts at obliterating it. To put it in his words, 'Social consciousness *reflects* social being—that is Marx's teaching. A reflection may be an approximately true copy of the reflected, but to speak of identity is absurd. Consciousness in general reflects being—that is a general thesis of *all* materialism. It is impossible not to see its direct and *inseparable* connection with the thesis of historical materialism: social consciousness *reflects* social being' (Lenin 1977: 303, italics in original). It is possible that Lenin was beguiled by his reading of Engels into misrepresenting Marx. But we still need to explain why so many intelligent interpreters of Marx, many of whom give clear evidence of having read his work, should misrepresent him in exactly the same way.

Marxists have in recent years found it increasingly difficult to apply consistently the distinction between base and superstructure in their analyses of society and history. The recognition of the problem has been followed by various responses. There are those Marxists, like the British historian E.P. Thompson, who would frankly admit that the distinction, once considered useful, no longer appears to be so, and may now be set aside in the interest of a further advance of knowledge (Thompson 1978).[18] Another kind of response is that of contemporary Soviet sociologists who retain the distinction between 'base' and 'superstructure', but introduce a third category of 'extra-superstructural' factors to accommodate items that do not clearly fall under either base or superstructure.[19]

Not all adherents of Marxism—or, for that matter, all followers of Lenin—have assigned the same fundamental significance to the distinction between base and superstructure. As against such a view, is the one which characterizes Marxism in terms of its emphasis on the totality. This was the emphasis of Georg Lukacs and those who developed what may be called a Hegelian as opposed to a positivist version of Marxism.[20] In such a version the relationship between social existence and social consciousness is a relationship between the whole and a part rather than that between two parts of which one is more important than the other.[21] It would be against the spirit of this approach to contrast 'economics' and 'psychology' with a view to asserting the primacy of the former over the latter.

Soviet Marxists have assigned fundamental importance to method, thereby meaning primarily the scientific method. There is also a great emphasis on method in the work of Lukacs—and, likewise, of Sartre (Sartre 1963)—but the term 'method' is here used in a different sense. For Lukacs method is, first and foremost, the dialectic, meaning the movement towards unity of subject and object. If it is true that men in society are governed by laws, it is also true that they themselves create these laws, and hence they can understand them best in the very act of their creation. As Marx asks, following Vico, 'And would not such a history be easier to compile, since, as Vico says, human history differs from natural history in this, that we have made the former but not the latter'? (Marx 1972: 352).

Lukacs' path-breaking work, *History and Class Consciousness* is not an attempt to subordinate consciousness to material forces. It is, if anything, a celebration of human consciousness as an active agent in the making of human history. As is well known, Lenin, who otherwise praised Bukharin, had remarked that Bukharin did not understand the dialectic. The dialectic as understood by Lukacs (or Sartre, or Merleau-Ponty) is, in turn, very different from the sense given to it by Lenin or by Engels.[22] For Lukacs there is no such thing as a dialectic of nature: the dialectic has a place only within human history which is more than merely a continuation of natural history.

Thus, method for Lukacs means, above all, the dialectic whose concern must be with the whole. As he puts it, '... dialectics insists on the concrete unity of the whole'; or, again, 'Concrete totality is, therefore, the category that governs reality' (Lukacs 1971: 6, 10). Method in Marxism, according to Lukacs (or Sartre), calls for the unity of theory and practice rather than any particular technique of observation or fact finding. The attempt to transform Marxism into scientific sociology is doomed to failure. Marxism grows with the growth of the revolutionary consciousness, towards which bourgeois social science takes a negative, if not hostile, stance.

History and Class Consciousness was directed against the Marxism of the Second International in which theory was claiming a life independent of practice. In the very year of its publication, another work, entitled *Marxism and Philosophy* was published by the German Marxist, Karl Korsch, also from an anti-positivist point of view. Korsch argued strongly against the kind of dualism that sought to drive a wedge between social existence and social consciousness: 'For the coincidence of *consciousness and reality* characterizes every dialectic, including Marx's dialectical materialism' (Korsch 1970: 77–88, emphasis in original). Korsch's work like that of Lukacs was denounced by Soviet Marxists. In an 'Anti-critique', published in 1930, Korsch traced back the roots of the dualism he had earlier attacked to what he considered to be Lenin's misrepresentation of Marx in *Materialism and Empirio-criticism* (Korsch 1970: 89–126).[23]

The preoccupation of Lukacs with human consciousness as an active agent in social transformation makes his theory and method very different from theories and methods which rest on ideas of external causality and determinism. Not surprisingly, Lukacs was attacked by the theoreticians of the Comintern for propagating 'voluntarism', a charge which he, again not surprisingly, repudiated. Whatever be the merits of these charges and countercharges, it is difficult, when comparing Bukharin and Lukacs—who criticized each other—not to be struck by their very different conceptions of the dialectic and of the laws which govern human conduct. The tension between determinism and voluntarism has become even more marked in the discussion of Marxism that has grown in western Europe in the last twenty-five years.

Among Marxists who have attacked determinism and asserted the primacy of the human will, none has enjoyed greater respect, at least since the time of Lenin, than Gramsci. Gramsci owes his unique place in contemporary Marxism as much to his highly original presentation of it as to the conditions under which he lived and wrote.[24] Like Lukacs, Gramsci also wrote a long critique of Bukharin's *Historical Materialism*, and this critique is important because it brings out the difference between his approach and the approach not only of Bukharin but of what became established as Soviet Marxism.

In the course of his critique of Bukharin, Gramsci wrote,

It is well known, moreover, that the originator of the philosophy of praxis [Marx] never called his own conception materialist and that when writing about French materialism he criticizes it and affirms that the critique ought to be more exhaustive. Thus he never uses the formula 'materialist dialectic', but calls it 'rational' as opposed to 'mystical', which gives the term 'rational' a quite precise meaning. (1971: 456–7)

Whether true or false, this view of Marxism is strikingly, if not startlingly, different from the text-book representation of it as being first and foremost a form of materialism.[25] Needless to say, it has implications for a critique of not only Bukharin's *Historical Materialism* but also Lenin's *Materialism and Empirio-criticism*.[26]

If we follow Gramsci, materialism is a metaphysics which obstructs historical understanding which is the only form of understanding appropriate to a subject concerned with human beings. Gramsci's approach to Marxism is a historicist approach consciously opposed to every form of positivism. The subject matter of history being radically different from the subject matter of the natural sciences, their methods must also be different.

Gramsci's historicism has appealed to many Marxists in the west, but by no means to all. A highly influential version of Marxism emerged in the sixties of the twentieth century under the leadership of the French structuralist, Louis Althusser. Althusser's structuralist interpretation of Marx sought to put back the emphasis on 'laws', 'determinants' and 'structures', as against a humanistic and historicist interpretation, on the basis of a sharp distinction between the earlier and the later work of Marx. In this version, the later, more mature and scientific work of Marx as exemplified in *Capital* should be seen as superseding his earlier work which, upto the period of *The German Ideology*, was permeated by 'humanistic' and 'historicist' categories.[27]

It will be clear from what has been said above that Marxism, as theory and method, has retained much greater unity and continuity in the Soviet Union than outside it. In western Europe several different versions of Marxism have succeeded each other, particularly in the last twenty-five years, and differences arising from national intellectual traditions, as between German and French Marxism or between French and English Marxism, are also discernible.[28] The co-existence of these various interpretations of Marxism—in some ways complementary and in others difficult to reconcile—enables Marxism to retain and perhaps extend its appeal among all those who have a real interest in the understanding of society and history.

The plurality of approaches within Marxism must be seen in the light of what has been and continues to be another important, if not intrinsic, feature of it, namely, the preoccupation of Marxists with orthodoxy. By this I simply mean that Marxists are concerned not only with the correct understanding of the world, but, over and above that, and to an unusual degree, with the correct interpretation of a particular body of writings. Thus, debates among Marxists, and between Marxists and their adversaries move along two intersecting scales: on the one hand whether, for instance, base in fact determines superstructure or psychology merely reflects economics; on the other, what Marx really meant by the various observations he made on such subjects.

Orthodoxy, as orthodox Marxists are ready to point out, is not the same thing as dogmatism. Dogmatism indicates unwillingness to reconsider one's initial position in the light of new facts or facts not considered earlier. Marxism would not have survived as an intellectual system had it refused to respond to the momentous changes taking place in the real world. The recognition of changes that call for the replacement of old ideas by new has been a conspicuous feature of European Marxism. And as one eloquent advocate of orthodoxy has argued, one may renounce many, even most of the substantive propositions formulated by Marx without ceasing to be an orthodox Marxist (Lukacs 1971).[29]

The idea of orthodoxy, which has its widest use in the domain of religion, is difficult to define in the context of Marxism which is secular and scientific in its orientation. Not all Marxists make a case for orthodoxy, explicitly and systematically, but the striking thing is that so many do. The orthodoxy of Kautsky, once widely acknowledged, was later repudiated by Lenin. Lukacs sought to give a new meaning to the idea of orthodoxy so as to harmonize it with Lenin's practice, but his formulation was condemned by Lenin's heirs in Moscow.

Not only are various forms of orthodoxy opposed to each other but orthodoxy as such is opposed to revisionism. The term 'revisionist' is difficult to define since it may be used in a loose sense by the advocates of one kind of orthodoxy to denounce or revile the advocates of another. But revisionists in the strict sense make no pretence at orthodoxy. They are those who call for a serious reexamination of the tenets of Marxism, including some of its fundamental tenets, while seeking to remain within the Marxist tradition.

The attack on the revisionism of Bernstein by Kautsky and the custodians of orthodoxy brought to light a fundamental contradiction in the Marxism of the Second International. For Marxism, as it was presented by the theoreticians of the Second International, was a positive science: it was the scientific aspect of Marxism that they most strongly recommended. Why should it be inherently wrong, as the orthodox seemed to say it was, to revise a body of knowledge that claimed to be a positive science? Marxist ideas of orthodoxy and revisionism are difficult to accommodate within the domain of positive science which regards the capacity for revision as a virtue and the claim of orthodoxy a defect.

The superior merit of Lukacs over Kautsky lay in this, that he did not seek to combine the claim of orthodoxy with the claim that Marxism was a positive science. For Lukacs (as also for Korsch and Gramsci), Marxism was not a positive science, not even a superior form of it, but stood in opposition to it. Orthodoxy in Marxism involved not a defence of but an attack on empiricism which, according to Lukacs, constituted the foundation of bourgeois social science. The obsession with facts as they are is a feature of the 'contemplative' as opposed to the 'dialectical' method which is the defining feature of Marxism.[30] Any attempt to revise Marxism in the name of facts as they are given 'must lead to oversimplification, triviality and eclecticism' (Lukacs 1971: 1).

Lukacs was the first to articulate in a systematic way a new view of orthodoxy in Marxism, centering not on scientific socialism but on revolutionary praxis. In 'What is Orthodox Marxism?' and in the other essays published together as *History and Class Consciousness*, he presented his case with unsurpassed verve and sophistication. Lukacs' view of Marxism as revolutionary praxis rather than scientific socialism found its echo in the writings of a number of his contemporaries, notably Korsch and Gramsci.

The shift in orientation from scientific socialism to the philosophy of praxis was precipitated by the momentous events of the Bolshevik revolution. Gramsci hailed these events in a newspaper article entitled 'The Revolution Against *Das Kapital*'. Korsch called for a closer union between revolutionary theory and practice, and Lukacs presented his new vision of orthodox Marxism. All three were calling for a fuller appreciation from Occidental Marxists of the significance, not merely the *practical* significance but also the *theoretical* significance, of the revolution made by Lenin and his associates.

History and Class Consciousness by Lukacs and *Marxism and Philosophy* by Korsch were both published in 1923. It seems to me that these two works (and the work of Gramsci) provide a far more powerful philosophical support for Lenin's practice than does Lenin's own philosophical treatise, *Materialism and Empirio-criticism*, published between the abortive revolution of 1905 and the successful one of 1917.[31] But Lenin's heirs in Moscow, those who had helped him to make the October Revolution and were still fighting bitterly to save it, thought otherwise. At the historical Fifth World Congress of the Comintern in 1924, Zinoviev led the attack on Korsch and Lukacs, denouncing their work as 'theoretical revisionism' (Fifth Congress, the Communist International, *Abridged Report*: 17).

The question still remains as to why the Soviet leadership reacted so sharply against the attempt to establish a new orthodoxy that would vindicate the revolution that was its own creation. Part of the answer lies in what may be described as the inertia of intellectual categories. The intellectual categories of Lenin's heirs were those established as authoritative by Plekhanov, in which matter was prior to mind and psychology expedient to economy; and the plain fact is that those who bring about a revolution in the real world do not necessarily bring about one in their own categories of thought. Without a fundamental change in those categories, the new proposals for orthodoxy were bound to appear 'idealistic' and 'voluntaristic' and to be rejected as such.

Lukacs, Korsch and other 'idealist deviationists' were not merely celebrating the Bolshevik revolution; they were presenting their arguments in a particular idiom that had its roots in Hegel's philosophy. Russian Marxism had absorbed very little of this idiom which might indeed appear as an encumbrance to those who saw the main intellectual task after the revolution to be that of codification. If, as Lukacs and Korsch were arguing, Marxism was the intellectual expression of the revolutionary movement of the proletariat, it had to be brought within the intellectual reach of the working class. Soviet Marxists might, with some justice, say that it was they, and not professors like Lukacs and Korsch, who were in reality carrying Marxism to the workers.

Codification might make Marxism easy for the workers, but it generates its own orthodoxy. The speed with which Soviet Marxism under Stalin displaced all other claimants to orthodoxy might have something to do with its intellectual form and content, but cannot be explained solely by that. Questions of orthodoxy never are fully resolved on the merits of ideas; they are settled in the end by the struggle for power.

Marxism is unique among modern intellectual systems not only in its insistence on orthodoxy, but in its attempt to create theoretical grounds for giving the party a determining voice on questions of orthodoxy. It is not enough to point to the part played by the Stalinist leadership in imposing a particular kind of orthodoxy through the use or threat of force; one must recognize also the legitimacy accorded to the party in the writings of Lukacs, Gramsci and others in deciding on questions of orthodoxy. Even if it is true that Stalin did not endorse the theories of Lukacs, or Gramsci the practices of Stalin, the two developments were taking place simultaneously in what appeared from the outside as broadly the same movement.

It is not unusual to view Marx as a social scientist, and to compare his intellectual system with the intellectual systems of other social scientists, for example, Max Weber or Keynes. But neither of these generated orthodoxies are at all comparable to the orthodoxies established in the name of Marx. In purely intellectual terms, the only possible comparison might be with the system created by Freud. But it was never a part of any Freudian orthodoxy to use a political party as the vehicle of its true expression. The practical and theoretical significance of the party in Marxism gives to Marxist orthodoxy a totally different character from all contemporary social science systems.

Those like Gramsci and Lukacs who, after the Bolshevik Revolution, sought to free Marxist theory from the strait-jacket of determinism imposed on it by the orthodoxy of the Second International, sought at the same time to give a central role to the party in the articulation of working-class consciousness. The party had some authority in deciding on questions of theory throughout the period of the Second International. But it was only after the Bolshevik Revolution that the essence of Marxism was linked to the revolutionary party with the aid of the most complex and ingenious theoretical reasoning.

Lukacs and Korsch attacked the orthodoxy of the Second International for representing Marxism as a positive science whose truth was independent of any political movement. In their view Marxism could have a valid existence only as 'the theoretical expression of the revolutionary movement of the proletariat', and never independently of it (Korsch 1970: 42). For Lukacs, as we have seen, method is all-important, but method consists not in a set of procedures for collecting and analysing facts but, above all, in adopting what he calls 'the standpoint of the proletariat'. It is this standpoint rather than any detached intellectual skill that is the guarantee of true insight. As Lukacs puts it, 'the knowledge yielded by the standpoint of the proletariat stands on a higher scientific plane objectively'; for only the proletariat is destined to become the 'identical subject-object of history' (Lukacs 1971: 163, 197).

But what is the standpoint of the proletariat? And what is the class consciousness of the proletariat? Lukacs is keen to point out that he is talking not about 'empirical' or 'psychological' consciousness, but about 'real' or 'historical' or 'imputed' consciousness:

Now class consciousness consists in fact of the appropriate and rational reactions 'imputed' (zugerechnet) to a particular typical position in the process of production. This consciousness is, therefore, neither the sum nor the average of what is thought or felt by the single individuals who make up the class (Lukacs 1971: 51).[32]

And it is here that the role of the party becomes decisive, for 'the party is the historical embodiment and the active incarnation of class consciousness', and, again, 'the party is assigned the sublime role of *bearer of the class consciousness of the proletariat and the conscience of its historical vocation*' (Lukacs 1971: 42, 41, italics in original).

Gramsci has been hailed as the exponent of a humanist form of Marxism, but it is to Gramsci that we owe the most persuasive attempt in theory at an apotheosis of the political party. *The Modern Prince* is one of the great works of social and political theory, and it is entirely free from the pyrotechnics characteristic of Lukacs' writing. Gramsci played a leading part in founding the Italian Communist Party, and his work derives its strength and appeal from its sincerity as much as its originality. When Gramsci spoke of working-class consciousness he did not mean an imputed consciousness accessible to only a select few; the actual or empirical worker and his view of the world never ceased to engage his attention.

We have to remember that in Gramsci's perspective the purely organizational side of the party was subordinate to its cultural and intellectual life. The party was to be not merely an engine for the capture of power; it was to be above all a school for the creation of a new culture, a new outlook and a new way of life. Men could not leave it to history to change things in accordance with some preordained law of progress. The initiative lay with them to create a new life for themselves in the pursuit of their own collective needs and aspirations.

Gramsci had a genuine belief in the efficacy of the human will and human ideas, and sought to give to these a central place in his conception of Marxism. There could be no revolution in real life without a revolution in ideas, and the revolution in ideas would not come about as a mere byproduct or after-effect of the revolution in material conditions. In all this the intellectual function was of crucial importance, but the intellectual function could not be performed from above or outside; it had to become a constitutive part of the working-class movement.

Gramsci thought of a new kind of intellectual, organically linked with the working-class movement, and a new framework for his intellectual activity, namely, the political party. He wrote, 'That all members of a political party should be regarded as intellectuals is an affirmation that can easily lend itself to mockery and caricature. But if one thinks about it, nothing could be more exact' (Gramsci 1971: 16). In Gramsci's view it was the party alone that could weld together the older 'traditional' intellectuals with the new intellectuals whose growth was organically linked with the growth of the working class.

Without active intellectual engagement the party would degenerate into a lifeless machine. But if intellectual activity was necessary to the health and well-being of the party, the party was no less indispensable to the kind of intellectual life Gramsci considered appropriate to Marxism. One cannot emphasize too strongly the central place assigned to the party in Gramsci's philosophy of praxis. The party *is* the 'modern Prince', the protagonist of revolutionary praxis in the modern world, and as such it has a historical mission of the highest importance: 'In men's consciences, the Prince takes the place of the divinity or the categorical imperative, and becomes the basis for a modern laicism and for a complete laicisation of all aspects of life and of all customary relationships' (Gramsci 1971: 133). It would be a grave error to think that the supreme role assigned to the political party in the direction of intellectual life can be detached from Gramsci's 'philosophy of praxis' without changing its character altogether.

These considerations leave us with a number of questions concerning contemporary debate of which I would like to raise only one in conclusion. It concerns the prospect of an independent Marxism in India today. I raise this question because I believe that the involvement of the party in Marxist thought, or even its control of it, in the Stalin years was not a mere aberration of Stalinist practice but a logical corollary of Marxist theory in at least some authoritative versions of it. The practice has changed, no doubt, but the implications for theory of this change in practice are not always candidly discussed.

Orthodoxy on questions of theory under the direction of a political party cannot mean the same thing today as it did during Stalin's time. The simple fact is that there is no longer any political party that can speak with the same authority to all Marxists that Communist parties all over the world, including India, did only a generation ago. There are divisions between national Communist parties even as there are divisions within the International Communist movement. Hardly any Communist party has today the moral authority to claim a determining role in settling questions of theory. Stalin's *Short Course* was intended to settle questions not only of practice but also of theory; it is hard to visualize another such work acquiring the same kind of authority in the eighties.

It is necessary to discuss the tension that has existed and continues to exist between what may be called 'academic Marxism' and 'party Marxism', and to examine its sources. There *is* an academic Marxism, distinct from party Marxism—and increasingly so—no matter how much its proponents might defer to the intellectual authority of Lukacs or Gramsci. Their relationship must be examined, not merely in a general and abstract way, but in the context of each national tradition with its particular intellectual culture and its particular political compulsions. It is often said that the social sciences have had very little autonomous growth in India, that their growth has followed paths laid down in Europe and America; there is truth in this, but the truth applies as much to Indian Marxism as to Indian social science.

If we look at the record since 1956, the intellectual contributions of independent Marxists will appear substantial, at least in western Europe. One thinks of Habermas in Germany, or Rodinson in France or E.P. Thompson in England. My own view is that the independent Marxist, mainly in the academic world but also outside, will extend his intellectual influence in the years to come, and in doing so will look over his shoulders less and less to see how the party reacts. Until now, at least in India, he has stood on somewhat uncomfortable ground, between the liberal academic who sees intellectual freedom as an end in itself and the orthodox Marxist who sees the authority of the party as supreme. The academic Marxist has perhaps less reason than he thinks to be on the defensive in his orientation towards the party. Marxist theory, since at least the time of Lenin, has combined the critique of bourgeois society with the exaltation of the Communist party. It has sought to make partisanship the basis of every kind of commitment. The spirit of Marxism requires that the critique of capitalist society be extended to other forms of society as well. Such a critique must have a basis in some kind of social commitment, but it is now too late to argue that that commitment can be guaranteed only by a political party.

Notes

1. 'Equivoque et inépuisable' is the title used for an essay on Marx by Raymond Aron (1970).

2. See the 'Supplement' by Engels to vol. 3 of *Capital*.

3. Marxist scholars have been from the beginning aware of this, and have tried to provide aids to the reading of *Capital*. See, for instance, the 'Introduction' by Korsch to the 1932 German edition of *Das Kapital*, republished in Korsch 1971. A more recent effort is Althusser and Balibar 1977.

4. This is not to suggest that Marx did not on occasion express himself with great self-assurance regarding his discovery of the laws of motion of capitalist society.

5. One hardly needs to be reminded of the three sources of Marxism—German philosophy, English political economy and French socialism—made famous by Lenin's pamphlet, *The Three Sources and the Three Component Parts of Marxism*.

6. The fact that Marxism, which, in its golden age, represented the highest expression of western intellectual culture, could establish itself only in what was intellectually and culturally the most backward part of Europe, had notable consequences for its further development. This point has been tellingly made by Leszek Kolakowski in his monumental *Main Currents of Marxism*. See also Deutscher 1966.

7. The contrast between Soviet and western Marxism has now become a commonplace among Marxists themselves. This was not so during Stalin's lifetime. Maurice Merleau-Ponty was perhaps the first notable Marxist to make the contrast between 'Leninism' and what he called 'Occidental Marxism' (Merleau-Ponty 1955). From the opposite camp, John Plamenatz made the contrast, with characteristic contempt for the Russian intellect. 'Passing from German to Russian Marxism', he wrote, 'we leave the horses and come to the mules' (Plamenatz 1954).

8. After the disenchantment with Stalin in the mid-fifties, there was the rise to prominence of Mao Tse-tung, with his celebrated Little Red Book. I do not discuss Mao's ideas at all as the discussion would take me too far afield to enable me to return quickly to my principal argument. But Mao's case would strengthen, not weaken, my argument that there are diverse authoritative versions of Marxism, difficult, if not impossible, to reconcile with each other.

9. I have been struck by the astonishing continuity of Russian culture as reflected in Russian prose literature. The sensibility to which Pasternak and Solzhenitsyn appeal is a Russian sensibility, and basically the same as the one to which Dostoevsky, Tolstoy and Turgenev appealed.

10. This point was made by Korsch after his break with the Communist Party. See his 'Anti-Critique', first published in 1930, in Korsch 1970.

11. It has become a fashion to contrast the shallow materialism (or even positivism) of Engels with the profound dialectics of Marx. See, for instance, Horowitz and Hayes 1975. See also Harrington 1976.

12. See Lenin's attack on V. Chernov for his 'attempt to counterpose Marx to Engels' in *Materialim and Empirio-criticism*, p. 84ff.

13. I find the argument for a complete misunderstanding of Marx by Engels or by Kautsky and the other pillars of the Second International to be weak and unconvincing. Marx was not a remote prophet, living in a distant age and out of reach of the people who became his authoritative interpreters after his death. The interpreters to whom the misunderstanding has been attributed lived in the same intellectual environment as Marx and shared the same intellectual presuppositions, and some of them knew him personally and even intimately. If Kautsky—and even Engels—had got Marx all wrong, how can we, at this distance in time and space, ever hope to reconstitute the true Marx?

14. It is no accident that so many of them—Plekhnov, Lenin, Bukharin—gave such a central place in their interpretation of Marx to the famous statement in the 'Preface' to *A Contribution to the Critique of Political Economy* which begins, 'In the social production of their life, men enter into definite relations that are indispensable and independent of their will.'

15. It received long, hostile reviews from both Lukacs and Gramsci. Lukacs's review has been republished in *New Left Review*, XXXIX, 1996 as 'Technology and Social Relations' (first published 1925); Gramsci's review is to be found in his *Selections from Prison Notebooks*.

16. The case for a 'natural science of society is most strongly made by Engels in *Anti-Dühring* to which, it must not be forgotten, Marx had contributed a chapter.

17. I would include not only Kautsky and adherents of his brand of orthodoxy, but also the Austro-Marxists, a good sample of whose work may be seen in Bottomore and Goode (eds) 1978. The scholarly contributions of the Austro-Marxists were substantial and, unlike Lukacs, Gramsci or Sartre, they took a positive view of empirical sociology; see, for instance, Neurath 1973.

18. Thompson has moved away from 'party' or 'orthodox' Marxism to a fairly independent position.

19. This position goes back to Stalin's famous intervention in the debate over the place of language. It has now become a commonplace of Soviet sociology. See, for instance, Afanasyev 1971.

20. The emphasis on 'totality' as against the 'base-superstructure' distinction is characteristic also of the unorthodox and somewhat personal Marxism of Jean-Paul Sartre (1976).

21. Kolakowski sums up the position thus: 'As the whole is always prior to its parts, so the determination of parts by the whole is more fundamental than that of some parts by others' (1978: vol. 3, 268).

22. Lukacs joined issue with Engels over the latter's concept of the dialectics of nature (Lukacs 1971).

23. It may be noted that *Materialism and Empirio-criticism* appeared in a German translation only in 1927, and was probably not accessible to either Lukacs or Korsch in 1923.

24. Kolakowski has written, 'It was undoubtedly thanks to his imprisonment that Gramsci was able to remain a member of the Communist party' (1978: vol. 3, 226).

25. It is now becoming increasingly apparent even to Marxists and Marxist sympathizers that there is a tension, perhaps an inherent tension, between materialism and the dialectic. See Merleau-Ponty 1955. For Lenin, of course, there was no problem in combining the dialectic with materialism: Marx and Engels had emphasized the *dialectical* side of dialectical materialism, but one might just as well emphasize its *materialist* side. See Lenin 1977: 309ff.

26. Gramsci castigates Plekhanov, 'who, in reality, despite his assertion to the contrary, relapses into vulgar materialism' (1971: 387), but does not, so far as I am aware, take issue with Lenin on his materialism.

27. See Althusser 1969. For a trenchant critique, see Kolakowski 1971: 111–228. See also Aron 1970: 193–354.

28. For an account of French Marxism in its social and intellectual setting, see Lichtheim 1966; for a lively contrast between French and English Marxism, see Thompson 1978: 'The Peculiarities of the English'.

29. But as against this, one may reasonably ask, as Bottomore has done, 'More generally, what is the sense of saying that Marxist orthodoxy consists in accepting Marx's method, if at the same time it should be the case that this method produces nothing but false propositions'? (Bottomore 1974: 105).

30. This is how Lukacs confronted the argument that facts seemed to go against the Marxist doctrine: 'If, in Hegel's terms, Becoming now appears as the truth of Being, and process as the truth about things then this means that the *developing tendencies of history constitute a higher reality than the empirical facts*' (1971: 181, italics in original).

31. This is not to say that Lenin hesitated to strike when the opportune moment came or that he did not produce arguments in support of such action. It must not be forgotten that Lenin spelled out the active role of the vanguard party in *What is to be Done?* before he wrote *Materialism and Empirio-criticism*. My point is a more limited one, namely, that there is a yawning gap between Lenin's political activism and his theory of knowledge, the presuppositions and implications of his materialist philosophy, which in fact became the established doctrine of the Soviet schools. This point has been noted by others before. Lichtheim, for instance, wrote, 'Though Lenin's *practice* was voluntaristic, his philosophy implied a belief in immutable laws impervious to human volition' (1966: 95, n.25, italics in original). The only thing that I would like to add is that Lenin's philosophy did not merely *imply* this, but hammered the point with singular tenacity.

32. Those with even a superficial acquaintance of the literature cannot fail to note in this an echo of Marx who wrote in *The Holy Family*, 'It is not a question of what this or that proletarian, or even the whole proletariat, at the moment *regards* as its aim. It is a question of *what the proletariat is*, and what, in accordance with this *being*, it will historically be compelled to do' (Marx and Engels 1975: 44, italics in original).

References

Afanasyev, V.G. 1971. *The Scientific Management of Society*. Moscow: Progress Publishers.

Althusser, Louis. 1969. *For Marx*. Harmondsworth: Penguin Books.

Althusser, Louis and Etienne Balibar. 1977. *Reading Capital*, 2nd edn., London: NLB.

Aron, Raymond. 1970. *Marxismes imaginaires; d'une sainte famille a l'autre*. Paris: Gallimard.

Bottomore, T.B. 1974. *Sociology as Social Criticism*. New York: Pauntheon Books.

Bottomore, T.B. and Patrick Goode (eds). 1978. *Astro Marxism*. Oxford: Clarendon Press.

Bukharin, Nikolai. 1969 [1921]. *Historical Materialism: A System of Sociology*. Ann Arbor: The University of Michigan Press.

Communist Party of Great Britain. *Fifth Congress of the Communist International: Abridged Report*.

Deutscher, Issac. 1966. *Ironies of History*. Berkeley: Ramparts Press.

Gramsci, Antonio. 1971. *Selections from Prison Notebooks*. London: Lawrence & Wishart.

Harrington, Michael. 1976. *The Twilight of Capitalism*. New York: Simon & Schuster.

Horowitz, I.L. and Bernadette Hayes. 1975. 'For Marx/Against Engels: Dialectics Revisited', *The International Journal of Critical Sociology*, vol. 1, no. 1, pp. 21–33.

Keynes, J.M. 1933. *Essays in Persuasion*. London: Macmillan.

Kolakowski, Leszek. 1971. 'Althusser's Marx', *The Socialist Register*, pp. 111–28.

—— 1978. *Main Currents of Marxism*. Oxford: Clarendon Press, 3 vols.

Korsch, Karl. 1970. *Marxism and Philosophy*. New York: Monthly Review.

—— 1971. *Three Essays on Marxism*. London: Pluto Press.

Lenin, V.I. 1969. *The Three Sources and the Three Component Parts of Marxism*. Moscow: Progress Publishers.

—— 1977 [1909]. *Materialism and Empirio-criticism*. Moscow: Progress Publishers.

Lichtheim, George. 1966. *Marxism in Modern France*. New York: Columbia University Press.

Lukacs, Georg. 1971 [1923]. *History and Class Consciousness*. London: Merlin Press.

Marx, Karl. 1972. *Capital*. Moscow: Progress Publishers.

Marx, Karl and Frederick Engels. 1975. *The Holy Family*. Moscow: Progress Publishers.

Merleau-Ponty, Maurice. 1955. *Les Aventures de la Dialectique*. Paris: Gallimard.

Neurath, Otto. 1973. *Empiricism and Sociology*. Dordrecht (Holland): D. Reidel Publishing Co.

Plamenatz, John. 1954. *German Marxism and Russian Communism*. London: Longmans, Green & Co.

Plekhanov, G. 1956 [1895]. *The Development of the Monist View of History*. Moscow: Progress Publishers.

Rodinson, Maxime. 1980. *Marxism and the Muslim World*. New Delhi: Orient Longman.

Russell, Bertrand. 1949 [1920]. *The Practice and Theory of Bolshevism*. London: Unwin Books.

Sartre, Jean-Paul. 1963. *The Problem of Method*. London: Methuen & Co.

—— 1976. *The Critique of Dialectical Reason*. London: New Left Books.

Thompson, E.P. 1978. *The Poverty of Theory and Other Essays*. London: Merlin Press.

3

Intellectuals*

The term 'intellectual' has various connotations. In one sense it refers to a certain quality of mind, to certain spiritual or even moral qualities: in short, to what people, or certain kinds of people, are. In another sense it refers to what people do, to certain occupational roles, or to a certain aspect of the division of labour. One might say that the first is the popular conception of the intellectual, and the second the sociological; except that the sociologist also presumes that the intellectual will not merely play his role, but play it with a certain kind of commitment. An American sociologist puts it, somewhat sententiously, thus: 'Intellectuals live for rather than off ideas' (Coser 1970: viii).

While some regard the quality of being an intellectual as a special or unusual gift, others regard it as a general or universal feature of the human condition. It was the second point of view that Gramsci expressed when he wrote, 'All men are intellectuals, one could therefore say: but not all men have in society the function of intellectuals' (1971: 9). There is a 'critical, creative and contemplative' side to the mind of every human being; and no human being, whether scholar, poet or philosopher, is critical, creative or contemplative in every one of his activities.

The intellectual faculty, if one may use such an expression, is not only in some form present in every individual, it is also in some sense valued by every culture. The anthropological study of primitive societies has greatly altered our perspective on the place of ideas as active, living elements in the human scheme of things. I particularly have in mind the work of Lévi-Strauss, which has shown how greatly the play

* Originally published in *Ideologies and Intellectuals*, Delhi: Oxford University Press, 1980.

of ideas is valued in societies with even the most primitive material technology (Lévi-Strauss 1966). Thus, it may be said that what Gramsci held to be true of all individuals, Lévi-Strauss has shown to be true of all cultures, primitive as well as advanced.

But the intellectual in the popular sense of the term is not universally acclaimed in modern societies. Appreciation of the moral and spiritual qualities typically associated with the intellectual goes hand in hand with a certain mistrust. Modern societies provide unique opportunities for intellectual self-expression. At the same time, the laws of the market as well as the apparatus of the state place important constraints on the freedom of the intellectual. When he falls out of step with these he might find himself being regarded as either parasitical or subversive.

Perhaps each culture has its own way of drawing the distinction between the 'intellectual' and the 'practical'. It cannot be said that the former necessarily enjoys precedence over the latter either in a society dominated by the business enterprise or in one dominated by the machinery of government. It is important not to lose sight of this fact even while acknowledging the great increase in modern times of those specialized roles, functions and activities we designate as intellectual.

While it is useful to remind ourselves that every human being is in some sense an intellectual and that every culture has some place in it for intellectual endeavour, it is also indisputable that intellectual activities are specialized to a far greater extent in some societies than in others. When such functions come to be located in specific social positions, we may speak of intellectuals as a distinct category of people and contrast them with other members of society. But even here there is a problem. For we think of the intellectual in terms of a vocation, and not merely an occupation. And no matter how we define our terms, broadly or narrowly, not all those who are in intellectual occupations have the appropriate vocation; and some who have that vocation might earn their livelihood from occupations that are only remotely connected with activities ordinarily considered intellectual.

With the specification of intellectual functions and their location in determinate positions, those who occupy such positions become increasingly conscious of their distinctive social identity. In other words, intellectuals come to think of themselves as a stratum or even a class, standing in relations of complementarity or opposition to other classes or other strata in society. It is in this light that we have to understand the significance of an observation such as the following: '... I hold that intellectuals as a self-conscious congeries of men arose only in the seventeenth century. They are a modern phenomenon, and they come into their own with the beginning of modern history' (Coser 1970: x–xi).

Intellectuals themselves are perhaps more immediately concerned with the content of intellectual activities, their originality and their excellence. But the content of intellectual activities cannot be understood in isolation from the context of social arrangements in which they take place. Intellectuals are inclined to seek for themselves a kind of freedom from the constraints of existing social arrangements which they know cannot be conceded to other persons in other walks of life. Are intellectuals entitled to greater freedom from social constraints than other members of society? What special claims can these other members of society make on intellectuals if, in fact, a greater measure of freedom is allowed to them?

The institutional arrangements in and through which intellectuals work vary enormously from one society to another. Correspondingly, there are variations in the ways in which societies mark out those categories of people who may be regarded as performing intellectual functions. The different terms employed themselves provide some indication of these differences in conception. Thus, the term 'intellectual', as used in Anglo-Saxon countries, has a narrower connotation than the term 'intelligentsia' more commonly used in East European countries.

It may be useful to begin with the widest available conception of the social category with whose definition we are concerned. In the Soviet Union, and in East European countries in general, society is commonly conceived of as being divided into three broad categories, viz., peasants, workers and the intelligentsia. There is some ambiguity about the characterization of these categories. Peasants and workers are described sometimes as 'classes' and sometimes as 'strata'. On the other hand, Soviet sociologists take pains to point out that in their society the intelligentsia are not a class but a stratum, even though their scheme might provide them with only a single stratum.

For East European sociologists the point of departure in the discussion of the intelligentsia is the argument that they are not a class but a stratum. The Polish sociologist Wesolowski argues thus: 'In Marxism the intelligentsia is a "stratum" and not a class.' This is so because, 'It is not distinguished with the aid of some antagonistic relation with another group—a class.' Further, 'It appears alongside the fundamental classes, particularly in capitalism, but also to some extent in earlier formations' (1979: 108). According to this argument, it is in socialist society that the 'non-antagonistic' character of the intelligentsia becomes most clearly apparent (Béteille 1969).

Given this conception of the intelligentsia as a stratum and not a class, various criteria may be used in providing a positive content to the category. Of the various features by which the intelligentsia may be characterized, 'the one generally emphasized is that of the non-manual nature of work. In the capitalist formation, the intelligentsia subsumes both employees and those working on their own account (e.g. doctors in state hospitals and those in private practice). Under socialism they all gradually become employees' (Wesolowski 1979: 108). Thus, what is seen as crucial in the definition of the intelligentsia is not their relation to the means of production but their place in the division of labour.

This broad conception of the intelligentsia is underscored in the work of the Soviet sociologist Glezerman who has enumerated the various types of persons included in the category. Thus, 'Most of the intelligentsia consist of office employees. These include all mental workers employed at state enterprises, offices, and so on. There is also a part of the intelligentsia employed in collective farms who are their members.' And again, 'But even among intellectuals far from all of them perform executive functions. Most of the intelligentsia consist of workers in education, science, medicine, accounting, and so on, who do not perform any executive functions' (1971: 146–7).

All students of the social category with which we are concerned have noted the rapid increase in its size in recent times. Thus, Glezerman writes of his own society, the Soviet Union: 'That the intelligentsia rapidly grows, absolutely and relatively, under socialism is beyond dispute' (1971: 146). The same point is made in a slightly different way by Edward Shils when he contrasts the life of the intellect in western Europe at the end of the seventeenth century with that life today. Nor is this just a contrast in the numbers of persons engaged in intellectual activity; it is, above all, a contrast in the volume and density of such activity. 'The sheer volume and diversity of production in the intellectual (including expressive) domain are incomparably greater than in any other epoch' (Shils 1972: 98).

There are obviously certain similarities in growth patterns between the two kinds of industrial society, arising from the compulsions of technological development; in both cases scientists and the institutions which train and employ them have grown at a very rapid rate. At the same time, it is not easy to make direct comparisons between them, partly because of differences in their institutional systems and partly because of differences in the classifications adopted in the two kinds of society.

Western sociologists, particularly in the English-speaking world, seem to prefer a rather more restricted conception of the life of the mind than the one employed by Soviet sociologists. Here it is not simply a question of another form of labour—'mental' as opposed to 'manual' labour—but, rather, of a peculiarly close and intimate relationship with the values cherished by society as a whole or by particular sections of it. It is from this standpoint that Coser writes, 'Not all academic men are intellectuals, nor are all members of the professions ... Intellect ... presumes a capacity for detachment from immediate experience, a moving beyond the pragmatic tasks of the moment, a commitment to comprehensive values transcending professional or occupational involvement' (1970: vii).

In the sense usually accepted in the west, the role of the intellectual is associated with what have been called 'critical, creative and contemplative' activities. As I have already indicated, there are problems in tying these activities down to any set of socially defined roles. Nevertheless, there are institutional systems which provide, or are designed to provide, a specific milieu for them. The scientific research laboratory is an obvious example. While such institutions no doubt existed in the past (e.g. the traditional universities), they have expanded and diversified enormously in the course of the last hundred years.

The growth and diversification in western countries of intellectuals, intellectual institutions and intellectual services in even the narrow sense is brought out in the following observation by Shils: 'The intellectual institutions, universities, technological colleges, research institutes, public and university libraries, bibliographic services, publishing houses, the better newspapers, reviews and periodicals, sound broadcasting and television, learned societies and academies, all engage great numbers of highly educated persons, many of whom are very productive, some of whom are creative at the level of genius' (1972: 98). There is differentiation also amongst those whom intellectuals serve. There are those intellectuals who provide highly specialized services to only a limited number of other intellectuals, and there are those who address themselves directly to mass audiences of millions of people.

It is true that intellectuals engaged primarily in 'critical, creative and contemplative' activities are a much more restricted category than the intelligentsia considered in the broad sense of non-manual workers in general. Even so, in the modern world they are such a highly differentiated category that it would be difficult to make an exhaustive enumeration of all their subtypes. Nor is it necessary to do so here. It is enough at this stage to draw attention to three broad categories of intellectuals: (i) poets, playwrights and novelists, or creative writers in the broad sense of the term; (ii) scholars and scientists, or intellectuals in the academic profession; and (iii) critics and journalists, including those in some branches of the mass media.

It must be emphasized that the categories listed above are neither exclusive nor exhaustive. Thus, the professor of poetry in Oxford might also be an outstanding poet; it is not easy to say of every essayist whether he is a 'creative' or a 'critical' intellectual; and many a scientist has achieved fame primarily through his journalistic writings. Nevertheless, if these people do not always have the same peculiar sensitivity to the core values of society that constitute the defining feature of the intellectual, it is among them that we are most likely to find those who do.

Do intellectuals create, interpret and transmit values and ideas even-handedly in the interest of society as a whole, or only in the interest of a particular section of it? We have seen that intellectuals, particularly in the modern world, are a highly differentiated category. But modern societies themselves remain deeply divided into classes and communities. What bearing do the divisions of society have on the recruitment of persons to intellectual roles and on the manner in which they play their roles?

In a sense intellectuals are amongst the privileged in all societies, although their privileges might appear more odious in some than in others. 'Mental labour' is more highly regarded than 'manual labour' in all societies, irrespective of the distribution of income between the two. It is a part of the modern intellectual's way of life to reflect on these privileges, and to criticize and condemn them in principle even while he clings to them tenaciously in practice.

It seems to me that there are two principal ways in which the intellectual in a class-divided society seeks justification for what he is and what he does. The first rests on some variation of the argument that intellectuals are not attached to any of the principal divisions of society, that they stand above or outside the conflict of interests between these divisions, and that it is precisely in a class-divided society that they play their most significant part. The second point of view is that, as 'mental' and 'manual' labour are but two forms of labour, the intellectual best articulates the interests of the working class as a whole against the vested interests of the exploiting class. The presuppositions of the two points of view are perhaps not as fundamentally different as their proponents make them out to be; and they both provide the intellectuals much scope for self-congratulation.

Among the liberal or bourgeois sociologists who have written on the intellectuals or the intelligentsia,[1] Karl Mannheim occupies an eminent position, and in his writings we get the clearest representation of what may be called the 'socially unattached'[2] character of the modern intelligentsia. Mannheim begins by contrasting the intelligentsia in a static society with the modern intelligentsia. In a static, traditional order the intelligentsia have a well-defined social position, and their thought flows along prescribed channels. With the passage into the modern world everything changes: 'The intellectual is now no longer, as formerly, a member of a caste or rank whose scholastic manner of thought represents for him thought as such' (Mannheim 1960: 11).

Mannheim underlines the inadequacy of any approach to the study of the intelligentsia 'which is oriented only with reference to socio-economic classes' (1960: 138). Modern intellectuals are of diverse social origins, and, correspondingly, their interests and orientations are also diverse. 'One of the most impressive facts about modern life is that in it, unlike preceding cultures, intellectual activity is not carried on exclusively by a socially rigidly defined class, such as a priesthood, but rather by a social stratum which is to a large degree unattached to any social class and which is recruited from an increasingly inclusive area of social life' (Mannheim 1960: 139). When the intellectual is able to move from one social class to another in the course of his own lifetime, he ceases to be imprisoned within the categories of any social class.

Curiously enough, a very similar kind of argument seems to have become a part of the conventional wisdom of Soviet sociology. This is precisely the argument used for contesting the view that there is a 'new class' in Soviet society or that the Soviet intelligentsia has become a 'new elite'. 'It should be added that the socialist intelligentsia is not a closed section, access to which is difficult for workers and peasants and their children. On the contrary, it has been formed and is replenished mainly by workers and peasants' (Glezerman 1971: 147). The implication of this argument is that only a self-recruiting group can have a defined set of interests and an intellectual orientation corresponding to it.

It would be a mistake to assume too close a correspondence between the social origins of the intelligentsia and their material interests, or their intellectual orientations. As Marx had pointed out, the Roman Catholic church managed for centuries to retain an impressive unity of intellectual orientation even though the clergy, being celibate, could not be a self-perpetuating group. It is well known that even in medieval times the Oxford and Cambridge colleges had ample provision for recruiting as both scholars and fellows were individuals from the most varied economic backgrounds.

A rather different vision of the role of the intellectual in modern societies may be found in the writings of the Italian Marxist, Antonio Gramsci. Unlike most Marxists of his time, Gramsci assigned primary significance to ideas and values, and to the conditions of their creation. For Gramsci the replacement of one social order by another involved not merely a redistribution of power, but above all the creation of a new civilization with a new world view; it is the magnitude of this endeavour that gives the intellectual his true significance in society and in history.

As we have seen, Gramsci employed a broad and somewhat flexible conception of the intellectual, often using the term in the general sense of 'intelligentsia'. He was interested less in the intellectual as expert or specialist than in the part he might play in shaping collective representations through an involvement in collective life. For Gramsci the creativity of the intellectual was linked inseparably to his involvement in collective life; the raw material of his mental constructions ought to be not detached observation but willed experience. The intellectual could not in any real sense be 'socially unattached', although he might have an illusion of being so.

Gramsci was aware that the intellectual might in fact become detached—or seek to become detached—from his social roots and, along with others like him, form a kind of free-floating category with allegiance to none and no social responsibility. This is how he was inclined to view what he called the 'traditional intellectual' in the modern world. Against this he opposed the 'organic intellectual' whose social milieu consisted not merely of other intellectuals, but of the entire class to which he belonged and whose world view he helped to create.

Gramsci's distinction between 'traditional' and 'organic' intellectuals, though rich in imagery and suggestion, is not always easy to follow. First, his notes on the subject are fragmentary and scattered, and the circumstances under which he wrote forced on him the use of euphemism and periphrasis. But there are deeper reasons behind the obscurity. For Gramsci incorporates a vision of the future in his descriptions of the past and the present. The 'organic intellectual' is thus an ideal type in a double sense; and it is not always easy to determine when Gramsci is writing about what is or has been, and when he is writing about what ought to be and will be.

The concept of 'organicity' is attractive in so far as it is suggestive of an alternative to an uncontrolled division of labour between 'manual' and 'mental' activities, and between the different kinds of mental activity. Nevertheless, it may be rash to take for granted the attainment of organicity in any human society, let alone a complex modern society with its multifarious needs and functions. There are moments when Gramsci's vision of the 'organic intellectual' seems to reflect the vision of Marx and Engels of a society which 'makes it possible for me to do one thing today and another tomorrow, to hunt in the morning, fish in the afternoon, rear cattle in the evening, criticise after dinner, just as I have a mind, without ever becoming hunter, fisherman shepherd or critic' (Marx and Engels 1968: 45).

Gramsci's ideal type of the 'organic intellectual' has to be understood in the light of his central preoccupation with the needs of the working class. Leaders of working-class movements have everywhere been haunted simultaneously by two fears: the fear that their movement will be dominated by intellectuals from other classes with no true spiritual kinship with the working class; and the fear that intellectuals originating in the working class will be tempted away from their own class by the attractions of professional life.

Both the richness of the notion of 'organicity' and the difficulty of operationalizing it become manifest when we examine it in the light of a reality such as the Indian. In Gramsci's own words, 'Every social group ... creates together with itself, organically, one or more strata of intellectuals' (1971: 5). Euphemism apart, we must consider, besides classes in the strict or loose sense of the term, groupings of very diverse kinds when we are dealing with a society as complex and heterogeneous as Indian society. The Indian intellectual who is organically disposed must consider not only the claims of his class but also those of his caste, his religious community and his linguistic region. To repudiate the latter claims in the interest of the former might lead to his being more rather than less detached from his immediate social milieu.

In countries like India it is precisely the claims of social groups such as castes and communities that stand in the way of intellectual endeavour and excellence. It is true that classes are groupings of a rather different kind from castes or religious communities or linguistic divisions, and that they have a special significance in the modern world. Even so, it is not easy to see exactly how the chemist in his laboratory or the historian in his seminar is going to balance the claims of his class against the demands of the job he has been appointed to do.

Mannheim's contrast between intellectuals in static and in dynamic societies tends to overlook the fact that in the former the intellectual is not infrequently an amateur whereas increasingly in the latter he is obliged to be a professional. This has implications for the intellectual's freedom of manoeuvre. A part of the freedom from traditional constraints that he gains by his passage from a 'static' to a 'dynamic' society —and perhaps a very large part of it—the intellectual has to surrender to the organization within which he has now to seek employment.

Thus, against Mannheim's statement about the 'absence of a social organization' among the modern intelligentsia, we have to counterpose the view of a more recent observer, Edward Shils: 'The trend in the present century, therefore, in all countries, liberal and totalitarian, has been toward an increasing incorporation of intellectuals into organized institutions' (1972: 13). The organized institutions within which intellectuals have to work differ greatly among themselves, but their growing importance calls for a reappraisal of the ideas held by liberal intellectuals about the nature of their own vocation.

The most dramatic changes in conditions of work may be seen among natural scientists who occupy in some sense a pre-eminent place among intellectuals in the second half of the twentieth century. Nuclear physicists, biochemists, molecular biologists and the host of other specialized scientists who have become an essential part of the modern world cannot do their work as amateurs or as independent and self-supporting individuals. They are today completely dependent for their work on the scientific research laboratory which has grown enormously in size and complexity and to whose discipline they must submit. The conversion of the independent scientist into an employee of the scientific research laboratory is a relatively recent historical phenomenon, but one which may be encountered equally under socialism and capitalism, and in developed as well as underdeveloped societies.

Till the eighteenth century it was possible—and perhaps not uncommon—for a scientist to make lasting contributions to human knowledge on the basis of experiments carried out in his attic or his cellar or his backyard. The conditions under which Benjamin Franklin (1706–90) or Henry Cavendish (1731–1810)—to take only two prominent eighteenth-century examples—conducted their investigations were such as to enable them to organize research on their own terms. Franklin made his pioneering contributions to the study of electricity in between periods of hectic activity as a statesman and a diplomat. Caven- dish was a man of means; but he lived in seclusion, and his epoch- making contributions to the theory of gases were basically the work of a single man.

The conditions of work in a modern scientific research laboratory, even in a poor country like India, are such that it would be unrecognizable to a Cavendish or a Franklin. It is important to keep the difference in mind because even when a scientist works under a completely new set of conditions, he might carry in his head the role model of a scientist from a bygone age. The difference between conditions of work then and now is not merely one of material resources, important though they are. The whole social organization of science in the modern world is such as to render obsolete the very idea of scientific creation in splendid isolation.

The experimental sciences moved into the colleges and universities in the nineteenth century,[4] and made a place for themselves alongside the older branches of knowledge. Their expansion and diversification brought about changes in the organization of academic life, at first slowly and then rapidly. At Cambridge and Oxford they contributed to the shift in the focus of academic life from the colleges to the university departments and laboratories. But the big changes were to come with the second World War, and then to manifest themselves most prominently in the United States and the Soviet Union.

The scientific research that culminated in the production of the atomic bomb at Los Alamos in 1945 was organized on a scale and conducted at a pace that had no precedents in the past. The story of the ill-fated director of the project, J. Robert Oppenheimer is too well known to bear repetition.[5] No two persons could be more unlike than this enterprising American scientist and his aristocratic English predecessor, Henry Cavendish. But the differences of personality are far less important than the changes in the social organization of science that had taken place between Cavendish and Oppenheimer. Oppenheimer's work put him in command over enormous resources, both material and human; but he became entrapped in the very organization he helped to create, and, when he sought to disengage himself from it, he was unable to do so without considerable sacrifice of dignity.

The fate that befell the atomic scientists working at Los Alamos was the culmination of a trend that many had foreseen. In a famous address in the University of Munich, Max Weber had said in 1918, 'The large institutes of medicine or natural science are "state capitalist" enterprises, which cannot be managed without very considerable funds. Here we encounter the same condition that is found wherever capitalist enterprise comes into operation: the "separation of the worker from his means of production"' (1948: 131). Even in 1918 Weber had noted that this trend had gone further in America than in Germany, and predicted that it would reach into every department of the German university as it was doing in the American.

In the second half of the twentieth century the scientific research laboratory represents an extreme case of 'the incorporation of intellectuals into organized institutions'. However, even today not all scientists work in large organizations, nor are all intellectuals scientists. There are—and hopefully will continue to be—poets, playwrights and novelists whose work depends more on their inner resources and who can therefore work more easily on their own terms. But the 'self-employed' intellectual or the intellectual who works for himself is increasingly outnumbered by those who work as employees in organizations. And even the poet, the playwright or the novelist—not to speak of the critic or the journalist—is increasingly dependent on large organizations for the distribution and sale of his work.

In India, and elsewhere, intellectuals who are employees of large orgnizations are often inclined to attribute their lack of control over their own conditions of work to the contradictions of the capitalist system. This is to mistake the species for the genus. In these matters conditions are hardly better under socialism, by which I mean the kind of system that prevails in the Soviet Union and in other East European countries. If anything, the conversion of the intellectual into employee is even more complete there. And it is now too late to pretend that because the scientific research laboratory is not privately owned there, the scientist's own conception of his calling and the goals of the organization in which he is employed are in a state of closer harmony.

It is only right that the intellectual should recognize the place of organizations in the modern world and the constraints they impose on those employed in them, whether as 'mental' or as 'manual' workers. But nothing will be gained from this recognition if it leads only to a flight into the past. It is all too easy to ignore in a mood of nostalgia the constraints on intellectual life imposed by all traditional societies. We can move forward only if we recognize that, while we have freed ourselves from many of the constraints of traditional modes of thought, freedom, whether for the intellectual or for any other member of society, can never be absolute or unconditional.

If it be conceded that intellectual activity in general cannot take place in isolation, then what are the social settings most appropriate to them? The social settings in which intellectual activities take place are multifarious, and not all are in the strict sense of the term institutionalized. I would like to discuss here two institutional systems which might be considered appropriate settings for intellectual activity in the modern world, namely, the university and the political party. To contrast university and party as alternative social settings for intellectual activity is also to contrast two different conceptions of such activity.

To many the university would seem to be an automatic choice as a social setting for intellectual activity. Many kinds of intellectual activity go on outside the university, and much of what goes on inside is hardly intellectual except in a purely formal sense. Nevertheless, one cannot easily think of any other institution in which so many people engage in such a variety of intellectual activities, self-consciously and as a part of their everyday life.

It is difficult to characterize the university in terms of any simple set of concrete activities or functions. There is first of all the ideal of university life: even this has changed vastly over time, and some feel that the reality has diverged so far from the ideal that too much attention to the latter is bound to obscure our understanding of the former. The proclaimed objective of the university is the advancement of learning, and most universities seek to achieve this by combining teaching with research, although in highly variable proportions. Secondly, university education is, or seeks to be, broad-based, covering the widest range of subjects, and including law, medicine, the natural sciences, the social sciences and the humanities. Thirdly, at least in modern times, the university is an open institution as regards the people it admits and the views it allows them to espouse.

There has been a phenomenal expansion in the university system in every part of the world since the middle of the nineteenth century. The number of universities has multiplied severalfold and the number of students in each university has also grown steadily, and, in many parts of the world, rapidly. This quantitative increase has been so vast and so rapid that it has led some to argue that the character of university education and of the university itself has been radically altered. There is also the question of the change in the character of the university in the course of its transplantation from its original home in the West to the countries of Asia and Africa.

The origins of the university go back in the West to the twelfth century with the establishment of foundations in Bologna, Paris and Oxford, with Cambridge following shortly after, that is, at the beginning of the thirteenth century. There were variations from the very beginning. University governance might be in the hands of the masters as at Paris and Oxford (the *universitas magistrorum*); or it might be in the hands of the students as at Bologna (the *universitas scholarium*). At Bologna the content of education was more literary and secular, whereas theology and speculative philosophy dominated at Paris and Oxford.

The relatively unchanging character of the pre-nineteenth century university system is seen best in England where Oxford and Cambridge remained as the only universities from the twelfth and thirteenth centuries till the nineteenth. This is not to suggest that Oxford and Cambridge themselves remained completely unchanged during their long term of existence. There were major changes in the relations between the university and the colleges in both Cambridge and Oxford. Changes took place also in the content of education: Latin was gradually displaced as the language of learning and teaching after the Reformation; the study of classical languages and literature, especially Greek, became established in the sixteenth century; and Cambridge took the lead in establishing mathematical studies in the seventeenth. Nevertheless, the changes that are most important from our point of view began even in Oxford and Cambridge in the nineteenth century.

Oxford and Cambridge are important not only because of their remarkable continuity over time, but also because they have stood as examples for universities in all English-speaking countries, including India. It must be remembered that both are small, exclusive and privileged institutions, and were very much more so till a hundred years ago. Smallness of size is important, particularly in view of the fact that in Oxford and Cambridge the academic community was, and continues to be, divided between the colleges where closeness of personal relations between fellows and scholars is prized as the most valuable part of academic life.

In talking about exclusiveness and privilege as features of Oxford and Cambridge, we must remember that these institutions are rooted in traditions that go back to the Middle Ages when the social world as a whole was a hierarchical one. In those ages it would have been considered absurd to think that university education was a democratic right which every member of society ought to enjoy irrespective of religion, class or gender. Admission was restricted in all sorts of ways, some of which might appear strange today: for instance, King's College, Cambridge, which was founded in 1441, admitted until the nineteenth century students from only a single school, namely, Eton. The same college also claimed till about the same time the privilege of getting university degrees for its students without their having to take university examinations. (A similar privilege was enjoyed in Oxford by New College.)

With the establishment of new universities in England in the nineteenth century, Oxford and Cambridge underwent reforms which have continued until the present time. They have altered in many ways without forsaking their traditional identity. They have grown in size, but not immoderately. They are more open now, admitting women as well as men, and both from a more varied background; but they are still able to pick out the best candidates, leaving the rest to the other universities. They continue to enjoy a number of privileges, but these are now used with greater discretion. They provide the best of modern education in a setting that has not abandoned all its medieval elements.

Thus, Oxford and Cambridge of recent memory appear as gracious places where academic excellence is pursued in a social setting marked by civility.[6] They appear neither as immovably hierarchical as they probably were during the first six or seven hundred years of their existence nor as aggressively competitive as so many of the American universities, at once better organized and more 'democratic', today appear to be. And no matter what the constraints to the free expression of thought might have been in medieval times or in the wake of the Reformation, their recent history has been marked by not merely the tolerance but the active encouragement of diverse—indeed, contrary—points of view.

Unlike Oxford and Cambridge, most present-day universities, and all those in Asia, are creations of the nineteenth and twentieth centuries. The demands that they have been created to meet are very different from those which gave rise to the medieval universities. The modern university in the second half of the twentieth century has to meet not merely the demands of academic excellence but also those of social justice. Those who are unable to pretend that there must be a pre-established harmony between the two must also recognize that, especially in countries like India, the claims made on behalf of intellectual excellence sound rather feeble to many ears against those made on behalf of social justice.

In the older universities traditions of intellectual excellence emerged slowly within a set of social arrangements which enjoyed legitimacy for centuries, but which would be totally unacceptable today and which therefore cannot be created *de novo* in the twentieth century. The new universities, particularly in poor countries like India, have to fight against time in order to establish standards of academic excellence in an atmosphere of implacable hostility to all forms of 'elitism'. They cannot easily resist the populist pressures for social justice by appealing to considerations of academic excellence, for they have very little of even that to show for themselves.

The modern university, particularly in the countries of the Third World, is located characteristically in the large metropolis. The universities of Calcutta, Bombay and Madras, the first to be set up in India, were located in the three major provincial capitals in contrast to Oxford and Cambridge, or even Harvard, Yale and Princeton. The problems of Indian universities, including those of large size and rapid expansion, cannot be understood in isolation from the problems of urban youth, particularly the problems of urban unemployment and urban unrest. It is well known that these universities are poorly equipped academically and otherwise; at the same time, they are being called upon to solve problems of a kind which even the best-endowed universities in the west were never expected to solve.

Until the nineteenth century the university was a kind of microcosm in which was reflected the larger social hierarchy; at any rate, it was not expected to change the basis of society from hierarchy to equality. On the other hand, one of the main reasons given for the expansion of higher education in India today is that it can be used as an instrument for dissolving the social hierarchy inherited from the past. This is the broad context within which the claims of academic excellence have to accommodate themselves to the claims of social justice.

It has thus come about that the purely academic has acquired even in the context of the university, a negative value, as something devoid of a social purpose, something lacking in relevance. In the Indian university today purely academic pursuits are under attack from without and from within. The external system, in the form of the governmental and semi-governmental agencies responsible for its funding, demands from the university tangible returns for the tax-payer's money on which it subsists. From within, there are pressures from unions of teachers and of students, and from other politically-organized bodies to put academic pursuits in the service of urgent social problems; academic life moves haltingly under threat of strikes from students' unions, teachers' unions and unions of non-academic staff, acting jointly in fraternal solidarity or severally in fraternal rivalry.

As the universities become overcrowded with students and with teachers, the more successful and the more ambitious academics look outwards for avenues of better employment. They try to go abroad or join the relatively small and quiet institutes of advanced study and research that have come up in the sciences and the social sciences (Béteille 1974). The point is not how many scientists and scholars try to do this or how many actually succeed; rather, it is that successful academics have begun to feel that today a truly academic-atmosphere is to be sought not within the university but outside it.

But the universities will survive their desertion by scholars of eminence in search of an atmosphere congenial to their work. The universities are here to stay, however much what is actually done within them might depart from what they were initially instituted to do. It is difficult to visualize any other institution with the same extensive capacity for establishing the daily routine of academic life. No matter how dull this routine is and no matter how frequently it is disturbed, no large-scale modern society, with its complex of scientific, technological, administrative and managerial requirements, can be kept moving without it. By and large, our scientists, our doctors, our civil servants—and our teachers—will be as good or as bad as our universities are; if our universities can only limp along, their performance too can only be halting.

While it may be true that 'ideas occur to us when they please, not when it pleases us' (Weber 1948: 136), it is also true that they are most likely to bear fruit in an environment marked by a certain density of *routine* intellectual activity. The university brings together large numbers of young people and provides a setting for their interaction during some very formative years of their life. This interaction contributes as much to the life process of the university as the formal instruction it is designed to impart. Perhaps in every age and in every country the young learn more from each other than from their teachers.[7] For a long time the university has provided to millions of young people a kind of privileged setting for the interchange of ideas.

Towards the end of his life Max Weber gave two addresses at Munich on 'Politics as Vocation' and on 'Science as Vocation'. Weber was no ordinary ivory-tower intellectual: he was intensely concerned with the interplay between the pursuit of ideas and the pursuit of power, between scholarship and partisanship, between science and politics. But however much they might be intermeshed in real life, Weber saw that the two were not animated by the same spirit. Indeed, to the liberal it is a matter of faith that science—or scholarship, or the pursuit of ideas—cannot prosper unless in principle it is conceded a measure of autonomy.

The faith of the Marxist is different. It is thus that we find a rather different conception of the relationship between science and politics in the writings of Antonio Gramsci. Gramsci wrote no less movingly about the intellectual than Weber; and he too had a vision of the intellectual, but it was a different vision. For him the central institution of the new civilization was to be the party, and it was in and through the party that the new intellectual was to achieve fulfilment.

In Marxist theory there is a close relationship between class, party and intellectual: one may say that the three constitute a kind of hierarchy in which class encompasses party and party encompasses the intellectual. The theory, conceived in this broad sense, lends itself to diverse interpretations and applications. Much of the actual discussion of the intellectual among Marxists centres around two issues: social background and party discipline. On both counts—the bourgeois or petty bourgeois background of intellectuals and their resistance to party discipline—the vast majority of Marxists since Lenin's time have had a highly ambivalent attitude towards intellectuals.

The great merit in Gramsci's approach is that it does not confine itself narrowly to the two questions of social background and party discipline, but poses the problem of the intellectual in its widest social and cultural context. He sees, for instance, that the content of thought is as important as the social background of the intellectual, and that there is no simple one-to-one relationship between the two. The relationship between the intellectual and the class structure is not a simple unmediated one, and Gramsci repeatedly draws attention to the 'complex of superstructures' by which this relationship is in fact mediated.

Every society, every class and every individual has a world-view, even though it often happens that we remain attached to a world-view which has fallen out of step with changes in the real world. The intellectual function consists of critically appraising existing world-views, in seeing how they relate to the real world of practical activity, in organizing their various elements into a meaningful whole; and, to paraphrase Marx, in creating a new world in imagination before constructing it in reality (Marx 1974: 174). The intellectual function is at once critical and creative, and it is rooted in practical activity: as we have already noted, Gramsci's conception of the intellectual is a broad one.

The intellectual in the broad sense must be distinguished from the expert or the specialist; and it might well be argued that even the best-trained specialist or expert might be as much a prisoner of false consciousness as a man of common education. The distinctive feature of the intellectual function lies then not so much in the facility for solving technical problems as in the capacity for piercing through the veil of false consciousness. The established routine of everyday academic life cannot guarantee the attainment of this objective; in fact it might become an obstacle.

It would be quite wrong to think that Gramsci simply believed that universities and schools were outmoded bourgeois institutions which might be easily dispensed with. In fact, he strongly believed that progress among the people at large was impossible without a continual rise in the level of their mental culture, and he acknowledged the part played by academic institutions, and even the Catholic church, in this process. Only, he maintained that the mere existence of schools and universities was not a guarantee that the intellectual function, as he conceived it, would be adequately fulfilled.

It is in this light that we have to view the guiding influence that Gramsci assigned to the party in the formation of the intellectual. It was the party alone which could place each routine task in the perspective of the whole, while relating theoretical speculation to practical activity; the party was necessary also for providing the framework of discipline essential to any kind of collective endeavour. In order to appreciate the force of this argument we must take account of Gramsci's vision of the party itself. As he saw it, the principal agent of history in the modern age—the modern Prince—could be no longer an individual but a collectivity, namely, the party; and the party could not play its historical role unless it became thoroughly intellectualized from within.

In order to understand the role assigned by Gramsci to the party in the formation of the intellectual, we must keep in mind his distinction between 'organic' and 'traditional' intellectuals. Very briefly, organic intellectuals arise in the course of the formation of a particular class, whereas traditional intellectuals cut across social classes and are to some extent detached from them. Gramsci naturally was concerned in particular with intellectuals whose creation is organically linked with the creation of the working class. Now, 'The political party for some social groups is nothing other than their specific way of elaborating their own category of organic intellectuals directly in the political and philosophical field and not just in the field of productive technique' (Gramsci 1971: 15); Gramsci's meaning becomes perfectly clear when for 'some social groups' we read 'the working classes'.

But the party does more than merely give organizational form to the intellectuals who emerge organically with the emergence of a particular class, in this case the working class. It provides a social setting which makes possible the incorporation of other kinds of intellectuals as well. 'In other words, it is responsible for welding together the organic intellectuals of a given group—the dominant one—and the traditional intellectuals' (Gramsci 1971: 15). Such a party should thus have a place not only for the worker turned intellectual, but also for the professor turned organizer of the working class movement.

It may happen that a political party brings together in a common endeavour people of diverse kinds, including writers, scholars and scientists. If the common endeavour is sufficiently compelling, it might override both distinctions of social background and distinctions of occupational position. But can such a common endeavour, of which the course and direction is charted by the party, retain a basically intellectual character? Gramsci writes, 'That all members of a political party should be regarded as intellectuals is an affirmation that can easily lend itself to mockery and caricature. But if one thinks about it nothing could be more exact' (1971: 16). Surely, this is an expression of faith rather than a true description of anything that one knows to have actually existed.

One must bear in mind that Gramsci's claims were made not on behalf of each and every party but of that party which was organically linked to the class which was to be the bearer of a new civilization.

Gramsci could not have had *all* political parties in mind when he asserted that 'all members of a political party should be regarded as intellectuals'. When Gramsci wrote this the party in power in Italy was Mussolini's Fascist party; one would have to extend the concept very far indeed to regard all its members as intellectuals.

Clearly, the model for Gramsci, as for millions of people during and since his time, was the Bolshevik party which, under Lenin's inspiring leadership, had steered the course of 'the Revolution against *Das Kapital*'. The leader of the party had been himself a formidable intellectual: pamphleteer, polemicist, philosopher, historian and economist; and he had also been a connoisseur of intellectuals—after his fashion. When Lenin detached himself from day-to-day politics and shut himself up in the Paris libraries in order to write *Materialism and Empirio-Criticism*, he acted after the example of Marx. Nor did Lenin shine in solitary splendour: there were others like him, such as Trotsky and Bukharin, who united the capacity for study and reflection with a tremendous zest for political activism. It was thus possible for even a man of Gramsci's piercingly clear insight to be beguiled by the Bolsheviks' early success in combining party work with intellectual work.

However, the marriage of knowledge and power in the Bolshevik party did not long outlive Lenin. Lenin's deeply ambivalent attitude towards intellectuals was replaced in Stalin by an attitude of deep distrust and hostility. The brutal suppression of intellectuals in the Soviet Union by Stalin and his ruthless use of the party machinery for the purpose have been recounted by a succession of authors apologetically, candidly, cynically, maliciously or passionately, depending on the inclination or the vantage point of the author concerned. It is one of the many ironies of the history of Marxism that all this was happening at precisely that moment when Gramsci in his prison was giving expression to his vision of a new world, to be created by a party whose historical prototype was the party that had made 'the Revolution against *Das Kapital*'.

Not many parties have even aspired to combine 'intellectual' activity with 'practical' activity on the scale attempted by the Bolsheviks. Liberal parties, or the general run of parties in liberal democracies—such as the Conservative and the Labour parties in Britain, or the Republican and the Democratic parties in America—have in general been satisfied with a much more modest intellectual role for themselves. In a few western countries, such as France and Italy, the Communist party has kept up a fairly high level of intellectual discourse, but hardly anywhere have parties succeeded in 'welding together' in a free and permanent union 'the organic intellectuals ... and the traditional intellectuals'.

In India the Communists have been virtually alone even in attempting to relate their everyday political practice to some kind of a theoretical framework. The Marxian system provides them with an intellectual apparatus for examining the structure of the world in which they live and the course and direction of its change. It enables them to reflect and speculate, at least occasionally, on matters that are beyond their immediate practical concern. And they have the example of party leaders who have contributed to knowledge and whose speculative ideas as well as practical actions are a source of inspiration to them.

For all this, in India the intellectual life of the Communist party taken as a whole is fitful, not to say feeble. The party cadres, with a few exceptions, acquire their knowledge of Marxian theory at second hand on the basis of limited reading confined to a small number of texts written by Marx, Lenin and Mao. The few exceptions are almost invariably people who acquired a wider and a deeper culture in Marxism in their student days in universities, not infrequently universities abroad: Oxford or Cambridge, the London School of Economics, or even an American university. And academic Marxists in their mature years seem to prefer being on their own, cultivating the dialectic in a manner that does not allow the discipline of the party to interfere with their individual freedom. The Communist parties—whether of the left or of the right—do not seem to have moved very far towards their goal of welding together 'the organic intellectuals ... and the traditional intellectuals'.

It is doubtful if even the modest intellectual life of the Communist parties can survive if the universities decay and disintegrate. If Marxism as a system of living ideas has found a place anywhere in India, it is in the universities rather than in the parties. The fact that this goes against one of the most cherished prejudices of the very people by whom it is kept alive should not be allowed to obscure the real contributions they make to the intellectual resources of their community.

In the modern age intellectual activity itself has acquired such a character that it has become increasingly difficult for the single individual to seriously pursue it on his own, in isolation from others. There is first of all the division of labour in the 'arts and sciences' to which economists, historians and sociologists have drawn attention from the end of the eighteenth century onwards. There is also the prevailing ideology of the age which frowns upon the 'ivory-tower intellectual' and favours a closer and more self-conscious link than was required in earlier ages between intellectual activity and collective life.

At the same time, the institutional setting required for the proper performance of intellectual activities in the modern world has not grown in countries like India; or, having grown for a brief span, it is now threatened with decay and disintegration. The confusion, disorder and unrest in India's colleges and universities are too well known to require detailed exposition; and some have begun to wonder whether these institutions, of alien inspiration as they are, have any future at all in the country. But we have to view things in perspective: the same doubt can now be expressed about a whole range of 'new' institutions whose continued existence we took for granted in 1950. It is true that India's universities do not function as universities were once supposed to function, but then neither do its legislative and judicial institutions always function as they ought to; and India's parties certainly do not function as parties are supposed to function.

It is not easy to acknowledge in one's own society the fragility of the institutional basis of so many activities without which no society can survive in the modern world. We tend to assign a particular cause—usually in the form of a particular weakness of character—each time we are confronted with breakdown in a particular institutional area. The politician blames the academic for his apathy; the academic blames the bureaucrat for his careerism; the bureaucrat blames the politician for his venality; and each one feels that he can do the other's job rather better, and gives free advice accordingly.

It is both a symptom of our lack of confidence in an institution and a source of its weakness that the division of labour appropriate to it is persistently disregarded. In India's institutions of higher learning there is an almost wilful confusion of academic, administrative and political functions. Academic success leads to administrative responsibility rapidly and almost inescapably, thus terminating academic achievement prematurely. Discharging the responsibilities of academic office requires not so much the use of administrative abilities as the deployment of political skills and resources. It is not as if academics do not engage in administration or in politics in countries like Britain and America; but the individual academic there has a measure of choice which is not available to the Indian if he is to succeed—or even survive—in the academic jungle.

A striking feature of India's academic institutions, and one which has contributed greatly to the disorder and confusion in them, is their recent rapid increase in numbers. It is as if we were determined to make good the weakness in their quality by multiplying their quantity. The number of universities, institutions deemed to be universities, autonomous and semi-autonomous laboratories, institutes of advanced study and centres of research has grown at a breathtaking pace since Independence. On the surface there might appear to be some kind of attempt at institutional innovation; but in effect there is very little genuine innovation. Either a new university decides to call its departments 'centres' and its faculties 'schools', or a new institute of research starts with a formal structure copied from some institute in England or America; in either case it takes only five to ten years for the familiar pattern to establish itself in the newly-created institution.

Two things happen when an academic system embarks on a course of reckless expansion. First, no particular institution is given the time to prove itself to be deserving of permanent or even long-term attention; it is nurtured for a brief span, and, when it fails to deliver the goods, resources and talents are made to flow into a new institution. Secondly, there is the chronic dependence of these institutions, initially for their expansion and then for their survival, on the government or other fund-giving agencies; as a result, within the academic institution itself, academic abilities are subordinated to administrative, entrepreneurial and political skills.

In order to create a social setting appropriate to intellectual activity it is not enough to have an organizational plan, as is required for building a factory. A university or a school is not a factory, and nothing could be more crass than to regard it as one.

If the university is to be a proper setting for intellectual activity it must become an institution; and an institution cannot be conjured into existence by either the planner's blueprint or the politician's slogan. An institution cannot simply be set up from the outside to be put at the disposal of anyone who might require its services; it has to be created by the people who themselves need to use it for their own fulfilment. It is in the very nature of an institution that there cannot be a recipe for creating one. It takes not only resources to build an institution, but also patience and care. Above all, we must pay heed to the dignity of institutions; for an institution, like an individual, requires not only a certain material base, but also a certain dignity for its health and wellbeing.

Notes

1. Mannheim seems to use the two terms interchangeably; see below.

2. The phrase is taken from Alfred Weber.

3. Compare Kolakowski's observation: 'Gramsci used the term "intellectuals" in a wide sense, practically equivalent to "intelligentsia" or the whole educated class' (Kolakowski) 1978: 240.

4. The eighteenth century was a period of general stagnation and decline in the universities in England, more marked in Oxford than in Cambridge.

5. For a highly readable account by a journalist see Jungk 1965.

6. There is a vast literature on the pleasures of Oxford and Cambridge. For a recent personal account by a social scientist who passed through both, see Hudson 1976: chapters 2, 3.

7. As a distinguished South American economist has written: 'Students, in fact, live in an intellectual community in which the role of the teacher is practically nil, but where books and ideas are passed around and minds opened to intellectual influences ... What matters is that students should have access to information and live in a community that is open to discussion.' (Furtado, 1973: 31)

References

Béteille, André. 1969. 'The Politics of "Non-antagonistic" Strata', *Contributions to Indian Sociology*, New Series, no. III.

—— 1974. 'Institutes of Research in India', *International Social Science Journal*, vol. XXVI, no. 1

Coser, Lewis. 1970. *Men of Ideas: A Sociologist's View*. New York: The Free Press.

Furtado, Celso. 1973. 'Adventures of a Brazilian Economist', *International Social Science Journal*, vol. XXV, nos 1–2.

Gerth, H.H. and C.W. Mills (eds). 1948. *From Max Weber: Essays in Sociology*. London: Routledge and Kegan Paul.

Glezerman, G. 1971. *Socialist Society: Scientific Principles of Development*. Moscow: Progress Publishers.

Gramsci, Antonio. 1971. *Selections from Prison Notebooks*. London: Lawrence & Wishart.

Hudson, Liam. 1976. *The Cult of the Fact*. London: Jonathan Cape.

Jungk, Robert. 1965. *Brighter than a Thousand Suns*. Harmondsworth: Penguin Books.

Kolakowski, Lezzek. 1978. *Main Currents of Marxism*. Oxford: Clarendon Press, vol. 3.

Lévi-Strauss, Claude. 1966. *The Savage Mind*. London: Weidenfeld & Nicolson.

Mannheim, Karl. 1960. *Ideology and Utopia*. London: Routledge and Kegan Paul.

Marx, Karl. 1974. *Capital*. Moscow: Progress Publishers, vol. I.

Marx, Karl and Frederick Engels. 1968. *The German Ideology*. Moscow: Progress Publishers.

Weber, Max, 1948. 'Science as Vocation', in Gerth and Mills (eds), *From Max Weber: Essays in Sociology*. London: Routledge and Kegan Paul.

Wesolowski, S. 1979. *Classes, Strata and Power*. London: Routledge and Kegan Paul.

4

Secularism and the Intellectuals*

The idea of secularism, like the idea of equality, is equivocal and at the same time inexhaustible. Particularly in India, secularism has come to mean different, even contradictory, things to different persons, and some have begun to believe that we should, in the interest of intellectual clarity, stop using the term altogether. But that is a counsel of despair, for the word has now become a part of not only our common vocabulary but also our Constitution. Besides, as the analogy with equality should remind us, it is not always a disadvantage when a term that represents both a concept and an ideal carries more than one meaning. It is the very ambiguity of the idea that makes it inexhaustible as a challenge and an opportunity for human beings.

The idea of secularism is ambiguous because secularism is not something out there, fully formed only awaiting description and analysis, but something that people strive for and, now it increasingly appears, also strive against. Where intellectuals are so strongly committed, one way or the other, about something that is itself in a state of flux, it is perhaps natural that they should misread the signals in ways that confirm their hopes or dispel their fears. But of course hopes and fears act in very complex ways in shaping concepts and giving direction to arguments relating to human affairs.

The recognition of the ambiguities inherent in ideas such as equality or secularism should not be taken as a licence to define terms and concepts according to our will and pleasure. The term secularism may be given more than one meaning, but not an infinity of meanings. I

* Originally published in *Economic and Political Weekly*, vol. 29, no. 10, 1994. I am grateful to Professor M.N. Srinivas for reading the paper and advising me on its publication.

shall be concerned in what follows with the meanings of a few related terms.

What makes the idea of secularism ambiguous is that a discussion of it involves questions of value as well as of fact. But the values we have to contend with are not merely the values of those remote and unknown persons about whom we write—the objects of our sociological investigations—but also our own values as well as the values of others like ourselves against whom we, as sociologists, argue. Naturally, all this makes the demands of objectivity more difficult to satisfy, but it does not make them more easily dispensable.

Since I write as a sociologist, I have to state that my view of sociology is that it requires as clear a separation as possible between empirical questions ('is' questions, or questions relating to facts, including the values that we seek to investigate as facts) and normative questions ('ought' questions, or questions relating to our own preferences among existing states of affairs, actual or possible) (Béteille 1992). While this is in my view desirable in every case and relatively easy in some cases, it is extremely difficult, though never impossible, in others. Where the separation of empirical from normative questions is particularly difficult, it is best for the sociologist to declare as clearly as possible where his own preferences lie so that even if he fails to keep apart what ought to be kept apart, his readers will know where to look for the bias in his statements.

I should state without further ceremony that my own bias, both as an intellectual and as a person, is for secularism. There are many reasons for this among which I would like to draw attention to only one. I am convinced that there exists a close affinity between secularism as a general orientation to the world and sociology as an intellectual discipline. Even a cursory examination of the history of the discipline will show that this is true (Evans-Pritchard 1965: chapter 3). It is not that the world does not reveal its meaning unless it is seen from the sociological point of view. Who can deny the value of the insights reached by the poet, the mystic or the theologian? But if there is anything distinctive in the sociological understanding of religion—or politics, or any other aspect of the human condition—it is the secular foundation of that understanding.

Religion is an important subject, and it has received the attention of a variety of intellectual disciplines: theology, philosophy, sociology, and so on. The theologian is concerned in a very important way with the truth of religious beliefs and the efficacy of religious practices; it would be hard for him to take the view that all religions are of equal value. The sociologist, on the other hand, takes the different religions as he finds them, and it is not his task to decide whether one religion is superior to another. The sociological perspective on religion is the perspective of someone who observes, describes, compares and contrasts from the outside rather than from within any given religious faith: it is a secular perspective (Béteille 1992). Therefore I find it strange for a sociologist to say that we should turn away from secularism or that we should put secularism in its place.

I must insist that the affinity between the sociological method and a secular orientation need not determine the conclusions reached by a secular-minded sociologist regarding the actual state of affairs, including the actual place of religion, in any society, including his own. However greatly such a sociologist may value secularism, he cannot tailor the evidence to declare that secularism is advancing when in fact it is declining. It is true that some sociologists may through an excess of enthusiasm give more weight to evidence of the advance than of the decline of secularism, but there is nothing in the method that compels him to reach a conclusion towards which his own inclination as a person may tempt him.

The idea of secularism has lost some of its shine in the years since independence among the Indian intelligentsia who were its principal if not sole proponents in the country. It has taken some particularly hard knocks in the last five years or so. Secularism had become a shibboleth in Nehru's India, and it is the intellectual's obligation to bring every shibboleth under scrutiny.

What we are witnessing today is a little more than the normal intellectual scrutiny to which every received opinion must be submitted. There has been a decided change in the political environment, and the current intellectual revaluation of secularism is partly a symptom and partly a consequence of this change. Some at least of the intellectuals who had taken secularism for granted two or three decades ago have begun to look at the idea more closely, and now they find it wanting. I mention this not in order to point to one or another intellectual in particular, but to draw attention to what I believe to be a significant change in our intellectual environment. There is no doubt that the conscious promotion of secularism as an ideal is largely the work of intellectuals; but its social critique is also the work of intellectuals.

Surely, an intellectual has a right to change course in regard to secularism (or any other ideal or value), but he must then ask what his own life—as economist or historian, or sociologist—would have been without the support of secular institutions.

Our two leading sociologists have recently expressed themselves either negatively or in sceptical terms about secularism and its prospects in India. In an article published in *The Times of India* on 9 July 1993, Professor M.N. Srinivas called for a new philosophy for India to meet its recurrent social and political crises. 'And that philosophy', he stated, 'cannot be secular humanism. It has to be firmly rooted in God as creator and protector, and the sustainer of human societies.' In a similar tone, Professor T.N. Madan has observed, 'Now, I submit that in the prevailing circumstances secularism in South Asia as a generally shared credo of life is impossible, as a basis for state action impracticable, and as a blueprint for the foreseeable future impotent' (Madan 1987: 748).

Those who now view secularism with an increasingly critical eye are often inclined to regard it as an artefact if not a particular vice of the intellectuals. I am not talking about persons with a political purpose or agenda but about those who are themselves intellectuals. Srinivas (1993) puts secularists, rationalists and unbelievers in the same basket, and draws attention to the fact that although they constitute a very small minority they are able to maintain a high public profile. 'Intellectuals in the academia, media and the bureaucracy are the pillars of rationalism, and they enjoy the support of the communist parties even though the latter have recently discovered religion.'

T.N. Madan sees secularism as not just the creation but the imposition—or the attempted imposition—of a small modernizing minority over the rest of Indian society. 'Secularism is the dream of a minority which wants to shape the majority in its own image, which wants to impose its will upon history but lacks the power to do so under a democratically organized polity' (1987: 748). Madan is a critic of modernity, and he appears to hold secularism responsible for disrupting the integrity, the unity and the wholeness of the traditional world. He believes that secularism was the outcome of a historical change in the intellectual climate in the west, and that the attempt to adapt it to the Indian environment is a snare and a delusion.

While it is true that its secular character was explicitly confirmed by the forty-fourth amendment in 1976, the Indian Constitution was from its inception secular rather than religious in its basic framework. It did not adopt a hostile attitude to religion as such or to any religion in particular, but, rather, sought to give equal protection to all religions within the framework of the rule of law. The final appeal in it is to a structure of impersonal rules rather than to any religious authority. In that sense the Constitution is both 'rationalist' and 'modernist', not only in regard to secularism but also in regard to equality and liberty. It cannot be too strongly emphasized that the Constitution of India makes a departure from tradition in its stress not only on secularism but also on equality and liberty.

Now, it may be argued that the Constitution as a whole, with its stress on equality, liberty, secularism and so on is the artefact of a minority determined to impose its will on the people of India whose concerns are of a very different nature from the ones embodied in it. It is certainly true that those who wrote India's Constitution did not constitute an average of the Indian population in any statistical sense of the term. At the same time, it would be safe to say that though a minority and in no real sense an average of the Indian population, those who wrote that Constitution were more representative of it than the authors of the *Dharmashastra*. It would be peevish to find fault with a Constitution or a plan for a new way of life on the ground that it is the work of intellectuals who constitute a miniscule minority.

Nor is it reasonable to denigrate a Constitution on the ground that many of its basic components have had their origin in traditions other than our own. Surely, the test of an idea or an institution should be its capacity to meet our present needs and not its provenance. If an idea or an institution is unable to meet our present requirements, it should be discarded, whether it has come from outside or emerged from within. Just as we should not hesitate to reject something from our own past that has now become anachronistic, so too we should not hesitate to accept something from another part of the contemporary world that is well suited to our present requirement: geography can never be a decisive test of the social value of an idea or an institution. No civilization has ever prospered either by holding on to every idea and institution inherited from the past or by completely insulating itself from all that is exogenous. It is an anthropological truism that a culture that fails to borrow useful arts from other cultures and adapt them to its own requirements becomes stagnant and ossified.

Intellectuals can be easily unsettled by being called rootless, particularly if they see themselves as being socially committed. Epithets such as 'cosmopolitan' and 'rootless intellectual' do more than merely damage the self-esteem and the self-confidence of those who seek to espouse and promote new ideas and institutions. They have been in our time used with devastating effect to silence and torment numberless persons. The miniscule minority of Indian intellectuals who have questioned settled traditions from a secular point of view have, at least in recent decades, sailed fairly smoothly; they should not be too surprised if they face rough weather in the years ahead.

Intellectual issues cannot be settled with reference to majorities and minorities. Intellectuals, or at least those who function as intellectuals, are always in a minority in every society. The proponents of secularism, in so far as they are intellectuals, are in a minority. But the critics of secularism, to the extent that their critique has an intellectual content, are also a minority. That should not matter very much because in India today it is still possible for both sides to sit together and decide where they agree and where they disagree; and where their disagreement is over ideas and values, and where it is over words only.

The discussion of the subject under consideration has been marked by a certain profusion of words, and, particularly in India, by their unlicensed, not to say promiscuous, use. Professor Madan (1994) has rightly drawn attention to the great confusion that is caused by the cavalier use of words such as 'secular', 'secularization' and 'secularism'. I would have preferred to avoid 'secularism', for the suffix here—as in terms such as Marxism, modernism, rationalism, empiricism, structuralism, feminism, and so on—tends to convey a doctrinaire tone, and it should be possible to argue the case for secular ideas and institutions without adopting a doctrinaire standpoint. However, the term has acquired such wide currency that it would be futile to attempt its exclusion.

It would be useful to distinguish between a social process that unfolds itself on its own, as it were, without being driven by any overall plan or design, and an ideology that some members of society strive consciously to espouse and promote. If we look at secularization in Indian society with this distinction in mind, it will be obvious that not all of it has been the work of a minority of intellectuals determined to impose their will on the unsuspecting masses of people. Such secularization as has taken place in India in the last hundred years has been only partly a matter of conscious or directed social change; a great deal of it has come about without any conscious direction. If secularism is an ideology, then secularization is not the outcome of that ideology alone, but of a variety of material forces in addition. Intellectuals should not overestimate their capacity to either advance or impede the course of secularization, for, although consciously-designed ideologies do contribute something to social change, they do not contribute everything.

One might argue that it should be possible in principle to give an account of secularization as a social process without entering into the merits of secularism as an ideology. In practice, it would be extremely difficult to keep judgements of value separate from judgements of fact in such an account. Everyone will agree that secularization, to the extent that it is taking place in contemporary India, does not follow a single, uniform course. There are currents as well as countercurrents. The reach and depth of the process cannot be accurately measured. The evidence is often fragmentary, and the fragments do not all point in the same direction. Where the facts are nebulous or unclear, one must take recourse to judgements, and these judgements are bound to be coloured, at least to some extent, by the values of the investigator. Therefore, it is unlikely that the partisans for secularism and their opponents will reach the same conclusions regarding the extent or the causes of secularization.

To draw attention to the difficulties we face in seeking objective accounts of the process of secularization is not to suggest that we can dispense with such accounts, or that those that exist are of no objective value. The best sociological account of secularization is in my belief still the one we find in Srinivas's (1966) Tagore lectures delivered thirty years ago. Here we get a finely-balanced account of a complex and many-sided process in which the temptation to dwell on one single current (or source) is studiously resisted. Nowhere are we given to believe that secularization is solely or even mainly the work of a miniscule minority of intellectuals. That would in fact be quite out of tune with Srinivas's general approach as a sociologist in which no large or complex process is ever explained by a single factor.

Srinivas attempts to do two things: firstly, to draw attention to the wide reach of the secularization process, and, secondly, to point to the great resilience of religious beliefs and practices in the face of that process. I believe that he is substantially right on both counts, and his contribution as a sociologist has been to show how two things that appear contradictory can nevertheless co-exist and, up to a point, even sustain one another.

What is 'secularization'? Srinivas provides an excellent working definition: 'the term "secularization" implies that what was previously regarded as religious is now ceasing to be such, and it also implies a process of differentiation which results in the various aspects of society, economic, political, legal and moral, becoming increasingly *discrete* in relation to each other' (Srinivas 1966: 119). In other words, secularization leads to changes in (a) the beliefs and practices of individuals, and (b) the nature of institutions and their mutual relations. In this definition at least, secularization does not lead to the elimination of religion, but to a state of affairs in which some ideas, practices and institutions cease to be regulated by religion. There is nothing in principle to prevent what is due to religion being at the same time more strongly acknowledged in other spheres of life that are outside the reach of secularization. After all, the strength of human sentiment and obligation is to be judged not solely by their extent but also by their intensity.

Srinivas rightly draws attention to the fact that secularization is a universal tendency and contrasts it with its more restricted counterpart in India, Sanskritization. 'Of the two, secularization is the more general process, affecting all Indians, while Sanskritization affects only Hindus and tribal groups' (1966: 118). He also associates secularization with westernization. Although the historical linkage between the two is obvious in India, it may not be wholly satisfactory to maintain as a principle that 'secularization is subsumed under Westernization' (ibid.). To take only one example, the United Kingdom is not a secular state, whereas China is, so that in at least one important respect, secularization has not gone as far in a western country as in a non-western one.

The realization that secularization is a universal tendency of the modern world should lead to the recognition of the many different forces and factors that work towards its growth and expansion. These forces and factors are not all equally active everywhere, and they have not all been at work for the same length of time everywhere. The range and depth of secularization vary from one country to another, and, within the same country, from one segment of the population to another, and this probably is how it will always be. The idea that secularization will inevitably shape every society in a single mould cannot be taken seriously from the sociological point of view.

Even a casual examination of the world as it is will show that nowhere has secularism led to the disappearance of religious beliefs, practices and institutions. Wherever an attempt has been made to use a doctrinaire secularism to eliminate religion—as in the USSR under Stalin or China under MaoTse-tung—it has proved to be a costly folly. But just as it has proved futile to use a militant secularism to drive out religious beliefs and practices, so also will it prove futile in the modern world to use religious ideology to drive out secular ideas and institutions. It is, I believe, a sociological truism that no modern society can as a whole afford to dispense with *either* secular ideas and institutions *or* religious beliefs and practices.

Srinivas draws attention not only to the many forces and factors behind secularization but also to its uneven development in Indian society. He notes in particular that 'Hindus were more affected by the secularization process that any other religious group'. Further, 'Different sections among the Hindus are affected in different degree by it ...' (1966: 119). He suggests that there are certain institutional features of Hinduism that make the progress of secularization easier among Hindus than among other religious groups. He was not the first to be struck by a kind of elective affinity between Hinduism, pluralism and secularism.

Of course, Indian society is not the same thing as Hindu society, and this makes it essential to begin with the changes in the external material conditions of existence that facilitate the advance of secularization among all Indians, irrespective of their religious faith. It is another matter that some of the forces and factors that work towards secularization serve also to give a new lease of life to certain religious practices. The development of transport and communication tends inevitably to weaken the rules of purity and pollution, but it also facilitates the activities of pilgrimage. It is to be regretted that few sociologists have followed the lead given by Srinivas in uncovering the details of this complex dialectic.

The massive growth of technology, the emergence of far-flung organizations for the production and distribution of goods and services and the expansion of administrative bureaucracies based on impersonal rules lead to the decline of many ritual observances, but they need not lead to the decline of all religious beliefs and values. When one speaks of secularization as a universal tendency, it is above all these external material forces and factors that one has in mind. But even here, it is most unlikely that every country will have the same technology, the same economic arrangements and the same structures of administration. It is true that all these things influence religious observances, but that is far from saying that religious ideas and values are determined by them.

How we view the prospects for the co-existence of religious and secular ways of life will depend in part on how we think of religion. It is possible, at least in principle, to define religion in such strictly doctrinaire terms as to either exclude or devalue every belief and practice that is secular in the sense of being non-religious; that would be a holistic definition of religion, more in favour among theologians than among the pious and the devout. What causes the most anxiety to secular intellectuals is a conception of religion which demands that every aspect of every individual's life be brought under religious scrutiny and control. But that is an extreme position, and few major religions have adopted it consistently or except in conditions of great internal crisis.

Again, one might view religion mainly in terms of ritual. No sociologist can deny the social significance of ritual, and, indeed, from the sociological point of view, a religion without ritual is as difficult to think about as a society without religion. At the same time, the place of ritual in the religious life is highly variable and subject to change over time. Secularization does bring about an attenuation of ritual practices, and those who are strict in their adherence to ritual may well regard this as a threat to religion itself, but when we view the matter in the light of comparative sociology, the threat appears largely illusory.

Srinivas has traced the course of secularization through changes in the rites and ceremonies of the Hindus. His first and most important observation is about practices relating to purity and pollution which occupied an important place in Hindu religion and society. 'The notion of pollution and purity has both weakened and become less pervasive in the last few decades as a result of the forces already mentioned' (1966: 122). The evidence of subsequent studies mostly points in the same direction. But this kind of evidence of 'secularization' still leaves open a fundamental question about the Hindu religion. Some would say that it has weakened Hinduism, although others, following Vivekananda or even Gandhi, might argue that it provides a more secure basis for the renewal of Hinduism.

Birth, marriage and death continue to be important religious occasions for Hindus, although changes are taking place in their modes of observance. The evidence seems to suggest some abbreviation of traditional rites, particularly for birth and marriage, and a certain shift in the balance between the 'religious' and the 'social' components of the observance. Srinivas remarks, 'The wedding reception is a recent institution—the word "reception" has passed into Kannada—and its great popularity is one of the many pointers to the increased secularization of Brahminical life and culture' (1966: 126). It is true that many ceremonies are now acquiring a different focus, but if this indicates 'secularization', that does not mean that it is necessarily at odds with religion.

One can find innumerable examples of the manner in which old elements are discarded and new ones incorporated in the life-cycle ceremonies and calendric festivals of Hindus—and to some extent other religious groups as well—all over India. Some of these new elements are by any definition 'secular', but there are new religious elements as well. This makes it extremely difficult to identify a single or uniform tendency in the transformation of the religious practices of the Hindus. While providing many examples of secularization, Srinivas rightly points out, 'It is easy, however, to exaggerate this increase in the secularization of village life' (1966: 137).

I would like to draw attention here to two important tendencies, although they are both extremely difficult to interpret. The first is the redefinition of religious occasions as 'social' occasions, and the second is the elimination of magical elements from traditional religious observances. Both are conventionally regarded as aspects of secularization.

In dealing with religious observances, we have to take into account not only what people do but also the meanings they assign to their actions. In the city of Calcutta, middle-class Bengalis, including prominent left intellectuals, celebrate Durgapuja with great pomp and ceremony, and almost certainly on a larger scale than in the nineteenth century. However, some of them at least point out that Durgapuja is a social occasion which enables people to recover their spirits, to renew their ties with relatives, friends and neighbours, and to replenish their wardrobes. This is indeed true. But a religious festival is and always has been a social occasion, everywhere and among all religious groups, though perhaps more conspicuously among Hindus and Catholics than some others.

It can safely be said that many elements of belief and practice came to be lodged in Hinduism—as also, for example, in Catholicism—that are better described as magical than religious. The distinction between religion and magic is of very great importance for sociological understanding. Every major student of the subject—Weber (1963), Durkheim (1915), Malinowski (1972), Radcliffe-Brown (1952) and many others—has addressed himself to the problem. It is true that a clear line has been very difficult to draw between magic and religion, but their distinction must be kept in mind in any serious consideration of secularization. If we then regard secularization as in part a process that leads to the elimination of magical elements from religion—or at least their reduction (Thomas 1971)—then the relationship between religion and secularization might appear in a somewhat different light.

Now, one might argue that many if not most of the practices associated with pollution and purity belong to Hindu magic rather than Hindu religion. Indeed, it may not be too fanciful to suggest that Vivekananda, or even Gandhi, would accept such an argument. The question that then arises is whether the reduction of those magical elements that is both directly and indirectly a consequence of secularization leads to the weakening or the strengthening of Hinduism. I will take only two examples to show how complex and at the same time how intriguing these questions are. Brahmin women were not allowed to enter the kitchen during their monthly periods, and untouchables were debarred from entry into the major Hindu temples. The weakening of these restrictions and the magical beliefs on which they mainly rested are undoubtedly linked with the process of secularization. Can we say that it has only a negative implication for the Hindu religion?

Secularization has other consequences besides the erosion of magical beliefs and practices, and I would now like to turn to the one that I consider to be the most interesting from the sociological point of view: I mean the slow, gradual and laborious process of the emergence of institutions that can only be described as secular in the sense that they are not significantly regulated by ideas, beliefs and practices associated with any of the traditional religions, such as Hinduism, Christianity and Islam.

I would like to return to that part of Srinivas's definition of secularization that relates it to the differentiation of institutions and their increasing autonomy. The differentiation of society, the growth of new institutions and their increasing autonomy is a long-term tendency of universal significance (Luhmann 1982), and in that respect secular in more than one sense of the term. I maintain that the growth of secular institutions such as universities, laboratories, hospitals, banks and so on, and their insulation from religion (and the state) are an important part of secularization, no matter how we define the term, and I find it difficult to understand why Indian intellectuals should view this tendency with antipathy.

I would like to dwell a little on universities and colleges as examples of the kind of secular institutions that I believe have an important part to play in the Indian society of the present as well as the future. These are the institutions that I know well from personal experience and also the ones in whose present and future well-being I have a special personal interest. My own experiences and observations relate particularly to the University of Calcutta where I was a student and the University of Delhi where I have taught for many years, each of which was in its time the leading university in the country.

The modern Indian university is in principle, and by and large also in practice, a secular institution. It is in principle also an autonomous institution. This means that it is free to organize its principal internal activities, namely, teaching and research, without regulation by religious authorities or by the state. The university is free to teach (or not teach) religious subjects such as Buddhist Studies or Islamic Studies. Academic work in those subjects, where they exist, is organized in roughly the same way and presumably in the same spirit as academic work in any other subject. There is no requirement that religious subjects should be placed on a higher or even a different plane than subjects such as physics, economics and sociology.

Theology was a subject of central importance in the medieval universities of Oxford and Cambridge which were not secular institutions in our sense of the term. Theology is still taught in these universities, but they do not enjoy pre-eminence any longer. In the United States, theology (or divinity) is taught in 'private' universities such as Harvard. But it is not taught in state universities such as the University of California at Berkeley, presumably because the state should not compromise its secular standing by encouraging the promotion of religious doctrine, although there is no bar on teaching and research in such academic subjects as 'history of religions' and 'comparative religion'.

Some European universities maintain religious functionaries, such as chaplains, on their payrolls, although with secularization their functions have become greatly attenuated. Maintaining religious functionaries on the payroll of the university would be an anachronism in Delhi and, so far as I am aware, in Indian universities generally. The Indian universities of today are modern and not medieval foundations, and they were designed by and large to be secular institutions from the beginning. This was not true of the medieval foundations of Cambridge, Oxford and Paris which were not only centres of theological learning but also actively implicated—Paris in particular—in the affairs of the Christian church. The European universities have undergone a long and laborious process of secularization, but some of the vestiges of their original condition remain.

The secular constitution of the University of Delhi[1] is plainly manifest in its Foundation Act of 1922. The Act makes it unlawful for the university to 'adopt or impose on any person any test whatever of religious belief or profession'. At the same time, the Act does not debar the university from providing religious instruction to those who desire to secure it. On the whole, the university has at least until now been remarkably free from the rancour caused by religious disagreement.

The Indian university is a secular institution in the further sense that individuals have equal opportunities to find places in the faculty and student bodies irrespective of religion, caste or creed. This is ensured by Section 6 of the Act of 1922 which says that the university 'shall be open to all persons of either sex and of whatever race, creed or class'. This is very different from past practice at Oxford and Cambridge which until the middle of the nineteenth century excluded Dissenters, Jews and followers of other religious faiths, requiring their members to subscribe formally to the Thirty-nine Articles of the Church of England. In Delhi, one can be an orthodox Sunni or an orthodox Sanatani and still find a place, by virtue of academic merit, as a student or a teacher in the university without prejudice to one's personal religious faith; it goes without saying that one is also free to be an atheist.

Indian academics place a high value on the autonomy of the university and are rightly concerned about threats to it. So far, they have seen the threats as coming mainly from the state and its organs, particularly the funding agencies. But in other places at other times, the religious hierarchy has presented an equally formidable threat to the autonomy of the university. I have already alluded to the surveillance maintained over university affairs in England first by the Catholic and then by the Anglican clergy. In our own time, the Shi'ite clergy have sought to maintain the same kind of control over the universities in Iran.

In my experience of university life in India, whether in Delhi or elsewhere, questions relating to religious faith or affiliation do not play a very important part either in the classroom or outside it. I have in my long experience of the Indian university, first as a student and then as a teacher, never felt threatened and rarely embarrassed for not belonging to the right religious group or to any religious group. I have tutored and supervised hundreds of students for more than thirty years, and they have come to me with all kinds of problems, including some very peculiar personal problems, but I have rarely felt that a student was troubled because of his religious faith or his religious affiliation by something that was happening within the university. I find it hard to imagine that such freedom from constraint could exist in a non-secular university by which I mean a university constituted according to Hindu or Islamic or Christian principles.

It is in this institutional context that the presence of the Aligarh Muslim University and the Benaras Hindu University might appear somewhat anomalous in contemporary India. To be sure, Paris was a Catholic university and Al Azhar a Muslim university, and they were flourishing institutions in the Middle Ages. But my feeling is that the time for such institutions is now long past, and I am not sure how many Indian intellectuals, including those who would like to see the drift towards secularization reversed, would welcome the replacement of the modern secular university by medieval religious ones in India.

The secular foundations of everyday activity that are characteristic of the Indian university may also be found, with appropriate variations, in a whole range of other institutions, such as laboratories, hospitals, banks, and so on. I would like to refer back yet again to Srinivas's observations about the growth of differentiation and autonomy than mark the progress of secularization. Each one of the institutions referred to above is governed by the rules of its own specialized practice—scientific practice, medical practice, or financial practice, as the case may be. These rules have no intrinsic relationship with those of any particular religion, or religion in general. To be sure, the former need not be contradictory to the latter, but nothing is gained for either religious faith or secular practice by trying to bring laboratories, hospitals or banks in line with the doctrines of one or another of the great religions.

Of course, it can be said that a hospital must constantly attend to questions of life and death, of suffering, pain and healing, and these have been of central concern also to every great religion. Nothing could be more foolish than for modern medical science to pretend that it knows all the answers to these questions. But it knows some of the answers and it can perhaps attend to a few of them a little more effectively than any other available agency. The important point is that what a hospital is able to do, it must be allowed to do on its own terms, and not on terms set down for it by some other kind of agency laying claim to a superior understanding of the fundamental questions of life and death.

The work of a modern hospital, whether in India or France, would be seriously jeopardized if questions of religious faith or affiliation were allowed to enter significantly into the day-to-day relations among doctors, patients, nurses and others. Ordinarily, one would expect to find in any large hospital in India, members of various religious groups among both doctors and patients. I believe that, like the universities, public hospitals are debarred from restricting the recruitment of doctors as well as the admission of patients on grounds of religious affiliation. It is true that there are hospitals that are funded and managed by religious bodies, but these are the exceptions that prove the rule, for even in them the content of medical practice and the nature of doctor–patient relations remain basically secular as in hospitals of the ordinary kind.

I have space here only to mention the variety of institutions, organizations and agencies associated with the expansion of the market on the one hand and of governance on the other. For all the sins that may be attributed to it, capitalism pays little attention to the distinctions of religion. It is true that those who operate capitalist enterprises frequently take advantage of the ties of religion (or other pre-existing social ties), but they do so in the pursuit of economic and not religious ends. To be sure, capitalism is not the only possible economic arrangement, but it is difficult to see how any alternative arrangement to it can be devised which reintroduces a basically religious orientation in all its multifarious activities and at the same time remains economically efficient.

In India, when intellectuals are not complaining about the market, they are complaining about the bureaucracy. Bureaucracy is an ugly word, a bad name for a kind of administrative arrangement that has become an ubiquitous feature of all modern societies. Its essential task is to provide a continuous organization of official functions in accordance with impersonal rules. It is true that this kind of organization is in practice easily perverted, and it is possible that future generations will devise more humane and at the same time more efficient arrangements for the discharge of official functions or learn to live altogether without them. But as things stand in present-day India, the alternative to bureaucracy in administration—the system it is struggling to replace and which constantly threatens to choke it—is patrimonialism.

Patrimonialism may not have any intrinsic connection with religious belief and practice, but historically it has been the characteristic administrative arrangement in a world permeated by religion. It would be difficult to assert that religion had necessarily a deeper hold in that kind of society, but it was almost certainly more widely (if also more thinly) spread across a variety of institutional domains. This is as one would expect in a society that has not to any significant degree undergone secularization in the sense given to it by Srinivas. It is only with the institutional differentiation brought about by secularization that administrative institutions can secure this autonomy from the prevalent beliefs and practices.

I have tried in the foregoing to give some idea of the implications of secularization in India and in general. There are two points that need to be kept in mind while considering the observations made above and the ones that are to follow. Firstly, the course of secularization is by no means an even one, and its success, whether desirable or otherwise, is by no means guaranteed for any society, certainly not the one in which we live today. Secondly, although secularization leads necessarily to the withdrawal of religion from certain areas of life, it does not lead to its disappearance or elimination, but may in fact give it a sharper focus, at least in some areas of life.

I have spoken at some length about secularization and about secular institutions, but have stepped lightly over 'secularism'. I must now address it directly. I have already indicated my discomfort over words that end with 'ism': *The Shorter Oxford English Dictionary* suggests that when applied to a doctrine, theory or practice, it is 'chiefly disparaging'. But as I have already said, apart from becoming a part of our common vocabulary, it has entered our Constitution, in a positive sense, and we have to consider whether it can at all be given a reasonable and acceptable meaning at least to some extent consistent with our present experience and future expectations.

From my description of the process of secularization and the constitution of secular institutions, it might appear that there is really nothing very much in them to which a reasonable person might object. Most such persons can be expected to concede that at least some secular institutions may be not only necessary but also desirable. I know very few intellectuals who would prefer a non-secular university to a secular one, or a non-secular press to a secular one. Why then would they balk at 'secularism'?

Although secular ideas and institutions tend to have a bias for moderation, secularism can be turned into a doctrine and an ideology, and, as a doctrine and an ideology, it has had its partisans and militants. Doctrinaire secularists have often taken a perverse pleasure in exposing and attacking all the elements of magic and superstition with which practically every great religion has been replete. And they have frequently done this in a manifestly biased way, singling out one religion as the target of their most vehement attacks, while showing an indulgent attitude towards others. As I have tried to argue, the attack on religion is not a requirement of the attachment to secular ideas and institutions; it can rarely, if ever, be even-handed; and it has led to the unfortunate belief that militant secularists are only communalists in disguise.

One of the peculiarities of secular intellectuals in India has been their general inability to accept the idea that religious believers can also be intellectuals. All intellectuals are for them, or the vast majority of them, by definition and without question, secular intellectuals. And yet, how can one deny that Shankaracharya and Thomas Aquinas, to take only two examples, were men of outstanding intellectual power? A hundred years of sociological study has shown beyond any doubt that the conception of religion as false consciousness is not only perverse but also childishly simple-minded. And yet, that conception dies hard among India's secular intellectuals.

The problem with religious beliefs, from the secular point of view, is not that they constitute false consciousness but that they require conformity to dogma. Belief and doctrine are much more closely linked in the religious than in the secular domain. The question therefore is not simply how tolerant militant secularism will be of religious beliefs and practices, but also of how much space will be allowed within society by doctrinaire religion for the growth of secular ideas and institutions. Religious beliefs tend to be not only doctrinaire but also sectarian, although it is certainly true that secular ideologies have never been fully free from doctrinaire and sectarian tendencies. It is sectarianism, historically more commonly associated with religious or pseudo-religious than with secular ideologies, that puts at risk the kind of differentiation and autonomy required by secularization.

Ecumenical movements in the present century have shown that it is indeed possible for religious ideologies to redefine themselves so as to become more accommodating towards each other and towards the secular world. It is a mistaken belief, very common among secular intellectuals in India, that only scientific ideas change and grow whereas religious ideas are condemned to remain stagnant. The great religions have everywhere and in ever-changing ways addressed themselves to the fundamental questions of birth and death, of misfortune, suffering and the renewal of life, and it is difficult to see how any kind of scientific or secular reasoning can displace religion from its own pre-eminent domain of ideas.

No matter what the ideal may be, the world we inhabit today is

Introduction

This collection deals with certain aspects of contemporary life in a sociological perspective. Although contemporary Indian society figures prominently in most if not all of the essays, they also have a more general purpose in applying and developing the concepts, methods and theories of sociology. Whatever may be the judgement on the merits of the present collection, I am convinced that the work of sociology has advanced sufficiently in this country for it to be able to make some contribution to the discipline at large. It is with this conviction that I plan to put forward before long a second collection of papers devoted to approach and method in sociology.

While the individual essays deal with a range of substantive issues, the underlying concern of the collection as a whole is with antinomies, and it is that underlying concern that gives to the book such unity as it has. By 'antinomies' I mean the contradictions, oppositions and tensions inherent in the norms and values through which societies regulate or seek to regulate themselves and continue their existence. Anyone who is engaged in the study of a complex and changing society must turn his attention, sooner or later, to these antinomies. This should not be taken to mean that an account of the norms and values of a society, no matter how detailed or exhaustive, can lead to a complete understanding of its operation; for that we need to know a great many things in addition, including the demographic, economic and other features of its morphology. But the focus of this collection is on the former and not the latter.

The antinomies of which I speak are social facts in the sense that they have social causes and social consequences, taking a variety of forms in different societies in different phases of their development. Such antinomies take their most acute forms in large and complex all of a follower's life, so that religion is constitutive of society' (Madan 1987: 751). From that point of view, the process of secularization outlined by Srinivas, with the increasing differentiation and autonomy of institutions, must indeed appear alarming. If the proponents of the religious point of view take their brief for totalizing (or religious holism) literally, religious sceptics or those with no religious attachments may, on the other hand, have serious reason to feel threatened.

In a very important sense, Madan is obviously right. The great religions such as Hinduism, Buddhism and Islam are no mere assortments of beliefs and practices relating to the sacred. Each has developed not only a system of doctrine but also a body of religious specialists whose task it has been through the ages to elaborate, systematize and rationalize the diverse elements in the religious life of the people. There is no great religion without its religious specialists, including theologians, and theologians have been notable, at least in the past, for their efforts to totalize the claims of religion.

Having granted the above, two points need to be indicated. Firstly, theology is not the whole of religion but only a part of it, and that too a highly variable part. I believe that it is notorious among those of a religious disposition that piety and devotion have not always been the strongest qualities of theologians most skilled in formulating the claims of religion in regard to the things of this world. And, surely, it is possible to consider piety and devotion as more central to religion than (*pace* Max Weber) the capacity for the construction, elaboration and systematization of the symbolic order of the scared.

Secondly, the totalizing aims to which Madan has referred vary greatly from one religion to another, and, within the same religious tradition, from one historical phase to another. Madan has gone somewhat against the current by stressing in particular the totalizing claims of South Asian religions, including Hinduism and Buddhism, whereas the conventional wisdom is to contrast the doctrinal severity of the so-called Semitic religions—Judaism, Christianity and Islam—with the more loose doctrinal texture of the eastern religions such as Hinduism, Buddhism and Confucianism. That certainly is the conclusion to be drawn from Gibbon's celebrated contrast between the ancient religions of the Romans on the one hand and Judaism, and more particularly Christianity, but also Islam, on the other (1910: vol. 2). The same point of view animates the contrast between monotheism and polytheism made by Gibbon's contemporary, the philosopher David Hume (1957, 1980).

Madan's inspiration, clearly, comes from Dumont rather than Gibbon or Hume. In recent times it is Louis Dumont who has argued with greatest force and persuasion that Indian society (or Hindu society) is the principal exemplar of holism and hierarchy in contrast with the individualism and equality characteristic of the modern west (Dumont 1966, 1977). Since I have repeatedly drawn attention to the flaws in Dumont's contrast (and in this, I believe, I have had some support from Srinivas) (Béteille 1986, 1987, 1990), I will avoid that line of debate here.

Having pointed to the provenance of Madan's sociological argument about India, I will let him speak in his own words. He draws attention to the holism characterizing the representation of Hindu society in the *Dharmashastra*. The things of this world, *artha*, are not ignored or overlooked, but they are assigned their proper and subordinate place in the larger scheme of things. 'The discrete realms of interest and power (*artha*) are opposed to and yet encompassed by *dharma*' (1987: 752). This observation may be interpreted in more than one sense, and it will be useful from the viewpoint of the sociology of religion to consider the various interpretations possible.

The observation that interest and power are opposed to *dharma* and yet encompassed by it may be interpreted in a weak sense, and such an interpretation will be suggested naturally if we adopt a broad conception of *dharma* to mean not religion in the accepted sense, but simply right conduct. If all that one means is that interest and power, however important, are distinct from a code of morality and must be regulated by it, it is difficult to see who could object to it whether from the religious or the secular point of view. It may still be important to assert that point in India today in view of the wide concern over what has come to be designated, somewhat infelicitously, as the criminalization of our economic and political life. All responsible citizens should support Professor Madan—and Mr Seshan—in reintroducing an agreed and morally-acceptable code of conduct in our economic and political life.

One can assume that agreement can be reached, at least in principle, between Hindus, Muslims, Sikhs and others about the desirability of such a moral code. Professor Madan may like to call it *dharma*, and others may call it by other names; hopefully, the secularist will also get a hearing for it should not be assumed that he is immoral as well as being irreligious. But there clearly is more to the hierarchical subordination of the secular to the religious than this, or so we may presume in view of the totalizing character that Madan attributes to the religions of South Asia. Now, it is true that many Indians, and not only Hindus, recognize *dharma* to be the kind of moral code to which they believe that interest and power should be subordinated. But they also recognize that Hindudharma is different from Islam and Christianity. It is with *dharma* as it is with 'secular'; we cannot impose upon it one single meaning to the exclusion of all others. We should keep its various meanings in mind and try as far as possible to see that they are not confused.

To be sure, religion—in the present case, the Hindu religion—is *dharma* in the sense of right conduct, duty, virtue, and everything that regulates, or ought to regulate, in accordance with moral principles of the widest amplitude, the narrow play of interest and power. But it is much more than that. It is also a large variety of beliefs and practices relating to what is considered sacred, inscrutable, inaccessible and set apart from everyday life by a community held together by those shared beliefs and practices. It would be disingenuous, particularly for the sociologist, to ignore the tremendous significance of the symbols that together give to every religious community its distinctive identity and make it different from every other community. Hinduism would not be a religion without its distinctive religious symbols; neither would Islam. The ineluctable fact is that religious symbols not only unite, they also divide. It is this that must give pause to the enthusiasm for the 'totalizing character' of religions in the face of the fact that we are all condemned to live in a world that must accommodate several religions, and not just one religion, no matter how worthy of admiration its moral code may be.

Despite the totalizing claims of each of the major religions, the co-existence of different religions with varying degrees of mutual tolerance has been a fact of historical experience, in India as well as outside. There is nothing inherent in the nature of things that guarantees the co-existence and the mutual tolerance. But if different religious communities have lived in some degree of mutual amity, however fragile or precarious, it has not been because of the totalizing claims of any one of them, but despite such claims. If the mutual amity is to be made more secure and durable, that end can be attained only by limiting and subduing the totalizing claims of every kind of ideology, whether religious or secular.

No religion ever in fact permeates or encompasses the whole of life. At least the evidence from the comparative sociology of religions does not point in that direction. Even in the simplest society there is some differentiation and autonomy of the non-religious from the religious. The hierarchical encompassment of the profane by the sacred—or the totalizing character of religion—is more an ideal than a fact of everyday experience. It is an ideal that has appealed most of all to the religious intellectual, or at least been articulated most forcefully by him.

What does it mean for the intellectual to articulate the totalizing character of religion? In the simplest terms, it means that religion must have all or it will have nothing. But that viewpoint has been invariably, and perhaps inevitably, articulated from within a particular religion and rarely if ever on behalf of religion as such or all religions collectively. It is doubtful that the totalizing claims of religion can ever be reconciled with any truly ecumenical movement among religions. Therefore, arguments put forward in the name of religious pluralism or tolerance that also assert the totalizing claims of religion or the claims of religious holism must be viewed with a large measure of scepticism.

It is not true that only religious intellectuals or theologians articulate totalizing ideological claims. Such claims may also be articulated on behalf of secular, even anti-religious, ideologies. The outstanding example in our time has been the claim articulated on behalf of Marxism by Soviet intellectuals and their counterparts outside the Soviet Union. But it is precisely this that led many external observers to characterize Soviet Marxism as a secular or a lay religion. The secular intellectual is, in my view, someone who accepts with all their implications the values of differentiation and autonomy, including the autonomy of religion within its own sphere.

My argument throughout has been that 'secularism', if we have to continue to use the term, is non-religious rather than anti-religious. It is not committed to any total or complete plan of orgnization for the whole of society in terms of a single consistent principle. Since it has always viewed with mistrust the totalizing claims of traditional religions, it must apply that mistrust to all totalizing claims made in its name or on its behalf. A secular perspective is not committed to the exclusion of religion from every sphere of life or even every important sphere of it. It acts against its own grain when it yields to the temptations of totalizing claims; and, in doing so, it damages the prospects for the establishment and growth of secular ideas and institutions.

It will be hard to deny that in contemporary India, secularism has suffered from bad advocacy. Its most articulate proponents, as Srinivas has rightly indicated, have been left intellectuals, and some of them have carried over to secularism the totalizing claims characteristic of

Marxism–Leninism. Others have on occasion swung to the opposite extreme and argued that what was required was not merely a tolerant attitude towards all religions by the state but their equal encouragement and promotion by it. The idea that society as a whole can accommodate various institutions, both religious and secular, is a sound one; the idea that secular institutions can accommodate all religions without limit, provided they do so on an equal basis, is unworkable and perhaps also meaningless. Those who wish to secure the foundations of secular institutions will gain nothing by prevarication. A university will not remain a secular institution if it tries to accommodate, no matter how equitably, a great assortment of religious beliefs and practices. The state will cease to be a secular state if it tries to carry every kind of religious burden on its shoulders.

Notes

1. My thanks are due to Professor Upendra Baxi for drawing my attention to the Delhi University Act of 1922.

References

Béteille, A. 1986. 'Individualism and Equality', *Current Anthropology*, vol. 27, no. 2, pp. 121–34.

—— 1987. 'On Individualism and Equality: Reply', *Current Anthroplogy*, vol. 28, no. 5, pp. 672–7.

—— 1990. 'Some Observations on the Comparative Method', *Economic and Political Weekly*, vol. 25, no. 6, pp. 2255–63.

—— 1992. 'Religion as a Subject for Sociology', *Economic and Political Weekly*, vol. 27, no. 35, pp. 1865–70.

Dumont, L. 1966. *Homo Hierarchicus*. Paris: Gallimard.

—— 1977. *Homo Aequalis*. Paris: Gallimard.

Durkheim, E. 1915. *The Elementary Forms of the Religious Life*. London: Allen and Unwin.

Evans-Pritchard, E.E. 1965. *Theories of Primitive Religion*. Oxford: Clarendon Press.

Gibbon, E. 1910. *The Decline and Fall of the Roman Empire*. London: Dent, 6 vols.

Hume, D. 1957. *The Natural History of Religion*. Stanford: Stanford University Press.

—— 1980. *Dialogues Concerning Natural Religion*. Indianapolis: Hackett.

Luhmann, N. 1982. *The Differentiation of Society*. New York: Columbia University Press.

Madan, T.N. 1987. 'Secularism in its Place', *The Journal of Asian Studies*, vol. 46, no. 4, pp. 747–59.

—— 1994. 'Secularism and Pluralism', *The Times of India*, 8 January 1994.

Malinowski, B. 1972. *Magic, Science and Religion and Other Essays*. London: Souvenir Press.

Nehru, J. 1961. *The Discovery of India*. Bombay: Asia Publishing House.

Radcliffe-Brown, A.R. 1952. *Structure and Function in Primitive Society*. London: Cohen and West.

Srinivas, M.N. 1966. *Social Change in Modern India*. Berkeley: University of California Press.

—— 1993. 'Towards a New Philosophy', *The Times of India*, 9 July 1993.

Thomas, K. 1971. *Religion and the Decline of Magic*. Harmondsworth: Penguin Books.

Weber, M. 1963. *The Sociology of Religion*. Boston: Beacon Press.

5

A Career in an Indian University*

I became a university teacher at the age of twenty-four and have been one ever since, remaining in the same institution in which I began my career in the academic profession thirty years ago. I think of this institution in various ways: sometime as the department of sociology and at others as the University of Delhi, but perhaps most often as the Delhi School of Economics. I have taught—or lectured—in various other institutions both in India and abroad, but have never been more than a visitor in any one of them.

The University of Delhi in the Late 1950s

When I look back on my early days as a university teacher, what strikes me is not simply that I myself was young then but that the institution which I joined was also young. I came to a brand new department, for it was set up in 1959, the year in which I joined it. The Delhi School of Economics had moved into its new building a couple of years earlier, having spent the first few years of its life in the recesses of the arts faculty building. The University of Delhi was itself new, at least as an institution of postgraduate study and research. Its first two professors were appointed in 1942, Professor V.K.R.V. Rao and Professor D.S. Kothari, and they were both in the university when I joined it, the former as its vice-chancellor and the latter as the head of its department of physics.

The place to which I came in 1959 was not only new, it was at the same time both small and spacious. I find it difficult to describe the

* Originally published as 'A Career in a Declining Profession' in *Minerva*, vol. XXVIII, no. 1, Spring 1990.

sense of space I felt when I first came to live and work in the University of Delhi. I had come from Calcutta where the university was crowded and cramped. There was no campus in Calcutta. The buildings were in different parts of the city, mostly in crowded areas. There were no staff quarters and hardly any gardens. The Delhi School of Economics had then a single building which looked imposing even though its architectural merit was slight. It stood on its own grounds where both trees and flower-beds were well maintained. The Delhi School of Economics was a privileged place, and I counted myself lucky to have a lectureship there at the very beginning of my academic career. Others were to become professors in the same institution while still in their twenties.

The sense of space was enhanced by the smallness of numbers. One did not have to contend with crowds in the Delhi School of Economics or, for that matter, anywhere in the University of Delhi. The department of sociology was very small. Until it became a 'centre of advanced study' in 1968, it had half-a-dozen teachers, a dozen or so research students and around fifteen students in each of the two M.A. classes. The department of economics was larger, with more teachers and more students, but, in the early years, lectures for M.A. students in economics were held elsewhere, and only those on the rolls of the Delhi School of Economics—about forty in each of the two M.A. classes—had tutorials in the school.

Because the place was spacious and the numbers were small, teachers were given individual rooms. I shared a room with two other lecturers in the department for a while, but within a couple of years I had my own room. I valued that room above most things, and without it the pattern of my academic life might have been very different. Indian academics cannot afford spacious homes, particularly when they are young, and it is difficult to do sustained academic work without security against intrusion. Teachers in Indian universities, especially in the humanities, do not generally have individual rooms, and their habits of work cannot be understood without taking that fact into account.

The Delhi School of Economics was not only a privileged place, it was also a place of academic distinction. The department of sociology was headed by M.N. Srinivas, who combined high academic distinction with enormous personal charm. I will not talk about his contribution to sociolcgy which is widely acknowledged. What is more important is the sense he conveyed to each one of us of the value of sociology and of the dignity of the academic profession. The department of economics, as I said, was larger, having had an earlier start. In the sixties, it had a great accession of strength, becoming easily the best department of economics in the country and, for its size, one of the best in the world. It was in that decade that the two departments, first of economics and then of sociology, became 'centres of advanced study'.

The Consequences of Expansion

A change came about in the atmosphere of the Delhi School of Economics in the sixties, beginning in the department of economics. When I came to the school, Professor Srinivas was the head of the department of sociology and Professor B.N. Ganguli of the department of economics; Professor Ganguli was also the director of the school. They were both men of great dignity, who commanded respect as much by their professional standing as by their scholarly attainments. Professor Ganguli was in every respect the most senior member of the institution. We all used to have tea in the afternoons in the staff-room, and when he walked in, as he occasionally did, we all stood up. Professor Srinivas had a proper sense of institutional hierarchy. He deplored the excesses of both traditionalism and modernism. He had great contempt for what he called 'the north Indian habit of feet-grabbing', that is, the custom—presumably more widely observed in the north than in the south—whereby junior academics greet their seniors in both private and public places by bending and touching the seniors' feet. But he also considered distasteful the back-slapping social style common in American academic circles. He was a Tamil Brahmin who had been an Oxford don.

The appointment in the sixties of a number of very young and very outstanding professors in the department of economics undermined the correspondence between academic attainment and professional seniority on which every institutional hierarchy rests. Some were dismayed by the fact that one of the new professors was not only in his twenties but did not have either a book or a Ph.D. degree, although his later achievements fully vindicated his appointment. The hierarchical spirit was replaced by a competitive one, although this did not immediately affect my own department. I spent most of my time with my students and colleagues in sociology, although I was personally well acquainted with the new professors in the other department. They were clearly playing in a different league and took little trouble to conceal that fact from their friends and colleagues.

Personally, I find an intensely competitive academic environment oppressive. It tends to turn one's mind to quick results and short cuts, and in the end to undermine what is of supreme value to scholarship, namely, the disinterested pursuit of the truth. At the same time, a competitive academic system has an advantage over a hierarchical one. It keeps up a certain pitch of activity and does not allow individuals to rest on their oars. There was a high pitch of intellectual activity in the Delhi School of Economics in the sixties, and it attracted scholars from all over the country and from many parts of the world. This intellectual traffic was not without its distraction but it was also exhilarating, particularly for students who were able to feel that they were at the centre of things or at least not very far from it.

Along with the competitiveness and the pitch of intellectual activity went a certain disregard for distinctions of rank. (I must insist that the disregard for distinctions of rank is healthy in an academic institution only when intellectual activity is at a high pitch, otherwise it degenerates into surliness and disorder.) When I first came to the University of Delhi most departments had a single professor who was also the head; he was usually a patriarch and often a despot. I lived in those days in a university hall of residence along with a dozen other lecturers from various departments who told me the most hair-raising stories about what they were required to do for their professors. The Delhi School of Economics was far away from all this. It did not by any means do away with all distinction, but academic distinction did not entitle anyone to push others around.

There was a self-consciously virtuous denigration of administrative office and rank, a kind of 'more-academic-than-thou' attitude among the professors. To be head of the department or even director of the Delhi School of Economics came to be regarded as a nuisance and a bore. This had its good side but it also led in the long run to a certain devaluation of the institution itself. Even today, any professor who is anyone in the Delhi School of Economics tends to look down his nose on administrative office—unless it is some very superior office in government.

It was in the Delhi School of Economics that the principle of rotation first gained acceptance. In 1962, Professor Ganguli left the school to become the first pro-vice-chancellor of the university, and Professor K.N. Raj succeeded him as both director of the Delhi School of Economics and head of the department of economics. He was a great enthusiast for the principle of rotation and immediately set about applying that principle to the office of the director. A few years later it was extended to the headship of the department of economics, and when Professor Raj became vice-chancellor for a brief period in 1969–70, steps were taken to introduce the principle of rotation in all the departments of the university. The principle of rotation has altered the character of the university department, having had consequences which were not all foreseen by its early enthusiasts. It can work successfully only when there is some commitment to liberal-democratic values, and that commitment cannot be created overnight.

As a young lecturer, I benefited greatly from the liberal atmosphere of the Delhi School of Economics. Much of that atmosphere still survives, despite the turmoil through which the university has passed in recent years. Distinctions of rank do not count for very much in the functional division of labour. In my own department, professors, readers, and lecturers all do much the same kind of work and participate on an equal footing in the process of decision-making. Every permanent teacher, irrespective of rank, has a room to himself, and the rooms are all of the same size and all furnished in the same way.

Physically, great changes have taken place in the Delhi School of Economics, as in the rest of the University of Delhi in the last twenty years. Although many plans were made, things did not work according to plan. The university as a whole has expanded enormously. There are now both many more students and many more teachers. In the Delhi School of Economics the open spaces have been taken up by several new buildings, generally mean-looking. The departments have become separated from each other, at least physically, and the place has become crowded. The shine has gone out of the institution, although it still retains the academic ethos that was built up in the fifties and sixties.

In those two decades, when the Delhi School of Economics was acquiring its character as a premier academic institution, the older universities in Calcutta, Madras, Allahabad and, to some extent, Bombay, were becoming more and more provincial. The four of us who made up the teaching staff of the department of sociology in 1959 all came from different parts of the country, and the staff of the Delhi School of Economics has on the whole maintained its all-India character. Unlike most other institutions in India, we continue to attract students from all parts of the country. This is an index as well as a source of the continued academic vitality of the Delhi School of Economics.

The Internal Life of the Delhi School of Economics

The Delhi School of Economics established high standards of teaching and research, and has been on the whole successful in maintaining those standards, despite the rising pressure of numbers and despite the loss of some of its most talented teachers. Certain material conditions are necessary for creating and maintaining a proper atmosphere for teaching; adequate classrooms for students, individual rooms for teachers: clean toilets for everyone, and a well-stocked library. But a great deal can be done on modest resources through the initiative and imagination of a small number of dedicated teachers. The Delhi School of Economics was fortunate in having such teachers in its early days, and the habits of work created by them still survive to a large extent.

University teachers are not assigned work-schedules in the way in which office or factory workers are. They have considerable autonomy in arranging their own programmes of work. This is not wholly free from disadvantage. In the absence of a well-established work-ethic, autonomy can be turned into licence, and teachers satisfy themselves by meeting only the formal requirements of teaching which are not, as in the case of schoolteachers, very heavy. It is not, however, only a question of work-ethic. Where the physical basis of regular and sustained work is lacking, teachers can easily slip into apathy and negligence. What I have in mind may be illustrated by contrasting the work habits of teachers in science and arts departments. Science teachers are obliged to work within the discipline of the laboratory for which there is no exact counterpart in the case of arts teachers. As a result, the latter tend to be more lax and irregular in their work than the former.

A room for one's own use is a great asset in this context. I use my room in the department of sociology not only for reading and writing but also for meeting students and colleagues. A great deal of the time of a university teacher, particularly in the humanities, is spent in discussion, much of which is unfocused or even aimless. The cumulative effect of this unfocused discussion is substantial. It is through such discussion that one often picks up new facts, new ideas and new ways of looking at both. Formal supervision, whether of M.A. or Ph.D. students, takes place in this intellectual context.

Within my own academic career I have assigned more importance to teaching than to research, and the teaching of M.A. students has been at the centre of my work. Over the years we have developed in the department of sociology a pattern of teaching for M.A. students which I believe to be one of the best in the world. We are not always fortunate in the M.A. students we admit, but when we get a good batch, teaching reaches a very high standard of excellence. It rests on a combination of three components: lectures, seminars and tutorials. I would like to describe briefly each of these in turn.

Teaching

Lectures are delivered according to a time-table drawn up in advance for each semester. A set of lectures, usually three per week for the semester, is delivered for every course, and this is typically the responsibility of a single teacher. A teacher in the department of sociology does not usually carry a heavy lecture load. When I first started teaching I usually lectured on two courses at a time, but the lecture load of a young teacher today is a little lighter. Attendance at lectures was in the earlier days compulsory for students but it is now optional. While I believe that attendance at lectures should not be made compulsory for students, an advantage of the older system was that it discouraged irregularity among teachers.

Because I was never required to carry an excessive lecture load, I have been able to devote much time to the preparation of lectures. An important factor behind this in my case was the personal influence of M.N. Srinivas. He convinced me, by both argument and example, that the gift of the gab was usually a liability in a scholar. He was not himself a very eloquent speaker, and he never tired of telling me what a poor lecturer his teacher, Professor Evans-Pritchard, the great Oxford anthropologist, was. As is well known, Indians are among the most eloquent speakers in the world, and Indian academics often rely on their natural eloquence, neglecting to prepare their lectures. I do not regret my natural lack of eloquence for it has forced me to take great pains over the preparation of lectures.

Both seminars and tutorials require more active participation by students and attendance at these, unlike at lectures, is compulsory. 'Participation' is a well-worn phrase, but any teacher who has struggled to engage his postgraduate students in active participation in serious academic work will know how difficult it is to keep them so engaged. Reading a seminar paper is a voluntary affair, and a student may have to be coaxed, cajoled and bullied into the task. Occasionally there are very willing students but these are not always the most able, and if the paper is very dull the class goes to sleep or many of its members quietly walk out. My experience of M.A. seminars is that students are inclined to be less kind to their fellow-students than even to their teachers.

Seminar topics for a particular course are assigned by the teacher responsible for the lectures in that course. Usually three seminars are held for every course. Since there are sixteen courses in all, a total of forty-eight seminars are held which means that, in a class of about fifty students, each student ought to get a chance to read a seminar paper during the two years devoted to an M.A. class. It rarely works out quite as neatly as that, and participation in the seminar varies widely from one M.A. class to another. Despite variations and shortfalls, the seminar still serves a useful purpose in enabling the teacher to get to know his class and the students to know each other.

The tutorial oragnizes interaction between teachers and students in small groups. It has been a tradition in the department of sociology that all teachers, irrespective of rank, take part in the tutorial programme, and I made it a point to take my normal quota of tutorial classes even when, as head of the department, I carried extra administrative burdens for three years. For the purpose of tutorials, the entire M.A. class of about fifty students is divided up into small groups which are assigned to the various teachers in the department, who act as tutors for their respective groups. Topics for tutorials are assigned by the teachers responsible for covering the various courses through lectures, and these are then taken up by the various groups with their respective tutors. Apart from other things, the tutorial system exposes the student to at least two points of view on a particular subject, that of the person lecturing on it and that of the tutor.

There are two sides to the tutorial: discussion and writing. Most students in most Indian universities are not trained to do either. It requires some skill and great patience in a tutor to get students to discuss an academic topic in a serious way. They do not come prepared to a tutorial class, and generally expect the tutor to give a lecture on the topic of discussion. A successful tutor manages to get at least a few of the students in his charge to open up and express their views, but in order to do this one has to range across a wide variety of subjects and to spend an enormous amount of time. One is often tempted to give up the whole exercise and to finish the business with a short lecture on the assigned subject.

The average student is not taught to write an essay in either school or college. Indians may be eloquent and voluble in speech, but they lack balance and measure in writing. It is not easy to get a tutorial essay out of a student, but when he submits the essay it is usually three times the specified length. Indian students write their answers at excessive length, and then invariably complain that the question was lengthy! It is not easy to create a habit of writing clear and concise essays in M.A. students who are already in their twenties, and have their minds on many things besides their tutorials.

I have tried to explain the importance of combining lectures, seminars and tutorials in the teaching of M.A. students. I hope I have conveyed some sense of the difficulty of doing this effectively for I do not believe that this difficulty is fully appreciated by the persons who make educational policy without being actively engaged in teaching. Over the last twenty-five to thirty years, the system has worked more or less satisfactorily in the Delhi School of Economics, especially in the departments of economics and sociology. But it does not work for most other subjects in the University of Delhi at the postgraduate level, and I doubt if it is even tried out in a proper way in other universities in the country. Incidentally, I was told at the Erasmus University in Rotterdam, where I spent some time as a visitor, that they did not have such a system as it would be too costly.

Apart from M.A. students, I have of course also had research students. Research students include both M.Phil. and Ph.D. students; I shall confine the discussion to the latter. It is difficult to devise standard procedures for the instruction of Ph.D. students, given the enormous variation in their abilities, aptitudes and interests. There is the research seminar which has a somewhat different format from that of the M.A. seminar. The research seminar can be quite useful to the Ph.D. student since it enables him to see how ideas take shape through the interaction of minds. But it can also be quite intimidating to the neophyte if he happens to get caught in a crossfire between academic heavyweights.

I have been somewhat handicapped in my academic career by the fact that I find seminars rather boring. I have not attended many seminars outside India, so I will speak only of those I have attended in India. Indian academics are not only very voluble, they are also supremely conscious of their status. At a seminar they often intervene, not because they have something to say but because they feel that their academic standing makes silence inappropriate. Much depends on how seminars are conducted; when they are well conducted, they can be an educative experience. I still recall vividly the time when the research seminar in the department was conducted by M.N. Srinivas. He was a superb chairman of seminars, who never dominated the discussion and made everyone feel that he might have something important to say.

Whatever may be the value of the research seminar, it cannot replace individual supervision of the student by the teacher. Here much depends on the personal equation between the two. I have never had a research student with whom my relationship did not at some point become strained, either because I felt that he was not doing enough work or because he felt that I was applying undue pressure. Managing a relationship with a Ph.D. student is not easy. Not only is he an adult person with his own convictions and his own sense of dignity, but there is always some area of inquiry in which his knowledge is, or ought to be, superior to his supervisor's. A Ph.D. student cannot be treated on exactly the same footing as an M.A. student; he has to be given a longer rope.

Research

I believe it was a mistake on the part of the University Grants Commission (UGC) of India to make a research degree a necessary qualification for all college teachers. Research calls for a very special kind of intellectual temper, and the research degree ought not to be devalued. For undergraduate teaching, a habit of extensive reading is far more useful than research on a specialized topic. It is true that knowledge becomes very rapidly outdated in the modern world, but the remedy for that is to provide undergraduate teachers with general facilities for keeping abreast of the literature, not to impose a uniform requirement that every teacher should secure a Ph.D. degree. This is not to say that a college teacher who is inclined to work for a research degree should not be encouraged to do so.

Research calls for a certain independence of mind, a quality which was never actively fostered in the traditional cultural environment of India. In a social world in which a young man expects his elders to find him a wife and an occupation one should not expect too much initiative in the pursuit of ideas. The majority of research students expect their supervisors to find suitable topics for them and suitable ways of dealing with them. There are, however, many exceptions in the Delhi School of Economics which is able to attract the best students in the country. I have myself had Ph.D. students who compare in sharpness of intelligence, though not in intellectual stamina, with the best I have known anywhere in the world.

The relationship between a supervisor and his research student is a difficult one because it has always a personal as well as an academic side. If a supervisor keeps too close a watch on his student, the student feels oppressed; if he is left wholly to himself, he feels rejected. My own students have on the whole felt rejected rather than oppressed, because I have made it a practice not to intervene personally in securing a job for a person on the ground that he was my student. While I do not wish to make a virtue of my inability to promote my own students, I cannot fail to point to the relationship between that kind of promotion and academic factionalism.

The New Situation

When I first started teaching I was not much older than my own students. A whole generation separates me from my present students. Many changes have taken place in the intervening years both in the institutional setting of academic life and in the orientation of the academic profession.

Students, teachers and *karamcharis* (non-academic staff) have increased at an exponential rate. Not only have numbers greatly increased, but the increase has been rapid, unplanned and under pressure. The massive increase in numbers has brought about qualitative changes in personal relations. Teachers who have been in the university for many years now feel that they have lost their grip on things.

Bureaucratization

When a university grows rapidly to a great size, academic life becomes difficult to manage on purely academic terms. The academic side of the university then inevitably loses out to the administrative and the political sides. This has happened in the University of Delhi, and it has been the general pattern in all universities throughout the country. Thirty years ago senior academics in the university, whether in the sciences or in the humanities, could hold their own if not with the vice-chancellor, then certainly with the registrar. It is now quite common to find heads of departments waiting upon a deputy registrar or a deputy finance officer. During the three years I served as head of the department, I did not visit even once either the registrar or the finance officer, but then my department probably suffered as a result.

The university administration has become a gigantic machine. When a teacher or a student applies for something—say, study-leave or the extension of his fellowship—he does not know at which end his application will come out. Notations are made on files by clerks, assistants, section officers and the rest on even the most trivial subjects. Everything is entangled in rules which are elaborate, unclear and mutually inconsistent. Nobody who is serious about teaching and research can hope to master those rules. Naturally, everybody wants to meet the vice-chancellor or the pro-vice-chancellor or the registrar or the deputy registrar to see if some way can be found of getting round the rules. Some way is almost always found of getting round them, but at the cost of an enormous waste of time and energy.

Everyone acknowledges that there are too many rules and that these are impediments to the smooth functioning of academic life. Committees are set up from time to time to streamline administrative procedures. These committees rarely take their work seriously and they recommend new rules and new procedures without ensuring that the old ones are discarded. The Indian approach to administration, in my view, is to create more and more rules, and to hope that some way will be found in the end to circumvent them. All this of course puts the academic at a disadvantage in relation to the administrator.

I do not wish to suggest that all professors are averse to administration. A life devoted solely to scholarship is extremely exacting and there are no assured rewards in it. Administration and committees provide escapes from the labours of research which must sometimes appear both endless and fruitless. Many academics shine on committees and, in a career of over a quarter of a century in the Delhi School of Economics, I have known several who have played important roles in governmental planning and policy-making. Most of these leave the university for good and only a few return to it, but those who return find it difficult to settle back into the dull routine of academic life.

The bureaucratization of academic life is a world-wide trend, but in a small postgraduate department of the kind in which I work, no one can seriously complain that administrative responsibilities interfere substantially with academic work. Even as head of the department I did more or less the same amount of reading, writing and teaching that I ordinarily do. If one is serious about academic work, it is better to be a victim of the administration than to join it in the hope of improving things.

What is time-consuming and exhausting is not academic administration but academic politics. Academic life has not only become more bureaucratized, it has become enormously more politicized. Although every teacher acquires some sense of this, its meaning became fully clear to me during the three years of my tenure as head of the department. Very broadly speaking, no major decision on any academic matter can now be taken solely on merit without consideration of the balance of power between students, teachers and *karamcharis*, and their various constituent parts.

The role of politics in academic life can be examined on two intersecting planes: first, on the plane of the department, faculty and the other constituent bodies of the university, and, second, on the plane of the unions of teachers, students and *karamcharis*.

Democratization

Like bureaucratization, the democratization of universities has been a world-wide trend, but while academics are eloquent in denouncing the evils of the former, they rarely express any misgivings about the latter, even when they have them. I have found it extremely difficult to engage academics in a candid discussion of the political presuppositions and implications of the democratization of academic life.

Let me begin with an example of the positive side of democratization. When I joined the University of Delhi in 1959, the typical post-graduate department had a very hierarchical character. Barring a few exceptions, the department had a single professor who was also the head, and remained in that position until he retired. The head of the department had a decisive say on all matters pertaining to his department: appointments, admissions, scholarships, syllabus, time-table, etc. There was enormous concentration of power in the hands of a single person and that person often acted as a despot. All this has changed vastly with the introduction of the principle of rotation and with the growing influence of the departmental staff council. There is more consultation now and the head can no longer act in a despotic manner. Older members of the university sometimes complain that democratization has robbed the departments of their coherence, and that loss of power has been accompanied by loss of interest among heads of departments. I believe that these are mostly problems of transition, and that from the purely academic point of view the new arrangement is an advance over the old.

However, democratization is not a panacea for every evil, and I will now give an example of its negative side. The academic council is the supreme academic body of the University of Delhi. There has been a sea change in its composition and character in the last twenty years. It has expanded greatly in size and has now a much larger component of elected teachers among its members. It used to be a sedate and dignified body in which a small number of university professors and college principals played an active part. It is now a noisy, disorderly and totally unruly forum dominated by university officials on the one side and elected teachers on the other. I cannot in my entire professional career recall anything more disagreeable than the hours I have spent attending meetings of the academic council. There is nothing remotely academic in the atmosphere of those meetings.

The academic council is now a fairly large body comprising, besides the vice-chancellor and his team—the pro-vice-chancellor, the director of the South Campus and the dean of colleges—the heads of post-graduate departments, a few other professors by rotation according to seniority, some principals of colleges, again by rotation according to seniority, and twenty readers and lectures, mostly from the colleges, elected by the teachers. A meeting of the academic council rarely passes without a confrontation, often very noisy and disorderly, between the vice-chancellor and his administrative team on the one side and the elected teachers on the other. Some of the latter are outstanding orators; they are very knowledgeable about rules and procedures, and are quick to pounce on the lapses of the authorities.

I have come to the conclusion that in the matter of public debate the two sides are unevenly matched in the academic council. It is a contest between four on one side and twenty on the other, and the vice-chancellor's team does not always include able spokesmen whereas eloquence is the strong suit of the elected teachers. It is true that heads of departments and other professors outnumber the elected teachers, but they tend to be silenced by the eloquence of their democratically elected colleagues. I do not wish to give the impression that vice-chancellors always play fairly in this game. They try to canvass support with the senior academics before a meeting, but this does not always work. In fact, my impression is that more and more of the new heads of departments tend to side with the elected teachers rather than the vice-chancellor. The only persons on whose solid support the vice-chancellor can count are the registrar and his subalterns who sit quietly in a corner of the large council hall, passing notes to the former since, not being members of the academic council, they cannot formally intervene in its debates, and of course they cannot vote.

Teachers and Administrators

Delhi University enjoys a pre-eminent position among Indian universities. This is partly because of its location in the capital city which enabled it, particularly in the two decades after independence, to attract talent from all parts of the country to its postgraduate departments. It is also a 'central university' and by far the largest among the central universities which means that it does not depend for funds on any state government but gets them directly from the University Grants Commission (UGC). More recently it has attracted national attention because of its very active teachers' union—the Delhi University Teachers' Association (DUTA)—which has played a leading part in negotiations with the UGC and the ministry of education for better pay and service conditions for university and college teachers, not only in Delhi but throughout the country.

A watershed in the life of the University of Delhi and perhaps of all Indian universities was reached with what has come to be known as the 'merit-promotion scheme'. The scheme as adopted in Delhi in 1983 offered promotion to lecturers to the next higher scale—reader in the case of university lecturers and the corresponding scale but without the title of 'reader' to college lecturers—after ten years of service if they had a Ph.D. and after fifteen years if they did not have one. There were some tests of qualification but these were generally made notional. What is more, readers in university departments who had put in a certain length of service became eligible for promotion to professorships. In the case of university departments, these promotions were made on the recommendation of selection committees which interviewed eligible candidates as in the case of the regular posts but acted, it is alleged, far more liberally. In the case of the colleges of Delhi University, the interviews were dispensed with and promotion became more or less automatic after the necessary passage of time.

The 'merit-promotion scheme' has not been applied in exactly the some way in the different departments of the University of Delhi. In the Delhi School of Economics individual readers were denied promotion (or did not ask for it) even after they had fulfilled the requirement of time, but this kind of thing is regarded as a scandal in the rest of the university. The merit-promotion scheme altered almost overnight the structure of the postgraduate department. Most such departments in the University of Delhi now have more professors than lecturers, whereas twenty years ago few of them had more than one professor each.

The concession made to the University of Delhi in the matter of promotions in 1983 was believed by some in the ministry of education to be temporary, whereas the teachers, particularly in the colleges, felt that it was a permanent gain achieved for them by their union. It is difficult to decide whether all parties acted in good faith or with whom, if anyone, the bad faith rested. It is true, nevertheless, that while all this was happening a committee was at work, formulating new scales of pay and new conditions of work for college and university teachers throughout the country. The announcement of the new scheme was followed by a country-wide strike by more than 200,000 teachers. The new scheme recommended higher pay but it also put restrictions on promotion. An uneasy compromise was reached and the all-India federation of unions called off the strike after a month. The compromise was not acceptable to DUTA, so the strike in Delhi continued for another month or more, and was eventually called off in an atmosphere of great bitterness.

The new arrangements have now come into force throughout the country, although it is still too early to say how they are going to work in the various universities. The demand for keeping open the avenues of promotion for lecturers has been conceded although new conditions have been introduced. Readers can no longer ask to be promoted as professors by merely completing a certain period of service.

The University of Delhi has now accumulated a large body of professors, partly through the extensive application of the merit-promotion scheme between 1983 and 1987. Because of the principle of rotation, many of the new professors are or will soon become heads of departments. Their attitude to academic administration and academic politics is somewhat different from the attitude of those who had become professors in the 1960s and 1970s. Many of them feel that they owe something to the democratic movement organized by DUTA. If they venture to speak against it they may be reminded that they are 'free-riders', for the movement was indeed organized and led by lecturers in the colleges rather than by readers or professors in the postgraduate departments.

The change in the character of the professoriate has not left unaltered the relationship between the academic and the administrative components within the university. The administration in the University of Delhi has expanded enormously. There are the offices of the registrar, the controller of examinations and the finance officer, and each of them has become a little empire in itself. Even under the best of circumstances it might be difficult for a senior academic to deal with an obstructive assistant finance officer. Now that heads of departments are in office for only three years at a time and many of them are there or believed to be there by grace of trade union action, such moral authority as their predecessors enjoyed over the administration has been greatly reduced.

At the University of Delhi, academics at every level complain endlessly of the obstructiveness of the university administration. It is not always easy to judge the merits of these complaints because they are often rhetorical and generally expressed in a highly stylized form. On the other side, one of the most senior administrators of the university, who entered it at a very young age as a junior clerk, used to tell me that the ruin of the University of Delhi began with the introduction of the principle of rotation for the headship of postgraduate departments. He was a discreet person who did not like to air such views in public; his juniors now speak openly of the sorry state of affairs to which some departments have been reduced by the merit-promotion scheme.

The Trade Union of University Teachers

A major part in the transformation of the social character of the university has been played by the teachers' strike. Between September 1982 and October 1987 there were three prolonged strikes by DUTA, each lasting for more than two months. The success of the first two strikes, in 1982–3 and 1985–6, surpassed the expectations of even the most ardent enthusiasts for industrial action by academics. The third strike, in 1987, did not achieve complete success because the all-India federation was eager to reach a settlement on terms that were not acceptable to DUTA but its social effect was not inconsiderable.

A strike for two or three months by 5000 teachers creates a very distinctive atmosphere in a university. That atmosphere has something of the quality evoked by Sorel in his *Reflections on Violence*, and I have seen many persons of sober temperament carried away by it. Meetings, rallies and demonstrations create a new sense of solidarity among teachers. A leadership of the young, animated by a fervent desire for social justice, comes to the forefront. Men of real academic distinction and those devoted primarily to teaching and research withdraw into the background, although some seasoned scholars find new roles for themselves as advisers and intermediaries.

The great achievement of DUTA between 1983 and 1987 was that it secured better salary-scales and easy promotion for thousands of teachers in colleges and postgraduate departments. It also showed the way to other unions throughout the country. Within the University of Delhi it had clearly established its political superiority over the constituted authorities; most teachers, including many heads of departments, principals of colleges and deans of faculties were for the movement and against whatever stood in its way. The vice-chancellor found himself in the awkward position of being both for and against the demands of his teachers.

Now the demand for better pay and assured promotion for teachers cannot be fully met from within the university for the simple reason that the university has very little money of its own. In India, although the university is technically an autonomous institution, governed by its own Act and statutes, it is financially dependent on the government, either the central or a state government. Delhi University, being a central university, gets almost all its money directly from the UGC, whereas the majority of universities, being state universities, are dependent on the state governments which have departments of education believed to be less understanding and less sympathetic than the UGC.

Despite the institutional autonomy of universities and despite the differences in the sources of financial support between central and state universities, it is now an accepted principle that university teachers should have the same salary-scales throughout the country. The UGC plays a major part in determining these scales, directly in the case of central universities and indirectly in the case of state universities. Although itself an autonomous institution created by an Act of Parliament, the UGC cannot make any major financial commitment without the consent and support of the central government; hence the ministry of education is a crucial actor in any negotiation involving fundamental changes in the conditions of academic employment.

Academic Standards and the University Grants Commission

Officials in the ministry of education are inclined to take the view that uniform scales of pay require uniform academic standards. It is a topsy-turvy world in which administrators worry most about academic standards and scholars about pay and promotion.

The ministry of education cannot, of course, impose academic standards on the universities or even talk directly with them about their academic standards. It is with the UGC that the responsibility rests for ensuring that academic standards are maintained throughout the country. Although the commission is made up largely of academics and makes extensive use of committees of academics, it has a secretariat of considerable and increasing size which largely determines how it actually functions from day to day. And, of course, it is entirely dependent on the central government for the grants it makes to the universities. Leaders of the teachers' movement in Delhi and outside have come to regard the UGC, not altogether without reason, as an appendage of government.

The UGC has had a difficult role to play, and few will say that it has played that role in an academically fruitful manner. It can hardly be expected to do so without the active and responsible participation of the academics who serve on its numerous committees. That participation it has on the whole failed to secure. It is not that academics refuse to serve on these committees but that they do their work fitfully and casually. Senior academics complain that their recommendations acquire strange forms by the time they come out as decisions of the commission; the commission, on the other hand, maintains that it never decides anything without the benefit of advice from distinguished academics.

The philosophy that governs the thinking of the UGC on academic reforms turns essentially around the idea of uniform standards. That the ends of science and scholarship may be better served by tolerating and indeed encouraging diversity is not a view that finds favour with the commission. I must hasten to add that the idea of uniformity is one that appeals not only to the commission's secretariat, but also to many academics, and I have found myself in a minority of one while arguing against it in academic committees within the commission. It nevertheless remains my belief that uniformity is a bureaucratic and not an academic virtue.

The UGC considers it a part of its responsibility to work towards uniform syllabuses for undergraduate and postgraduate teaching throughout the country. Naturally, it would be unable to do this without the active co-operation of at least some academics in each of the disciplines concerned. Of course, nobody can insist on such a syllabus being adopted by any university, but a department which is struggling for funds may in fact adopt it in the hope of attracting favourable attention from the UGC. How it actually uses the syllabus in its teaching is of course a different matter.

The Academic Profession and the Loss of Academic Autonomy

With the coming into force of the new scales of pay, the UGC has stepped up its programmes for creating and maintaining uniformity of standards among both students and teachers. These include tests of qualification as well as in-service training at various levels. They are viewed with misgiving by many academics and some of them have far-reaching implications for the institutional autonomy of the university.

The Ph.D. programmes of most university departments depend on fellowships for which, at least in the humanities and social sciences, most of the money comes from the UGC. The Delhi School of Economics has been able to attract good students from all over the country, and the commission has on the whole been generous in providing research fellowships for them. In the past the only condition it made—and it was not wholly unreasonable—was that at least half the fellowships at any one time should go to students from universities other than the University of Delhi.

We in the department of sociology have taken enormous trouble in identifying the most suitable students for admission to the Ph.D. course and for the award of fellowships. If anything, we spend more time in deciding whether to admit them than in recommending them for fellowships. We have found no substitute for a close personal knowledge of a student and his aptitude for research as the ground for his selection. The UGC has now introduced a national test which every applicant for a research fellowship is required to pass. Every applicant who passes the test need not be given admission, but the provincial universities will find it increasingly difficult to deny a place to someone who comes with a certificate from the UGC which he views as an entitlement to a fellowship.

Not content with this, the commission is now planning public examinations to test the eligibility of candidates for academic appointments throughout the country.[1] If this comes about, no university will be able to appoint a lecturer unless he comes with a certificate from the UGC. Many academic administrators have begun to feel that those who secure appointments as lecturers are not always qualified to meet their responsibilities. It is now possible to get an M.A. degree, and in some universities even a first class M.A. degree, without too much effort, and the standards of research degrees are notoriously uneven. While all this may be true, it is difficult to see how the commission can ensure quality control by conducting tests of eligibility for entry into the academic profession.

There is perhaps a deeper reason, one almost feels inclined to call it a moral impulse, behind the move to introduce tests of eligibility for entry into the academic profession. Teachers themselves use the higher civil service as a kind of yardstick for constructing their claims for better pay and opportunities for promotion. Entry into the higher civil service is through a public examination conducted by the Union Public Service Commission. Of the many thousands who take this examination, only a few hundred are selected for service. Success in a highly competitive public examination gives the Indian civil servant a keen sense of having had his worth tested and he feels that those who claim privileges similar to his should have their worth similarly tested.

It would be disingenuous to maintain that only the bureaucrats wish to bring the academic profession in line with the civil service; many college and university teachers see themselves in the image of the civil servant. It is well known that students come from all parts of India to enrol in postgraduate courses in Delhi because it gives them a better chance of competing in the civil service examinations. The postgraduate hostels in Delhi are filled with students who spend more time in preparing for these examinations than on the courses of study for which they are enrolled in the university. For some at least, it is a matter of chance that they become college or university lectures and not civil servants.

Those who become college lecturers do not always forget the fact that, had luck favoured them, they might have been in the Indian Administrative Service (IAS). There are many examples of individuals who start as lecturers and leave within a year or two to join the civil service, but very few examples of the reverse movement. I know someone who gave up a career in the IAS to become a lecturer in the department of physics in Delhi; thirty years after the event, colleagues still point to him as an example.

Successful academics in India move easily from teaching and research into academic administration. There they learn quickly to mistrust those who try to do their own work in their own way without proper regard for rank and status. They feel that the safest course is to have objective rules—for appointments, for evaluation and for promotions. They are troubled in their minds when someone becomes a professor at the age of thirty or when someone has to retire at the age of sixty as a lecturer. This way of thinking is not fundamentally in conflict with the thinking in the teachers' union movement.

What has struck me most about discussions in the teachers' union is the preoccupation with objective criteria, the obsession with foolproof procedures. Nothing brings this out more clearly than the insistence on 'time-bound promotion', or the demand that promotion for a college teacher should be guaranteed after ten years with a Ph.D. and after fifteen years without a Ph.D. That demand is the assertion of a bureaucratic and not an academic value. I am convinced that such a demand touches a sympathetic chord in the bureaucrat. It is true that there was much acrimony and some show of injured innocence on both sides during the bargaining over the new scales of pay. The unions wanted the promotions to come quickly and smoothly whereas the bureaucrats felt that the teachers should be made to sweat a little longer for their promotions. But that indicates a difference of interests, not one of ideas or values.

Conclusions

The changes that have taken place in the University of Delhi and in other universities were to some extent inevitable, given the changes taking place in the larger social and political environment. What is no less remarkable than the general turmoil and disorder in the university system is the survival of islands on which science and scholarship are still actively pursued by some individuals, either on their own or in small groups. Perhaps such individuals find a greater challenge in the very disorder of their environment, for it is certain that more published work, of greater variety if not always of better quality, now comes out of the University of Delhi than was the case thirty years ago.

What I have tried to bring out is the devaluation of academic institutions through actions for which academics themselves are to some extent responsible. They could have done better to protect those institutions from the forces by which they were threatened. Academics have no right to expect that a benevolent providence will place at their disposal a state and a society tailormade for the pursuit of science and scholarship. Indeed, a part of the inspiration and excitement of intellectual life comes from having to navigate against the current. At the same time, the creation and transmission of knowledge requires not only a framework of institutions but a measure of autonomy for those institutions.

At the time of independence in India, both state and society provided some space for academic institutions to grow in their own way. If they are now losing their autonomy, it is not solely because of external constraints over which they have had no control at all. The processes of bureaucratization and politicization, by which academic life is being squeezed out from two sides, have been encouraged to grow in the universities by academics themselves. They first went to the government for more and more money to enable the universities to expand at a pace that was often reckless. The government now wants to extract its pound of flesh by imposing strict procedures for 'quality control'. It is, I believe, a mistake to think that political parties opposed to the government will help the universities to recover their lost autonomy.

Academic autonomy can be preserved only if academics themselves show the will to preserve it. Neither the government nor the opposition has in India, or perhaps anywhere, much interest in protecting the autonomy of universities. It is not that academics care nothing at all about autonomy, but that so far they have not shown themselves to be sufficiently determined about it. They have wanted it in addition to a good many other things. They will show themselves to be determined and serious only when they are ready to ask for it at the cost of some of the good things in life.

Notes

1. Since then adopted by the UGC, as the National Eligibility Test (NET).

6

Universities as Centres of Learning*

Ideals of the University

Universities are now faced with adversity, not only in India but throughout the world. This was the message that came through at the roundtable on 'The Universities of the Twenty-First Century' held at the University of Chicago in October 1991 as a part of its centenary.[1] There, Michael Shattock from the United Kingdom, editor of the journal *Higher Education Quarterly*, spoke eloquently about the internal and external threats to the university (Shattock 1992). Even the American participants, from such premier universities as Harvard, Princeton and Chicago, drew attention repeatedly to the pressures on the university from various quarters. But the troubles of those universities, no matter how acutely felt by their representatives, appeared as small ones to an observer from India.

It is not for the first time in their long history that the universities are faced with adversity. The great European universities of Paris, Oxford and Cambridge had sunk to a very low level by the eighteenth century (Stone 1974). But a strong current of renewal developed in the nineteenth, beginning with Humboldt's great experiment in Berlin, and by the beginning of the twentieth century, the universities had recovered their preeminence as centres of science and scholarship in Europe, and begun to extend their influence to America and other parts of the world. The remarks that follow express a strong sense of the internal and external threats faced by the Indian university today, but they are not altogether without hope in the possibility of its future regeneration.

* Originally published in *Journal of Higher Education*, vol. 18, no. 3, Monsoon, 1995.

When those within the university begin to feel an acute sense of the problems by which their institution is threatened, their first response is to wish them out of existence; their second response is to look for enemies outside. While it is difficult to rank the different kinds of pressures—financial, political, bureaucratic, and so on—with which the university has to contend, the most serious threat to the university today, as I perceive it, is a loss of nerve. This is a problem that is internal, and not external to the university. It leads to a continuing distortion of focus in the activities undertaken within the university. No one can impose from outside the tasks that are proper to the university; but if it fails to define its own tasks with sufficient clarity, as it has increasingly failed to do, then it must necessarily submit to what is imposed on it from outside.

What are the tasks appropriate to a university? What should a university stand for? In the nineteenth century, when the English universities were coming back to a new life after a long period of slumber, many eminent Englishmen wrote eloquently about the idea of a university (Newman 1976). I will not dwell on what they said. It is enough to recall what Jawaharlal Nehru said to the convocation of Allahabad University shortly after assuming office as independent India's first prime minister.

> A university stands for humanism, for tolerance, for reason, for progress, for the adventure of ideas and for the search for truth. It stands for the onward march of the human race towards ever higher objectives. If the universities discharge their duty adequately, then it is well with the nation and the people. But if the temple of learning becomes a home of narrow bigotry and petty objectives, how then will the nation prosper or a people grow in stature? (Nehru 1949: 333)

Nehru's phrase was echoed by Radhakrishnan who wrote in the Report of the University Education Commission (1949: 34), 'Universities are the homes of intellectual adventure.' Today, we have to add that the adventure of ideas and the search for truth are hard pursuits, particularly in a country with so many urgent and pressing problems.

Nobody can be said to set the right value on the university unless he is prepared to maintain that the advancement of learning—the motto of the University of Calcutta, the first modern university in India—through the pursuit of science and scholarship is an end in itself. The social as against the purely personal significance of the disciplined pursuit of science and scholarship is difficult for most persons to see when they have no connection or only an indirect one with those pursuits;

in this, as in many other matters, Nehru was an exception. The university is a remote presence for most Indians who have to live without the benefit of even primary and secondary education. The middle classes who are the opinion-makers in this country, as in most countries, want good education for their children. By this they generally mean education that will secure them lucrative employment. They do not easily perceive the connection between successful careers in business or government and the slow and laborious study of such subjects as medieval history, comparative sociology, structural linguistics, the uncertainty principle or chaos theory.

Yet there is a connection between those pursuits and the long-term health and well-being of society. If India has survived so many vicissitudes, it is in no small measure due to its rich, complex, even arcane—some would say too arcane—intellectual heritage in which the life of the mind was valued for its own sake. It is perhaps no great misfortune that a middle class on the make—aggresssive, competitive and full of dreams of upward mobility—should view the universities from the narrow angle of their self-interest. The real threat to the university comes when so many of its own members—more and more professors, and perhaps the majority of vice-chancellors—fail to see things in proper perspective or are too demoralized and timorous to assert that the adventure of ideas and the search for truth are also socially commendable objectives. Their own lack of conviction makes them cynical and fatalistic, not only about their immediate environment but about the world as a whole.

The adventure of ideas and the search for truth, the advancement of learning and the pursuit of science and scholarship might also contribute to material advancement and social justice in one way or another, in the short or the long run. But the university, like any other institution, can undertake to do only certain things and not everything directly. If it does well at least those things that are put in its special care, then it does well by society. It cannot do well by society by neglecting its proper sphere of work for the pursuit of other and more immediately attractive goals. In my experience, it is the scientists and scholars who have been left with little to contribute to science and scholarship who speak most energetically and eloquently about the economic utility and the social relevance of their work. In India, promotion comes easily to such persons, and they are the ones who occupy the highest public offices having to do with education and research. Men and women with practical good sense might listen to them, but they do not take them seriously. There are many arenas in society—the business enterprise, the party office, the administrative department—for solving urgent practical problems; the university is not one of them.

Teaching and Research

The distinctive orientation of the modern university, starting in 1809 with the University of Berlin, is to be found in Wilhelm von Humboldt's ideal of Einheit der Lehre und Forschung, or the unity of teaching and research. Not every university realizes this ideal in practice, and it is now common, at least in the United States, to refer to only the front-ranking universities, such as Harvard, Princeton, Stanford, Ber- keley and Ann Arbor as 'research universities'. In India, the first universities, at Calcutta, Bombay and Madras had little to do with research, or for that matter with teaching, in their initial of phase of development (Béteille 1981, 1995). They were affiliating bodies whose main responsibilities were the framing of syllabi, conduct of examinations, and the issuance of degrees and diplomas. Even today, certification continues to be an important concern of every Indian university and in some cases, it is their only significant concern.

The first post-graduate departments where teaching and research were actively and fruitfully combined were set up in the University of Calcutta under the leadership of Sir Ashutosh Mukherji (Banerjee et al. 1957). It was here in the 1920s that the outstanding work of such scientists as C.V. Raman, Satyendranath Bose and Meghnad Saha was done. In the humanities, there were such distinguished scholars as Surendranath Dasgupta, Jadunath Sarkar and Suniti Kumar Chatterji. I will say nothing about their contributions to science and scholarship, but only point out that their work was done on the most slender of material resources imaginable. Their work was driven not by considerations of economic utility or social relevance,[2] but by the most passionate engagement with 'the adventure of ideas' and 'the search for truth'.

Other Indian universities at Allahabad, Benares, Dacca and elsewhere followed the lead of Calcutta in developing post-graduate departments in which teaching and research were effectively combined. After independence, a large number of new universities came into being, and the University Grants Commission (UGC), set up in 1956, seems to have taken it for granted that teaching and research should be combined in every university. Today, there are more than 150 universities in the country, and they are all expected to undertake teaching and research. But the practice is, in most cases, very different. There are many universities in which very little research worth the name is conducted. It is not simply that the quality of research is poor, but that what passes for research has very little to do with any kind of purposeful intellectual activity. Most of it appears in the form of Ph.D. dissertations and conference papers that meet only the formal requirement of research outputs, and not even that in every case. Research students soon learn that they can copy or paraphrase work already published elsewhere, and professors who do no substantial work can always say that they are engaged in directing research.

There are university departments where serious research is still undertaken but they are few in number. Today, research in even the social sciences, not to speak of the natural sciences, is expensive. Thus to escape the possible charge of discrimination, even the 'good' departments are starved of funds because the available resources, meagre as they are, have to be divided between universities as evenly as possible. The UGC committees responsible for the distribution of research funds consist mainly of academics, but few of them are prepared to speak against the wastage involved in allocating funds for research to institutions where no research is done because they wish to avoid being accused of elitism. In these circumstances, research as such comes to be viewed, both within and outside the universities, as economically unproductive and socially wasteful. To say that research cannot be driven by considerations of utility is not to say that it should be unmindful of wastage.

If a university is to be judged by its capacity for combining teaching with research, there are now many universities in India that are universities only in name. We cannot wish these out of existence, but we must begin to seriously consider whether in any large and heterogeneous society such as ours, every university should even be expected to do the same kind of work. The demand for education upto the B.A. or even the M.A. level is not likely to decline in the foreseeable future. There are many universities in India that can meet that demand more or less capably and conscientiously. To deny them the credentials of a university would be unrealistic and perhaps also unjust, but to keep the pretence that they are all doing the same kind of work that is being done today at the University of Delhi or the Jawaharlal Nehru University and was done in earlier years at Calcutta and Allahabad would be no less unrealistic and unjust.

In India, wherever institutions of the same kind are set up under public auspices, the general drift of thinking is that they must all have the same resources and facilities irrespective of their actual quality or performance, or none should have them. Differences among institutions grow in course of time, but the energy to monitor those differences and to act in accordance with them seems to be lacking. When resources appear abundant, all are given a share; when they appear scarce, all are made to suffer equally. As things stand today, only a few universities in the country have the intellectual capacity to perform as research universities, irrespective of the material resources that may be available to them. Unless resources are made available selectively and with discrimination, the little research that is still done in the good universities will be driven away from them into other and more specialized institutions. To abandon the idea of the research university as a place where research and teaching are done in close association will do great injury to the tradition of learning in India.

It will be a sad mistake to regard the teaching university as a thing of little value. Teaching, no less than research, is or ought to be viewed as a part of the adventure of ideas and the search for truth, and I say this from the experience of someone who has always given priority to teaching over research. Teaching and research call for different kinds of resources, and also different temperaments. I am not suggesting that those who wish to do research in the teaching universities should be prevented or discouraged from doing so. But there are many universities where few have shown that inclination. To keep up the pretence that everyone in a university is under obligation to do research only encourages senior members of such universities to dispense with the obligations of teaching.

Specialization and Co-ordination

The ideal of the university as it has developed in India has been not only to combine teaching and research, but also to do so in the widest range of disciplines. The modern university is a place of specialized teaching and research, but one which keeps together a large variety of disciplines and also encourages active cross-fertilization between them. Today the questions with which we are faced are how large this variety should be, whether there should be a core of intellectual disciplines, and, if so, what that core should be.

I would like to dwell a little on the range of intellectual disciplines that a university aspires to accommodate and the kind of specialization that has become integral to the pursuit of knowledge in the modern world. The unity of knowledge, to the extent that such a thing exists, can no longer be realized in the work of any single individual, no matter how gifted, but can be realistically pursued only within institutions. Historically, no institution has played the part that the universities have in holding together the various disciplines in an era of explosive specialization. Those who look askance at disciplinary specialization as being alien to the vocation of the intellectual as well as those who maintain that specialization alone can meet the technical demands of the modern world are both enemies of universities.

A hundred years ago, Émile Durkheim, one of the founders of modern sociology, had noted the rapid growth of specialization in the pursuit of knowledge: 'The time lies far behind us when philosophy constituted the sole science. It has become fragmented into a host of special disciplines, each having its purpose, method and ethos' (Durkheim 1984: 2). On the whole, he welcomed this trend as being not only inevitable but also beneficial. 'The man of parts, as he once was, is for us no more than a dilettante, and we accord no moral value to dilettantism. Rather, do we perceive perfection in the competent man, one who seeks not to be complete but to be productive, one who has a well-defined job to which he devotes himself, and carries out his task, ploughing his single furrow' (ibid.: 4).

Addressing an audience of students at the end of his career, Max Weber too pointed to the relentless progress of specialization: 'In our time science has entered a phase of specialization previously unknown and ... this will for ever remain the case. Not only externally, but inwardly, matters stand at a point where the individual can acquire the sure consciousness of achieving something truly perfect in the field of science only in case he is a strict specialist'.[3] And again, 'Only by strict specialization can the scientific worker become fully conscious, for once and perhaps never again in his lifetime, that he has achieved something that will endure. A really definitive and good accomplishment is today always a specialized accomplishment' (Gerth and Mills 1946: 134, 135).

Where science and scholarship are driven by the constant pressure of specialization, knowledge faces the constant threat of becoming fragmented. Weber brooded over the possible damage this might do to the spirit of adventure in the pursuit of ideas. Durkheim was more optimistic in his belief that differentiation would be accompanied by complementarity, and that this would not only benefit the parts but also enrich the whole. For Durkheim, complementary difference was a more dependable source of vitality than sameness, in intellectual life, as in social life generally.

Of course, complementarities between highly differentiated intellectual pursuits might develop spontaneously, as it were by trial and error. An intellectual pursuit is never undertaken by any individual in complete isolation from other individuals. At the very least, the ideas of one intellectual influence other individuals and are in turn influenced by them, so that a certain amount of mutual correction and co-ordination of ideas comes about even in the absence of any larger organizational plan. In addition, there are, of course, occasions, agencies and institutions designed specifically to ensure such co-ordination on a continuing basis. Historically, the university has provided the most important institutional locus for facilitating and maintaining co-ordination of intellectual activities on an extensive scale.

Intellectual Disciplines: Training and Apprenticeship

Taken as a whole and in the broadest sense, the university is a place for the adventure of ideas and the search for truth. But the pursuit of science and scholarship in a modern university is a disciplined pursuit, requiring long periods of training and apprenticeship. As one moves from lower to higher levels in the academic system, there is a sharpening of intellectual focus. An academic apprenticeship is an apprenticeship in a particular discipline rather than in the pursuit of science and scholarship as such. Sometimes a person might move from one discipline to another, but at any given time, it is the discipline that anchors the work of the individual scholar or scientist. Universities are organized according to disciplines into faculties, schools, departments and centres, and no one can move at will from one faculty to another or even from one department to another.

An academic career begins with a long period of apprenticeship in one of the recognized disciplines. Today this is seen most clearly in the sciences. There the choice of discipline is made at a fairly early stage, and, although lateral movements are possible, it is customary to make such movements either towards the beginning of one's career or much later in life, after one has made some contribution in a particular disciplinary field. Ordinarily, a person who seeks to make a career in science begins by attaching himself to a particular laboratory whose work is directed by a senior scientist. There he learns the techniques of his craft under the guidance of his senior and in association with his peers. Doctoral work in the sciences has to find accommodation in the larger division of labour within the laboratory. Even a doctoral degree is now no longer sufficient to begin one's own independent programme of work; before embarking on that, one has normally to spend a further period of time doing post-doctoral work in someone else's laboratory.

Apprenticeship in the humanities and social sciences is less tightly structured than in the natural sciences. In these disciplines, even the doctoral student enjoys greater freedom in choosing his own subject of investigation and pursuing it in his own way, and the extension of the apprenticeship through post-doctoral work is more the exception than the rule, at least in the Indian university system. Nevertheless, there is a period of apprenticeship here as well, for a Ph.D. degree earned through research under an approved supervisor is coming to be viewed as a necessary qualification for academic appointments in most postgraduate departments.

The period of apprenticeship is one in which the neophyte's mental energies are concentrated on a particular body of data, concepts and methods. It is a mistake to believe that the observation and description of facts in a disciplined way comes naturally to everyone who is driven by curiosity. The new entrant to a discipline learns that the facts with which he has to deal have a life of their own, and that they cannot be altered at will or mixed together indiscriminately. He also learns that the development and refinement of concepts is a cumulative process, sustained by the work of generations. Finally, there are methods and procedures that can be mastered only through a long and laborious apprenticeship.

Being trained to work as an independent scholar or scientist in a discipline means that one is socialized in a certain tradition of work. It also means that one learns to avoid making mistakes, new ones as well as ones that have been made before. No amount of training can by itself enable someone to make a new discovery. But we know from experience that new discoveries are seldom made without tedious and costly mistakes. Working in and through a discipline is a way of minimizing those mistakes. It is also a way of relating the work of the individual scholar or scientist to a larger endeavour.

Intellectual Disciplines: Core and Periphery

A university has or is expected to have a 'universal' character in more than one sense. It is a site for teaching and research in a variety of intellectual disciplines. The requirements of teaching ensure that specialized intellectual pursuits do not become completely detached from a wider base of knowledge. The modern university is 'universal' in the further sense that it is an open institution (Rüegg 1992; Béteille 1992) where admissions of students and appointments of teachers are made on the basis of universalistic criteria, without consideration of caste, creed or gender. At least in modern India, the universities were among the first public institutions where women were accommodated in significant numbers, as students initially, and then increasingly also as teachers (Béteille 1995).

Whatever may be its ideals, no university can in fact give its due place to every single intellectual discipline. There have been a great many variations between places and a great deal of change over time. The English universities did not accommodate law and medicine until the nineteenth century, although those disciplines held a prominent place in the Italian universities such as Bologna and Salerno since the Middle Ages. Theology was perhaps the most important discipline in the medieval universities of Paris and Oxford, although it has now a marginal place in Oxford, and no place at all in many universities. State funded universities in the United States, such as those at Berkeley and Ann Arbor, do not provide religious instruction, although they might accommodate such disciplines as Comparative Religion and History of Religions. In the United States today, opinion is divided on whether such subjects as Black Studies or Ethnic Studies or Gender Studies should be recognized as university subjects (Bloom 1987; Shils 1992).

Universities have in the past been slow in acknowledging and accommodating new branches of knowledge and learning. Many of the subjects that now have an important place in teaching and research have found places in universities only since the nineteenth century. Prior to that, they either did not exist or were not considered as university subjects. Most of the major developments in the social sciences in the nineteenth century took place outside the universities. David Ricardo, Alexis de Tocqueville and Herbert Spencer had little to do with universities as either students or teachers. Yet, they helped to shape intellectual disciplines that soon became central to the work of the universities.

If the nineteenth century university, particularly in England, appears excessively conservative, the contemporary American university seems to show an eager appetite for every conceivable subject. These tendencies are not always driven by the 'adventure of ideas' or the 'search for truth'. Political considerations—the desire to trim one's sail to the prevailing winds—and commercial considerations—the desire to augment the university's income—play their part, although they may be masked, often only thinly, by tendentious arguments about the need for innovation. When this happens repeatedly and on a wide scale, the university is likely to lose its focus as a centre of learning.

As historical experience abundantly shows, it is difficult, if not impossible, to determine once and for all the intellectual core of the university in terms of a set of substantive disciplines. What constituted the core at one time became peripheral at another, disciplines that hardly existed in the past have now come to inhabit the core. The core can be identified only with reference to the existing body of systematic knowledge and the possibility of its further systematization in the foreseeable future. The governing principle, at any rate, should be the scope for systematic knowledge, and not reasons of state or the logic of the market.

The intellectual core of the university as it has developed in India is to be found in what are broadly described as the arts and sciences. They cover such disciplines as literature, history, philosophy, mathematics, physics, chemistry and biology. These are the basic disciplines, not only at the level of undergraduate teaching but also from the viewpoint of the most advanced and specialized research. Other disciplines, such as law, medicine, engineering, management and music have also been accommodated in the Indian university, but they do not constitute its intellectual core in terms of either teaching or research, and are indeed often pursued at highly advanced levels in specialized institutions outside the universities in the proper sense of the term.

Academic and Practical Values

It can of course be argued that it is subjects such as medicine, engineering and management that are of direct and immediate practical value in the modern world, and therefore those subjects rather than the academic ones such as literature, philosophy and mathematics should be most actively promoted in universities today. Practical concerns have begun to weigh very heavily on the university, and the conception of it as an 'ivory tower' is under attack from all sides. I do not know a single Indian academic who is prepared to make out a case in public for the university as an ivory tower, and, yet, such a conception of it is not in principle indefensible.

It has now become a matter of habit not only to distinguish between the practical (or useful) and the academic but also, and invariably, to treat the latter as of lower value than the former. It would be understandable if the habit were confined to businessmen, politicians and administrators, but it seems in fact to be equally common among academics. When people, including professors, say that something is only of academic interest, what they mean is that it is of no real interest at all. A little bit of self-doubt is always to be commended, but the wholesale denigration by academics of what is essential to their vocation cannot have a generally beneficial effect on themselves or their work.

The demands of science and scholarship have never stood in a simple or direct relationship to the demands of practical economic or political life. In the words of Parsons and Platt (1973: 33), 'Concern with knowledge and its advancement is analytically independent of its practical uses.' Even where scientific pursuits have had enormous practical consequences, they were not always foreseen by the persons who were engaged in those pursuits. The real value of the best scientific work, as indeed of the best work in the humanities, is that it alters our perceptions of the possibilities inherent in nature, society and man. The pursuit of science and scholarship has continuously shifted the horizon of human possibilities through the laborious and systematic accumulation of knowledge. The universities carry the responsibility not only of creating new knowledge but also of transmitting the accumulating knowledge to successive generations. It is the recognition of this that led some of the ablest minds to argue that the university must keep moving on the two legs of teaching and research.

Why has it become so easy to put scholars and scientists out of countenance by saying that they live in ivory towers? Was this always so? Or is the contempt for the ivory tower a specific feature of the modern world? A life of contemplation as against a life of action was not always viewed as a thing of little value. Detachment from the affairs of the world was indeed carried to its ultimate limit in the Brahminical intellectual tradition, and the present extreme hostility towards detached intellectual pursuits in India may in large part be a reaction against that very tradition.

But nobody can really pretend that the Indian university today is a haven of contemplative calm. It is marked by a pervasive turmoil and disorder that seems to become more intense with every passing day. Anyone who values sustained and disciplined intellectual effort has to work against the current and to expend a considerable part of his energy merely to keep his head above the water. I am not talking now of creative or original work in science and scholarship, but merely of the effort to keep abreast of new knowledge in a particular field in order to transmit it in a spirit of critical detachment. Only those who have the stamina to persevere in that effort can have some sense of the utter vacuity of the clamour from outside to be creative and original or to be socially useful and relevant.

It would be unrealistic to expect too much from our universities as they are constituted today. They have to contend with too many problems that are extraneous to the pursuit of science and scholarship, and we cannot wish those problems out of existence. Vice-chancellors, deans and principals—those from whom academic leadership is expected—are beleaguered persons who have very little time to devote to academic matters, and if they manage to read a few books in their spare time, they should be applauded.

Originality and Tradition in Science and Scholarship

I do not visualize much original work in science and scholarship emerging from our universities in the immediate future. Moreover, we should not discount the negative effects of the pressure for originality in research. One unfortunate outcome of it is the menace of academic fraud, not only in India, but in many parts of the world. A large number of research dissertations are produced every year and are awarded the highest degrees of our universities. As I have indicated earlier, the research embodied in these dissertations is often of doubtful value. Apart from the poor quality of the research, texts are often extensively copied, and results occasionally faked. The worst part of it is when this is done with the complicity of the supervisor and the examiner turns a blind eye to palpable evidence of fraud. This would not be possible on the scale on which it appears to exist if supervisors and examiners did not themselves occasionally engage in academic fraud on a higher level under the pressure to publish research papers and monographs.

The question will naturally be asked, if little original work is being done in the universities, then why talk about the 'adventure of ideas' and the 'search for truth'? This is an important question that should not be swept under the carpet. First of all, the traditions of science and scholarship are of value in themselves, and must be sustained and nourished at some cost, even considerable cost, if that becomes necessary. Enlightened Indians who take a critical view of the many sins of the universities, real and imagined, must seriously ask themselves whether their society can afford to turn its back on those traditions; and, if not, then how successfully they can be kept alive in the absence of an appropriate institutional setting.

It may sound jarring to modern ears to find science and scholarship juxtaposed with tradition. Yet even a casual examination of how scientists work, not only in India but in the most advanced countries in the world, will show how closely their work is embedded in the traditions of scientific research (Shils 1981). Science and scholarship must necessarily depend on traditions because their work is in a fundamental way cumulative; no scientist or scholar today sets out entirely on his own, but builds on the work of his predecessors. The mistake is to think of tradition—whether in science, scholarship or religion—as merely a mechanical repetition of *mantras*. When I speak of a tradition of science and scholarship, I have in mind something living that is renewed, even reshaped and recreated, through everyday practice. That tradition develops habits of thought and work over a long period of time. It does not exist everywhere, and where it exists, it is not immune to decay and degeneration.

Undoubtedly, where new ideas are being continuously forged, the tradition of science and scholarship will present a particularly vibrant aspect, but it need not die for want of original work of a high equality. There are many different ways, and not just one singl· way of participating in the adventure of ideas and the life of the mind. Steadfast loyalty to the demands of disciplined enquiry, rather than originality, is what counts in the vocation of science and scholarship. To devote a lifetime of disciplined enquiry to the solution of an intellectual problem and to then find that an elegant solution to it has already been found by someone else is also a way of participating in the life of the mind. To hold a brand new idea in one's grasp—even if it is someone else's idea—and to share its contents with eager minds—if only a handful of students or colleagues—that too is a way of participating in the adventure of ideas. In the world of ideas, it is the philistines who ask only for results.

Universities as Trustees

I have spoken of the traditions of science and scholarship, and of the university as providing an institutional home for the preservation, protection and cultivation of those traditions. The university is in that sense much more than a teaching shop or an agency for the efficient completion of research projects. What I would like to stress here is that the traditions of science and scholarship need an institutional home even when, or perhaps specially when, they are relatively dormant. There will be no call to argue for the social significance of the universities when those traditions are active and vibrant in them: nobody seriously asked what social purpose was being served by the University of Calcutta in the twenties or by the University of Delhi in the sixties. The mere presence in the University of Calcutta in those days of its great scientists and scholars, and in the University of Delhi in a later period of such persons as T.R. Sheshadri, P. Maheshwari, D.S. Kothari, M.N. Srinivas and K.N. Raj would ilence such questions.

Now there is a change of fortune in the Indian universities, and they have to answer for themselves. In their present predicament, they can think of only the present, and of neither the past nor the future. The overwhelming feeling in the universities, at least among those responsible for their governance, is that *if only* the current financial crisis can somehow be overcome or circumvented, the future will look after itself. But the life of the university as a repository of knowledge and a centre of learning is different from that of its individual members: it does not live for the day, but for the future.

Universities are important in the modern world because they serve as repositories of knowledge for present as well as future use. There is no dearth of individual talent in our country, but such talent is generally infructuous in the absence of an environment for its disciplined cultivation and use, or it comes to fruit in the person of the dilettante who has a passing thought to fit every occasion. No individual scholar or scientist today can carry in his own head every fact or idea that he may require to use; and it saves an enormous amount of time and energy to have the results of one's enquiries checked and corrected at every step by others who are engaged in similar enquiries.

A certain tradition of disciplined enquiry can be maintained, even when it is not being substantially extended, through the regularity and routine of everyday academic work. I have stressed the importance of this kind of work in the maintenance of the tradition of the universities. Its long-term cumulative effect is not easy to demonstrate, but the tradition it helps to maintain does place within easy reach of its bearers, facts and ideas that it would be impossible today for any single individual to master on his own. What use the majority of students—and teachers—make of what is still easily available within the university, and in some respects only within the university, is another question. To be sure, the mere existence of the resources of intellectual life does not ensure their active use: one can easily find examples from our universities of libraries where books gather dust and laboratories where equipment gathers rust. Intellectual resources, no less than material ones, decay through disuse, and when the traditions of science and scholarship dry up in our universities, even our best intellectual talent will have to compete on unfavourable terms with intellectual talent in other countries that have done well by their universities.

When a society prospers by virtue of its material technology, that is readily discernible. But no less important to its general well-being is its capacity to keep abreast of the most advanced forms of knowledge. No doubt, at the individual level, it is now possible to secure some of that knowledge in centres of training in countries other than one's own: the massive outflow of talent from our colleges and universities to centres in the United States and Europe shows it only too well. But that is hardly a solution to the problem at the social level. A society so large and so well-endowed intellectually as ours must maintain within itself the traditions of science and scholarship for future use by its own members, no matter how freely it allows the movement of ideas and persons across its frontiers.

The proper way to view universities is as trustees for society of a valuable component of its resources. The American sociologist Talcott Parsons has characterized the academic system as a fiduciary system, whose 'primary societal function is to act as a trustee of cognitive culture and the interests associated with it' (Parsons and Platt 1973: 18). It is true that in recent decades in India, neither students nor teachers have acted like trustees. The predominant tendency has been to use the universities instrumentally, by students to secure degrees and diplomas with minimal intellectual effort, and by teachers to secure pay and promotion for as little academic work as possible. These developments have led to a steady decline in the value placed on the universities by those outside them. But there is no indication whatever that any other institution can take over the role of trustee that the universities have played in our society and play in all societies that value the long-term and disciplined cultivation of knowledge.

Polymorphous Nature of Higher Education

Because the pursuit of science and scholarship is part of a tradition which entails shared activity, the nature and types of institutions available for that pursuit are important. There is, as I have indicated, no dearth of intellectual talent in India, or of even a genuine respect for learning, including modern science and scholarship. There are indeed many able persons with a genuine vocation for science and scholarship who seek to draw on the resources of their own as well as other cultural traditions. The real source of anxiety does not lie here, but in the failure to build and sustain institutions for the pursuit of science and scholarship. Given the way in which knowledge is organized in the modern world, the individual scientist or scholar cannot proceed far without the support of an institutional structure. Although India has an ancient intellectual heritage, the traditions of its universities do not go back very far in time. There was a period when they appeared to be doing well, but the massive and thoughtless expansion of the fifties and sixties took a heavy toll on the fledgling traditions of the Indian universities, and, today, for a variety of reasons, their fate seems to hang in the balance.

Although universities, as I have described them, are an important, not to say an indispensable, part of the modern world, higher education today is and must be institutionally polymorphous. As Edward Shils has put it, 'Indeed higher education, in Great Britain, Germany, the United States, Italy, the Scandinavian countries, has always been polymorphous. There have been specialized colleges of particular sciences, engineering colleges, commercial colleges, mining academies, colleges of chemistry, teacher training colleges and many others' (Shils 1992: 242). This diversity of location is only one indication of the great importance of higher education and of institutions of learning in all modern societies.

Where so much attention is paid to higher education and the advancement of learning, it is natural to find continuous efforts at institutional innovation. By the end of the eighteenth century, the European universities had touched their low—water mark. Most of the developments in science and scholarship were taking place outside the universities. Henry Cavendish (1731–1810) left Cambridge without taking a degree and did his pioneering work in physics and chemistry in the peace and quiet of his spacious London home. Edward Gibbon (1737–94) left Oxford in disgust, and completed his monumental work on Roman history single-handed and in isolation from the influence of universities. The situation was similar throughout Europe. Clearly, the universities had exhausted their capacity to provide a congenial home for science and scholarship, and new beginnings had to be made.

I will mention here only the two most important attempts at institutional innovation, associated with the names of Napoleon in France and of Wilhelm von Humboldt in Germany. Napoleon's reform sought to bypass the universities by creating special schools—the *grandes écoles*— for training a new kind of professional for the services of the state. These institutions, particularly the École Polytechnique and the École Normale Supérieure, have emerged as highly successful centres of study and training, but, although the French universities remained in the doldrums for many decades, they recovered much of their prestige and influence by the end of the nineteenth century. Humboldt's innovation was to change the university from within, and the new university set up under his guidance in Berlin in 1809 established the principle of the unity of teaching and research, and became a model for many universities, first in Europe and then in the United States. Today, it is in the United States—at Harvard, Princeton, Stanford and Chicago—rather than in his own country that Humboldt's model of the university seems to be working most successfully.

Here I would like to note in passing that both types of institutions of higher learning, the *grande école* and the 'research university' were throughout the nineteenth century very small and very selective institutions. The *grandes écoles* continue to this day to be small and selective, even elitist, despite Napoleon's formula of 'careers open to talent' (Smith 1982; Suleiman 1978).

Particularly since World War II, a great many new centres of advanced study and research have been created outside the universities. The natural sciences provided the lead, and other disciplines followed. Notable among these are the various units of the Centre Naionale de la Recherche Scientifique (CNRS) in France and the Max Planck Institutes in Germany. In India, there were first the national laboratories, notably the National Physical Laboratory and the National Chemical Laboratory, and then the twenty-seven social science institutes under the aegis of the Indian Council of Social Science Research.

There is no reason why all scientific or scholarly work at even the most advanced level should be done only in institutions of a single kind. Hitherto, the universities have provided the most important setting for conducting study and research in a certain way, and I have tried to argue that they should continue to play their part in maintaining, cultivating and extending the traditions of science and scholarship in the present and the future. Other institutions will play their part in other ways. It is not altogether easy in the light of this to understand the recent scramble to get some of these institutions recognized by the UGC as 'deemed universities'. It is perhaps a sign of a deep ambivalence among our scholars and scientists that some of those who think the worst of the universities would nevertheless like to be recognized as university men and women. To be fair, there are on the other side academics busily engaged in contriving all kinds of courses and programmes to show that universities too can contribute to socially useful productive work.

University Funding

If we acknowledge the value of having a variety of institutions for training, study and research, we have to ask how and by whom they are to be supported. If there is to be public support, then what should be the criteria for allocating public funds among these various types of institutions? Here I will consider the question only in relation to the universities, although we cannot ignore the possibility that more money for universities might mean less money for other institutions, and vice-versa.

The universities are now facing a financial crisis throughout the country. They have faced other kinds of crises in the past, but nothing is taken as seriously in a university as a financial crisis. This is because they have neither the ability to raise new resources nor the energy to manage their meagre resources economically.

The financial crisis in our universities is an expression of a deeper moral crisis that may be encountered in almost every type of public institution in the country. Over a period of nearly fifty years since the country became independent, these institutions have acquired the habit of being prodigal at the expense of the Consolidated Fund of India. Nobody will say that the universities have been lavishly funded, but funds have been made available in a manner that has bred laziness and irresponsibility. The universities were encouraged to believe that all their expenditures would be underwritten by the government, but the government rarely gave money with good grace. In the end, the government always gave the money, not on the scale expected or required, indeed often arbitrarily and quixotically, and in course of time, the universities became abjectly dependent for money on petty bureaucrats, neglecting all other sources, internal and external, for augmenting their revenue.

A change has now come about in the policy environment, and the universities have begun to feel the pinch. There is even talk of privatization. This adverse turn of events may have some beneficial effect on the universities if it teaches them to husband their resources with care and a sense of responsibility. No agency other than a corrupt and ineffectual government bureaucracy is likely to provide a continuing supply of money where it is so wastefully expended. The trick of wasting public money and then seeking immunity in the name of 'academic autonomy' has been played out. In any case, it is unlikely to work with private donors. The universities must first learn to cut out waste in the use of existing resources, and then seek to raise new resources. Here it is not a question of economically useful or socially relevant intellectual pursuits, but one of efficient as against wasteful use of resources. A small but active department of philosophy may use its resources much more economically than a large department of chemistry where equipment lies unutilized and little work is done.

Cutting back on waste is a very different thing from cutting back on basic disciplines in favour of applied ones, for resources may be as wastefully used in the one as in the other. It does not mean cutting back on medieval history to make room for hotel management, or cutting back on physics to make room for computer science. Hotel management and computer science are no doubt important in their own right, but they do not belong to the core of the university as a repository of knowledge and a centre of learning . Indeed, such practical and applied subjects can be more efficiently handled in specialized institutions outside the universities. This is not a time for the universities to take on new responsibilities that they are ill equipped to discharge. They should return to their old commitments, towards which they have been apathetic and neglectful, and pursue them with some energy and sense of purpose.

If privatization means that the universities should turn away from the basic pursuits of science and scholarship in order to give more attention to easily marketable courses and programmes, then such privatization can only bring disaster to the universities. The universities in India must continue to do what they were established to do—the advancement of learning—and what they are best capable of doing. They must for the present continue to act as repositories of the traditions of science and scholarship, and keep those traditions alive in the hope that in the future they too might add something of their own to them. They must resist demands and temptations to take them away into domains in which they have little capacity to act effectively. The universities were not created to serve either the state or the market; they were created to serve future generations.

A society that values the traditions of science and scholarship, the 'adventure of ideas' and the 'search for truth' can ill afford to make the universities fend for themselves. The state has some obligations to the universities that it must clearly acknowledge. It must also acknowledge that part of the poor performance of the universities in recent decades has been due to its own thoughtless pressures on them. The universities have been expected to keep masses of potentially turbulent young men and women off the streets; to provide 'meaningful education' to young persons from families with little experience of learning; to train people for administrative, managerial and professional employment that has expanded very slowly; and, on top of that, to contribute directly to the attainment of economic development and social justice. Some of these unrealistic expectations have been encouraged from within the universities by thoughtless and self-serving vice-chancellors, deans and professors. Today, their inability to meet these expectations has become only too plainly visible. No amount of help from outside can dispel the atmosphere of apathy and indolence to which academics have become accustomed in our universities. They must change themselves, and decide what they stand for and what they are prepared to do. Only then can they expect society to meet its obligations to the universities.

Notes

1. The symposium was published in a special issue of *Minerva*, vol. XXX, no. 2, Summer 1992.

2. Some scientists, Saha in particular, later worked tirelessly for the promotion of science ir the cause of nation building, but I am talking about the impulse behind their work when they were most active as scientists.

3. The term 'science' here translates the German word 'Wissenschaft' which

covers all branches of systematic learning; Weber's observation related particularly to the social sciences.

References

Banerjee, Pramathanath et al. 1957. *Hundred Years of the University of Calcutta*. Calcutta: University of Calcutta Press.

Béteille, André. 1981. 'The Indian University: Academic Standards and the Pursuit of Equality'. *Minerva*, vol. XIX, no. 2, pp. 282–310.

—— 1992. 'Comments', *Minerva*, vol. XXX, no. 2, pp. 206–10.

—— 1995. 'Universities as Institutions', *Economic and Political Weekly*, vol. XXX, no. 11, pp. 563–8; see chapter 7, this volume.

Bloom, Allen. 1987. *The Closing of the American Mind*. New York: Simon and Schuster.

Durkheim, Émile. 1984 [1893]. *The Division of Labour in Society*. New York: The Free Press.

Gerth, H.H. and C. Wright Mills (eds). 1946. *From Max Weber: Essays in Sociology*. New York: Oxford University Press.

Nehru, Jawaharlal. 1949. *Speeches, 1946–49*. New Delhi: Government of India, vol. 1.

Newman, John Henry. 1976 [1852]. *The Idea of a University*. Oxford: Clarendon Press.

Parsons, Talcott and Gerald M. Platt. 1973. *The American University*. Cambridge, Mass.: Harvard University Press.

Rüegg, Walter. 1992. 'The Traditions of the University in the Face of the Demands of the Twenty-First Century', *Minerva*, vol. XXX, no. 2, pp. 189–205.

Shattock, Michael. 1992. 'The Internal and External Threats to the University of the Twenty-First Century', *Minerva*, vol. XXX, no. 2, pp. 130–47.

Shils, Edward. 1981. *Tradition*. Chicago: University of Chicago Press.

—— 1992. 'The Service of Society and the Advancement of Learning in the Twenty-First Century', *Minerva*, vol. XXX, no. 2, pp. 242–68.

Smith, Robert J. 1982. *The École Normale Supérieure and the Third Republic*. New York: State University of New York Press.

Stone, Lawrence (ed.). 1974. *The University in Society*. Princeton: Princeton University Press, vol. 1.

Suleiman, Ezra N. 1978. *Elites in French Society*. Princeton: Princeton University Press.

University Education Commission. 1949. *Report*. Simla: Government of India Press, vol. 1.

7

Universities as Institutions*

An institution is a social arrangement that has not only a certain form and function but also a certain legitimacy and meaning for its individual members. Its form and function are what we may observe from outside; but viewed from within and by its members, what count for as much, if not more, are questions of meaning and legitimacy. I would like to discuss the university in contemporary India as an institution. Conducted with proper care and attention, such a discussion might open a window onto many aspects of Indian society today.

The life of a society, if the metaphor be permitted, is in a significant sense the life of its many and diverse institutions. Sometimes old institutions decay through loss of legitimacy and meaning even though many of their morphological features survive. The opposite may also be true; a new social arrangement may be given the outward form of an institution, but it will not function as one if its members find little or no inner meaning in it. Let me repeat an observation I have made elsewhere (Béteille 1992): an institution is not simply any social arrangement, but one which has a certain meaning for its members such that they acknowledge its moral claims on them and are willing to submit to its demands, at least some of the time, even when they find those demands to be contrary to their individual interests.

* Originally published in *Economic and Political Weekly*, vol. XXX, no. 11, 1995. This is a revised version of the second of the two Sudhir Kumar Bose Memorial Lectures on Institutions delivered at St Stephen's College in February 1992. I am grateful to the authorities of the college, and in particular Dr Rajinder Gupta for the invitation to deliver the lectures and for their hospitality during the occasion. I would also like to thank Professor Veena Das who chaired the two lectures for her observations and suggestions at that time and subsequently. In particular, it is due to her persuasion that I revised the second lecture for publication.

By the test I have just proposed, is the University of Delhi an institution? Is St Stephen's College an institution? The direction of my enquiry should be clear. St Stephen's college—or, for that matter, any college in the University of Delhi—has the external characteristics of an institution. Those external characteristics are of very great importance and have to be carefully observed and described. But we have to move beyond that to the other question: what does it mean today for a student or a teacher to be a member of a college or a university department in Delhi?

It is difficult to answer the questions I have posed without entering into the details of the everyday life of the university, its colleges and post-graduate departments. But before I attempt to do that, I would like to place those questions in a wider social context. A large and complex society such as the Indian has a highly differentiated institutional system: there are many and various institutions in it, some securely established, others on their way out, and yet others struggling to become established. These last have become a source of concern to many in India today. The present exercise may be regarded as an attempt to give expression to this widely-felt concern from the sociological point of view.

The transformation of Indian society since the middle of the nineteenth century has been associated with the growth of a large number of public and semi-public institutions that are either new or differ substantially from those that prevailed in the past (Béteille 1991). The new institutions differ from the old not only in their morphological forms but also in the values that give them meaning and legitimacy. To be sure, India had institutions of learning in the past, but a modern college such as St Stephen's—or a modern university such as the University of Delhi—differs from those both in its external characteristics and in the norms and values by which its members are required or expected to abide.

Independent India set itself the objective of economic development within the framework of a democratic political system. Whether one stresses the plan or the market, and whatever combination of the two one recommends, there can be no sustained economic development in the absence of appropriate institutions; and unless there are effective institutions to mediate between citizens and the state, there can be no democracy in any meaningful sense. The old social arrangements inherited from the past can no longer meet all the demands of economic efficiency, and even less those of good citizenship. It is said by one and all that the old hierarchical and paternalistic values have become obsolete. But the new values that are to replace the old ones cannot exist, still less act, in a vacuum; they need new institutions for their sustenance and expression.

I would like to stress here the variety of institutions and the importance of this variety for a dynamic economy and, even more, for a democratic polity. A democratic polity requires not only parties and other political institutions, but different kinds of these that are to some extent in competition with each other. A dynamic economy requires not only banks and other financial institutions, but a variety of these to offer services on competitive terms. The same argument may be extended to educational institutions. Schools, colleges, universities and other educational institutions are not only different from political and financial institutions, they also differ among themselves. Today, one of the advantages of the American university system over the European is that the former accommodates a richer variety of institutions, 'private' as well as 'public', than the latter.[1]

Institutions have in general a longer life span than individuals. Sometimes they decay over time and become attenuated or even extinct. Or they change and adapt themselves to the changes taking place in the wider society. For example, the Indian family is changing and likely to change further, but it still remains recognizably the same kind of institution despite these changes. I may refer here to the universities and colleges in Europe. Some of these are medieval foundations, going back to the twelfth and thirteenth centuries. The universities have changed enormously in time but can still be recognized as universities today. The fate of the colleges has been somewhat different. The University of Paris, one of the two founding universities of Europe, had a number of important colleges in the past, but they all disappeared in course of time (Rashdall 1936; Stone 1974). In Oxford and Cambridge, on the other hand, the colleges made a more successful transition from medieval to modern times, and, though vastly different from what they were in the past, remain active as institutions to this day.

The integration of institutions, whether of the same kind or of different kinds, is a complex and difficult subject into which I cannot enter here. It is sufficient to note that many different kinds of institutions—old and new, traditional and modern, sacred and secular, private and public—have in fact co-existed in one and the same society at different times in different places. To be sure, institutions may be mutually incompatible, but their incompatibility has to be established not so much by applying formal rules as by examining the historical record.

Finally, we have to remember that, although every institution demands some loyalty from its individual members, the same individual is characteristically—and not incidentally—a member of several institutions. For instance, a permanent member of a college is typically, though not universally, also a member of a family and sometimes a member of a church or some other religious institution as well as a member of a party or some other political institution. Here again, the conflict of demands may sometimes be acute as, for instance, when the same individual is a member of the Catholic church as well as of a Communist Party, but both individuals and institutions are capable of a great deal of accommodation in these matters. In the past, in Cambridge and Oxford, domestic life was considered incompatible with the life of fellowship in a college, so fellows were not permitted to marry. For instance, the economist Alfred Marshall had to give up his fellowship of St John's College when he married (Pigou 1956); but the demands of the college on its fellows eased somewhat over time, and it is no longer considered necessary for them to remain celibate. What is more, St John's College now admits women to its fellowship, a development that Marshall would have deplored.

I would now like to take up for consideration universities (and colleges) as institutions characteristic of modern India. Their importance in the modernization of Indian society—its economic and political transformation—hardly requires emphasis. At the same time, I would not like to claim any pre-eminence for these among other institutions such as courts, legislatures, parties, banks, hospitals and so on, that are also a part of the modern Indian scene. If I select a particular kind of institution, it is because I believe that I can present my argument best by a close examination of a single type, and I know academic institutions a little better than most other institutions.

Universities and colleges in India are modern institutions. Unlike domestic and religious institutions, they do not derive their sanction from 'immemorial tradition'. Since universities and colleges as academic institutions typically pride themselves on the antiquity of their traditions, the fact of newness is important. Most parts of the University of Delhi, including the majority of its colleges, have come up in the last two or three decades. The university itself came into existence in 1922, although its two oldest colleges both belong to the end of the nineteenth century. It is sometimes felt that in contemporary India universities and colleges have expanded too rapidly and too haphazardly under demographic, political and other pressures to enable them to create secure institutional foundations for themselves.

Delhi University has emerged as a large and sprawling institution with many parts that do not appear to fit together harmoniously or at all. No proper history of it exists, and it is difficult to give even an adequate description of it in sociological terms. Yet the transformations undergone by the University of Delhi in the last forty years might be a subject of great interest to the sociologist and the social historian concerned with the study of social change in modern India.

The two principal component parts of the University of Delhi as an academic institution are the colleges and the post-graduate departments. There are in addition halls of residence, libraries, laboratories, statutory bodies such as the executive and the academic councils, and separate departments dealing with administration, examinations, finance, and so on. The different parts of the university have grown unevenly, some very rapidly, and Delhi University is losing the unity and coherence it had in the fifties. An important aspect of the university as an institution is that its individual members—whether students or teachers—should have some sense of it as a whole. Not many persons can say confidently or honestly that they have such a sense about Delhi University today, and in that regard it is now different from what it was forty years ago and what the Jawaharlal Nehru University still is today.

The growing loss of identity in the University of Delhi is due in part to its great and rapid expansion, but there may be other, deeper reasons as well. The individual colleges and post-graduate departments, though perhaps not all of them, retain a larger degree of self-identity, and they are in any case the principal seats of teaching and research in the university. Today one gets a better sense of the life in an academic institution by examining a college or a post-graduate department than by trying to look at the university as a whole. I must point out that there is nothing inconsistent in speaking of the University of Delhi as well as any of its colleges as institutions, since institutions are often nesting systems in which the fundamental features of the whole are replicated in the parts and sub-parts.

In their foundation, the colleges are prior to the university, not only in Delhi but also in Calcutta, Bombay and Madras where the first three modern universities were established in India. In Calcutta, throughout the nineteenth century, the centres of academic life, where students and teachers met and interacted, were in Hindu College (later Presidency College), St Xavier's College and the Scottish Churches College rather than in the University of Calcutta (Banerjee et al. 1957). Lord Curzon noted this lack of institutional focus in the University of Calcutta, then the premier university in the country. He observed, 'How different is India! Here the university has no corporate existence ... it is not a collection of buildings, it is scarcely even a site. It is a body that controls courses of study and sets examination papers to pupils of affiliated colleges' (Government of India 1971: 498).

Attempts were made in the early part of the twentieth century to make good the deficiency by creating a focus of institutional life in the universities of Dacca, Benares, and later Delhi. Lord Curzon's observation on the absence of buildings and building site was taken to heart. The idea that every university must have its own campus has now come to be generally accepted. In post-independence India, the establishment of a new university has generally been associated with much building activity. But while campus and buildings may be necessary to give the university an institutional look, they are not sufficient. In any case, the new university soon outgrows the buildings with which it started, and the regularity with which they are allowed to run down is a symptom of the university's inability to find and retain its institutional focus.

The older universities were set up to be examining bodies rather than bodies of scholars engaged in study and research. Attempts to change this began in the early part of the present century. The University of Calcutta took the lead under the vice-chancellorship of Sir Ashutosh Mukherji by creating strong post-graduate departments in the arts and sciences (Banerji et al. 1957). It became the centre of a vigorous intellectual life in the twenties, thirties and forties, but lost its focus soon after independence. The University of Delhi came into its own as an institution in the fifties and sixties, but has now entered a phase of decline. There are many reasons behind this, but here I will only point to the constant threat to the institutional focus of the Indian university from the pressures of certification. Examinations are no doubt important, but when a university subordinates its other concerns to the concern for certification, there cannot but be a loss of institutional focus.

The University of Delhi, like the Universities of Calcutta, Bombay and Madras, conducts hundreds of examination, and awards thousands of degrees, diplomas and certificates every year. It is believed, though difficult to prove, that large and growing numbers of students enrol themselves in the University of Delhi mainly if not solely in order to secure its degrees. One cannot say how widespread this tendency is, but where it becomes the general pattern, the university will, despite campus and buildings, become what the University of Calcutta was when it started, an examining body with little or no corporate existence.

Today it may be easier to find a corporate identity in the colleges, or at least in some of them, although these may be in a minority among the thousands of colleges that now exist in the country. I shall turn presently to the social side of this corporate identity, which is its most important aspect, but before that I would like to make a few observations on its physical locus.

While going through the history of St Stephen's College, I was struck by the continuous concern of the authorities to provide the college with buildings of its own (Monk 1935). The college started in rented premises but soon moved to its own buildings near Kashmiri Gate in 1891. There was no University of Delhi then. Shortly after the new university was established, the college, which became affiliated with it, began making plans for buildings on the campus, but it took a couple of decades for it to move into its present location. St Stephen's College is by common consent one of the few physically attractive places remaining in the University of Delhi, although there were several such places only thirty years ago. Few colleges in India have the resources of St Stephen's; nevertheless, the others might have done a little better, if they had cared a little more for their institutions, about the maintenance and upkeep of their premises.

Why is the physical aspect of a college important? Certification and even formal instruction in the classroom are only a part, and perhaps not the most important part, of the life of the college as an institution. A college is above all a place for the interchange of ideas on every conceivable subject among teachers and students, and that interchange cannot be effective without long and continuous interaction. To be sure, those who are driven by the passion for ideas will make a place for their expression anywhere. But I am talking about institutions and not exceptional individuals, and the task of the institution is precisely to provide its ordinary members with a setting that they find both physically and socially congenial. A college which is physically incongenial will be unlikely to keep its ordinary members longer than is minimally required by the rules of attendance. As we know very well, that requirement, for both students and teachers, has turned out to be remarkably elastic.

I now move from the physical to the social, and start with Curzon's lament about the lack of a corporate existence. We might ask in what sense a university or a college may be regarded as a corporation. I do not wish to enter into technical legal questions, but we might consider the celebrated dictum of Sir Henry Maine—incidentally, one of the early vice-chancellors of the University of Calcutta—that 'Corporations *never die*' (Maine 1931: 104, emphasis in original).

Of course, Maine knew very well that it is not literally true that a corporation cannot die: what he wished to convey by the phrase was a sense of the enduring identity of the corporation, or its capacity to outlive its individual members. I can be reasonably certain that St Stephen's College—or even the University of Delhi—will not cease to exist in my own lifetime. But there is more to it than that, for one can see the college extending into the future and retaining its identity even after all its present members have been replaced by new ones.

Every institution must have the capacity to maintain its collective identity despite the continuous replacement of its old members by new ones, but that capacity is particularly manifest in the university and the college. In the typical case, the students greatly outnumber the teachers. Between a third and a quarter of the former leave the college or the university every year and are replaced by new ones. The student body of the college today is completely different, or almost completely different from the body five years ago yet it is the same college. Teachers have a lower turnover, and that is why they have an appearance of permanence whereas the students appear as transients, although in the long run, or from the viewpoint of the institution, everyone is a transient.

A college or a university derives many of its distinctive features as an institution from its characteristic age-structure. It differs from all the modern institutions to which I have earlier referred by virtue of the predominance of the young. The relations between the generations is of great significance in every society, and especially in one in which important changes are taking place. Changes are taking place not only in social relations and in attitudes and values, but probably also in the very meanings that people assign to youth and age. I will make my point with a rapid digression. Many years ago, I was taken aback to read in a very popular text-book on social stratification 'that in American society one is generally considered better, superior, or more worthy if he is ... Young rather than Old' (Tumin 1967: 27). That did not correspond at all with my understanding of my own society, but I soon realized that the meanings assigned to youth and age are neither invariant nor unchanging. If those meanings are changing today, there is no public domain in which the change can be more easily observed than in the college or the university.

The same text-book on social stratification observed that one is generally considered better, superior, or more worthy if he is 'Male rather than Female' (Tumin 1967: 27). Here, by changing themselves from within, the universities and colleges have played a crucial part in introducing changes in attitudes and perceptions throughout society. The universities were predominantly, if not overwhelmingly, male institutions until very recently, not only in India but everywhere. Removing the restrictions on the admission and appointment of women, and their incorporation into the institutions of higher education have been among the most significant changes of the twentieth century. Towards the end of his life, Edmund Leach, known for his radical views as a young anthropologist but later criticized for joining the establishment, said in an interview that it was after all while he was Provost of King's College that women were first given admission into that bastion of male privilege (Kuper 1986). He wished to be remembered for the part he had played in that outcome, and, I believe, with good judgement.

Young men and women unrelated by ties of kinship and community can interact more freely in the university than perhaps in any other domain of society. If it has done nothing else, it has at the very least created a new basis for the relationship between men and women in contemporary India. In the past, whether among Hindus or Muslims, the life led by women was either hard or confined, or both, and that is probably true of most women even today. It is mainly in the college or the university that, as a young adult, a woman can enjoy a little freedom to explore new social relations and to construct a new social identity. In the past, in all social classes a woman was already burdened by the cares of domestic life by the time she was seventeen or eighteen, today, if she has the luck to enter university, a new life might open up for her at that age. The university has provided a new ideal of womanhood even if only a handful are able to give that ideal a concrete shape.

Success in academic competition creates a new sense of confidence in women, although we must not exaggerate the extent of change that this can bring about in the actual relations between men and women. Ours is in many ways a deeply conservative society, and conservatism takes its most obdurate form in the attitudes of men towards women.

Academic and other achievements do not automatically bring about equality in social relations, and women are reminded at every turn of their subordinate position in society and its institutions. Yet, I believe that it speaks well of our colleges that here in Delhi the best women undergraduates prefer mixed colleges for their study to colleges only for women.

I now turn, though only briefly, to the thorny question of institutional hierarchy. I have spoken deliberately of the inequality between men and women in order to point out that, although it is pervasive in Indian society, it is neither necessary nor desirable in an academic institution. If the college cannot remove or reduce the inequalities in the relations between men and women that its members bring into it from the wider society, it fails as an academic institution to that extent. But that does not mean that all forms of inequality can or should be removed from the college. Certain forms of it are constitutive of an institution as a stable arrangement of persons engaged in a set of co-ordinated activities. But the inequalities constitutive of, say, the family are not the same as those constitutive of the college; and certainly the inequalities inherent in the institution of caste—and also those largely accepted in our traditional institutions of learning—can have no place in a modern college or university.

I would like to draw attention to only two sources of inequality characteristic of the college or university as an institution. The first is associated with the regulation of activities and the maintenance of discipline; and the second with competition and its outcome. Every institution must take steps to ensure that its daily tasks are smoothly performed and must therefore invest some of its members with more authority—and also more responsibility—than others. It is difficult to visualize a college in which teachers and students—or even the principal, the senior teachers and the junior teachers—all enjoy equal authority. It can be easily argued from general principles that the co-ordination of the wide range of differentiated activities that take place in a college—and even more in the university as a whole—requires some regulatory mechanism which in turn requires some inequality in the distribution of authority (Béteille 1977).

Discipline in any institution is maintained largely through internal sanctions without the use or even the threat of punishment. Where the use or the threat of punishment becomes the usual rather than the exceptional method of social regulation, one might hesitate to speak of it as an institution. No institution can work without some exercise of authority, but the constant exercise of authority leads to a loss of its legitimacy, and where authority loses its legitimacy, the institution is bound to decline.

A university or college is a place of achievement through success in free, if not always fair, competition (Béteille 1987: 157–84, 212–32). It is also a place of academic distinction; or at least its members are expected to strive to make it one. This means that it must not be apprehensive of inequality as such, but be prepared to accept those forms of it that follow from the application of the criteria that it values. It must take the responsibility of sorting the good students out from the bad ones. Above all, it must not be afraid to distinguish between bright, capable and enthusiastic teachers and those who are dull, incompetent and lazy. A university will fail in its essential responsibility to discriminate among students according to academic standards if it refuses to apply those standards in discriminating among its teachers.

One cannot speak of the university or college as an institution without confronting the question of academic standards. There cannot be any fixed or invariant standard of academic excellence and, above all, it cannot be imposed on the university from outside. Universities and colleges differ enormously in their resources, both material and human, and one cannot speak of academic standards without reference to those resources. A college with modest resources cannot maintain the same academic standards, in absolute terms, as, say, the University of Chicago. But the two institutions can both maintain the same high standards, in relative terms, if they use their respective resources with equal care and imagination.

What matters in the end for the institution is not whether it achieves academic excellence but whether it values it. Even our best may not be as good as the second-best in some other institution, but we must not for that reason fail to discriminate among those that we do have. A college thrives on the enthusiasm of its students, and that enthusiasm is smothered if they are all treated alike, irrespective of quality or performance.

Teachers should be prepared to apply academic standards rigorously and impartially not only to their students but also to themselves. The academic selection process is central to the life of an academic institution which is threatened whenever that process is called into question or loses its credibility. It is a fact that there is today in the University of Delhi, as in most Indian universities, pervasive mistrust of the integrity of academic selection committees. That mistrust, irrespective of the grounds on which it is based, strikes at the very heart of the meaning and legitimacy of the college and the university as academic institutions.

How extensive is the lack of integrity of academic selection committees in India today? Let me say at once that the facts are extremely difficult to establish, for, to quote Max Weber's ominous words, 'No university teacher likes to be reminded of discussions of appointments, for they are seldom agreeable' (Gerth and Mills 1946: 133). It is true that academic selection committees make mistakes, but it not true that those mistakes are always made because they act in bad faith. Although they do sometimes act in bad faith, the greater fault with academic selection committees, in my limited personal experience, is not their corruptibility but their conservatism. I have rarely been able to persuade a selection committee to recommend a younger candidate with less experience and fewer publications against older and more experienced candidates with more publications, even when we were all agreed that the younger candidate had greater academic merit than all the others.

More and more people seem to believe that there is something subjective, hence arbitrary, if not capricious, about all judgements of academic merit. It is therefore better, they say, to go by 'objective' criteria such as seniority, class of degree, and number of publications in making academic selections. In the end, they tend to settle for what is, after all, the most objective criterion, namely, the length of service measured in years, months and days, irrespective of the quality of that service. The academic selection process is then reduced to a routine which has the advantage of administrative convenience, but deprives it of all meaning from the academic point of view.

The fear of exercising and being subjected to academic judgement is rationalized by the argument that academic distinctions, like all distinctions of rank, are invidious. I have heard persons in prominent public positions say that such distinctions are a legacy of colonialism, or a form of elitism, and ought to be abolished. Many a pillar of our academic establishment has learnt to mask intellectual timidity by the use of populist rhetoric. Neither the timidity nor the rhetoric augurs well for our universities and colleges, for no academic institution can be sustained on the ideology of Levellers.

The passage from growth to stagnation and decay has been repeated with almost unfailing regularity in practically every Indian university and in most colleges. What is more, the time taken for this passage appears to be getting progressively reduced. When I left Calcutta where I had been a student in the University College of Science to join the University of Delhi as a teacher, the contrast between the two institutions made a great impression on me (Beteille 1990, 1995). Calcutta is India's oldest university. Although it was founded in 1857, it began to function as a centre of post-graduate study and research only in the early years of the twentieth century, and it soon acquired a reputation throughout the country. But by the late fifties it was already in a state of decline. The authorities had failed to look after the physical upkeep of its buildings, libraries and laboratories, and protests, demonstrations and strikes were beginning to undermine the regularity and routine of academic work.

In the late fifties, Delhi University was in the ascendant. It had the advantage of having a proper campus which the University of Calcutta lacked. It appeared both spacious and well-maintained, and teachers and students were moving into it from all parts of the country. But within twenty years it had outgrown its capacity to maintain itself, and the contrast between Delhi University today and as it was in 1959 is as great as that between the Universities of Calcutta and Delhi at that time.

Today the predominant impression of the typical Indian university or college is one of disorder and apathy. The two reinforce each other. The disorder is most clearly visible when large numbers of persons congregate, especially during protests and demonstrations, but it is also seen in the confusion over admission procedures, examination schedules, and even teaching time-tables. A common response to the disorder in an institution is withdrawal by its members, and very few institutions tolerate absenteeism to the extent that universities and colleges do among teachers as well as students. There are not only students who attend courses fitfully and intermittently, but also, and increasingly, professors who are professors only in their spare time.

Every college and university has an administrative staff, and some colleges are in fact well administered and maintained. Universities are generally larger, and their administration and maintenance more difficult. Moreover, academics set a high value, at least in principle, on 'academic autonomy', and the university is organized in such a manner that much of the responsibility for its administration and maintenance rests, at least formally, with the faculty. But increasingly, the members of the faculty are unavailable for that kind of routine work because of lack of time, or lack of interest or lack of energy.

Beneath the surface of apathy and disorder there is an undercurrent of aggression that finds expression in periodic outbursts. A factor that contributes to these outbursts of aggression is that among all public institutions, the universities are the ones that are most open and exposed. For one thing, the university campus is frequently and increasingly invaded by what are euphemistically called 'outside elements'. Moreover, the university brings together socially heterogeneous components, men and women, and persons of diverse castes and communities. As I have observed, for some women the university is preeminently a place of freedom, and in our fundamentally conservative society, this is deeply resented by many men and also by some women. Again, it is not very easy to adjust to the redefinition of the social relations among persons from diverse strata that the university or college necessarily demands.

In popular writing on the university, all the attention is paid to the acute forms of aggression as manifested in campus violence, and hardly any attention is paid to its chronic forms. Yet these chronic forms of aggression have in the long run a debilitating effect on the life of the institution that tends to escape the notice of even its concerned members.

Very few colleges in India retain an aesthetically pleasing appearance, and I cannot think of any university as a whole that does so.[2] Peeling walls, broken window-panes, leaking taps, unswept corridors and filthy toilets meet the eye everywhere, and the sad thing is that teachers and students become so easily inured to the dirt and decay. The university authorities say that they cannot do very much since they are hamstrung by financial cuts which become more acute every year. There is no doubt a problem of financial shortage, but even more acute is the problem of managing and husbanding scarce financial resources. University authorities appear at one and the same time helpless when it comes to augmenting income and profligate when it comes to spending money.

The university campus is aesthetically unattractive partly through neglect and lack of care, but also on account of deliberate and wanton misuse of its spaces. Furniture is broken and window panes are smashed not only on occasions of collective outburst, but as a matter of routine by individuals letting off steam. Outer walls and even inner ones can never be kept clean, since it is the clean ones that are specially targeted for political slogans and moral exhortations. Another expression of this kind of aggression is the defacement of books and periodicals that has become endemic in virtually all university and college libraries.

The chronic aggression finds expression in the surly tone habitually adopted by students, *karamcharis* and teachers whenever disagreement has to be expressed in public. I will say little here about students but confine my observations to the employees of the university. Firstly, there are the specifically political occasions, such as strikes, rallies and demonstrations where discontent is aired and demands presented in the most violent language, not only by *karamcharis* but also by teachers. No doubt the tone of anger is often simulated, but it is infectious. Here, a decisive change has come about in the culture of university and college teachers in the last three decades. Vice-chancellors and principals are often singled out for the choicest abuse by the leaders of the teachers' movement; I have been told that there is nothing personal in this, it is just the political culture of the mass movement from which the university cannot remain isolated.

Violent and abusive language is not confined to strictly political occasions as when trade-union leaders negotiate with the authorities. I can speak from experience about the Academic Council of the University of Delhi, and from hearsay about similar bodies in other universities. I will say nothing of the level of academic ability displayed in the discussions, but only about their tone. That tone is now marked by a conspicuous, even deliberate, lack of civility. At meetings of the Academic Council, those professors who still value civility as a virtue sit silently for most of the time, and quietly slip out as soon as they can decently do so. Many scholars and scientists have begun to feel that it is no longer possible to participate in the decision-making bodies of the university and maintain their self-esteem.

The persistent abuse of vice-chancellors, noisy scenes in the Academic Council, and the generally uncivil tone of public discussions violate the dignity of the university as an institution. It is not enough to be mindful of the dignity of individuals, we must also be mindful of the dignity of institutions. In the past in India people took great care of their traditional institutions, particularly their domestic and religious institutions. When the first universities and other modern institutions came up in the nineteenth century, there was some sense of their dignity, and the need to preserve and nourish it. That sense seems to be now evaporating. This is only another symptom of the loss of meaning and legitimacy which I set out to discuss.

Successful professionals in India—scholars, scientists, doctors, architects, accountants, and others—tend to attribute the apathy and disorder in the institutions in which they work to the malign influence of politicians. There is no dearth of examples of unscrupulous interference by politicians in appointments, promotions and transfers in practically every kind of public institution, and few will deny that our political morality has reached a very low ebb. But there are many issues here that cannot all be despatched by being self-consciously virtuous. Politics is not just something 'out there', the creation and instrument of a separate species called 'politicians' who act on professional pursuits only from outside. It has come to lodge itself within our universities, laboratories, hospitals, and other public institutions. If by politics is meant the use of power for achieving particular ends in accordance with certain accepted codes, it is difficult to see how public institutions can be wholly insulated from it. Scholars, scientists, doctors and others who are quick to condemn politics in public life often fail to acknowledge their own involvement in activities that are also a form of politics.

If the university is to be a self-governing institution, it must make room for some form of politics within it. The lofty attitude to politics adopted in public by many scholars and scientists is misconceived, and it is often hypocritical. As institutions, universities have always been jealous of their autonomy, and their leaders have needed political support both within and outside to protect their autonomy in the face of threats from church, state and other powerful agencies. No one who cares for the university can say that its autonomy does not have to be fought for, or that it can be defended and strengthened without any regard for politics. What is true of the university as a whole is true also of its individual parts, for faculties, departments and colleges also need to protect their autonomy from unwanted and unjustified intrusion by the powers in the university, and that too cannot be done without engaging in politics in some sense of the term.

Having said all this, one must also say that the politics of the university need not, perhaps should not, be organized in the same way as the politics of legislatures, parties and trade unions. Democratic politics requires for its sustenance not only a certain kind of political constitution but also a certain kind of political culture. In a country with a rich intellectual tradition but no democratic institutions, it was hoped that the universities would play a leading part in the creation of that culture. They have on the whole failed to do so. Today, academic politics is not an example for the politics of the wider society; it has allowed itself to be swallowed up by that wider politics. Leaders of teachers' unions have not enhanced their own dignity or the dignity of the university by becoming petty instruments of the Congress (I), the CPI (M) and the

BJP. And they could hardly protect the autonomy of the university by surrendering their own autonomy to their parties.

Today, the problem with academic politics in India is that it is all politics and hardly academic. Few leaders of teachers' unions have any credibility as scholars or scientists, and many of them are indeed teachers in their spare time. Academic politics today is about 'empowering' teachers for securing better pay, guaranteed promotion and easy conditions of work; it has lost all connection with the content of science and scholarship. Universities ought to have representative, even elected bodies in which some amount of political bargaining is to be expected before decisions are reached on academic issues. Academic issues hardly figure in the political bargaining that takes place in organs of the university with a large elected component. Those issues are now not only neglected, they provoke derision from activists among teacher politicians.

Vice-chancellors, deans, principals, and occasionally even leaders of teachers' unions say that the universities have been undone by politics, but by politics they generally mean what other people do, not what they themselves do. They also say from time to time that the government should step in and cleanse the universities of politics, but they say so without much conviction, for they know at bottom that such intervention is more likely to increase than to reduce the part played by politics. Embattled vice-chancellors turn sooner or later to political instruments in order to contain the political forces by which they see themselves threatened. They try to befriend ministers and officials on the one side and leaders of the unions of teachers, *karamcharis* and students on the other, hoping perhaps to use the one against the other, but ending frequently, and perhaps deservedly, as victims of both.

When an institution becomes politicized beyond a point, every problem in it seems a political problem, and no problem seems solvable except in political terms. The head of a university has to spend most of his time and energy in dealing with politicians and officials from outside, and leaders and representatives from within. He cannot, even if he wishes to, spend much time in discussing academic subjects with scholars and scientists, and not many vice-chancellors even appear to wish to do so. In this way, university vice-chancellors come more and more to resemble precisely those adepts in the art of the possible who appear to be their worst adversaries.

Politics cannot be expelled from the university or from any institution that values self-governance. At the same time, it cannot determine the agenda of an institution whose basic aim and purpose is the pursuit of science and scholarship. There are some who believe that the university can be set back on its natural path by a single decisive political act that will expunge all corruption and all injustice from it. That is a mistake. Every living institution has to accommodate some corruption and some injustice as a part of its ordinary existence. The real challenge is to remain loyal to the ideals of science and scholarship in a world that offers other and more immediate attractions.

Notes

1. This point came up repeatedly at the round-table discussion on 'Universities of the Twenty-First Century' held at the University of Chicago on 4 and 5 October 1991 on the occasion of its centennial. See *Minerva*, vol. XXX, no. 2, Summer 1992.
2. A notable exception is the University of Panjab at Chandigarh.

References

Banerjee, P. et al. 1957. *Hundred Years of the University of Calcutta*. Calcutta: University of Calcutta.

Béteille, A. 1977. *Inequality among Men*. Oxford: Basil Blackwell.

—— 1987. *The Idea of Natural Inequality and Other Essays*. Delhi: Oxford University Press, 2nd edn.

—— 1990. 'A Career in a Declining Profession', *Minerva*, vol. XXVIII, no. 1–20, pp. 1–20; reprinted as Chapter 5 in this volume.

—— 1991. 'Distributive Justice and Institutional Well-being', *Economic and Political Weekly*, vol. 26, nos. 11 & 12, pp. 591–600.

—— 1992. 'Caste and Family in Representations of Indian Society', *Anthropology Today*, vol. 8, no. 1, pp. 13–8.

—— 1995. 'My Formative Years in the Delhi School of Economics, 1959–72' in D. Kumar and D. Mookherjee (eds), *D. School: Reflections on the Delhi School of Economics*. Delhi: Oxford University Press.

Gerth, H.H. and C.W. Mills (eds). 1946. *From Max Weber: Essays in Sociology*. New York: Oxford University Press.

Government of India. 1971. *Education and National Development: Report of the Education Commission, 1964–66*. New Delhi: NCERT.

Kuper, A. 1986. 'An Interview with Edmund Leach', *Current Anthropology*, vol. 27, no. 4, pp. 375–82.

Maine, H.S. 1931. *Ancient Law*. London: Oxford University Press.

Monk, F.F. 1935. *A History of St Stephen's College, Delhi*. Calcutta: YMCA Publishing House.

Pigou, A.C. (ed.). 1956. *Memorials of Alfred Marshall.* New York: Kelley & Millman.

Rashdall, H. 1936. *The Universities of Europe in the Middle Ages.* Oxford: Clarendon Press, vol. 1.

Stone, L. (ed.). 1974. *The University in Society.* Princeton: Princeton University Press, 2 vols.

Tumin, M.M. 1967. *Social Stratification.* Englewood Cliffs: Prentice-Hall.

8

Civil Society and Its Institutions*

Concepts and Terms

The idea of civil society—or at least the term 'civil society'—has acquired a certain currency in discussions of society and politics in India. It was not widely used in the Indian context until very recent times, and those who use the term now do not always make its meaning clear, often leaving the reader in some perplexity. The general impression conveyed in these writings is that civil society is something desirable, that it should be given room for expansion and protected from forces hostile to it.

In the tradition of western writing on the subject going back to the eighteenth century, civil society is a historical and not a universal category of human existence. It is not something that exists everywhere or has existed at all times. European writers of the eighteenth and nineteenth centuries, such as Adam Ferguson and G.W.F. Hegel, made some effort to identify and describe the conditions under which civil society came into existence in the west, even though they might not all use the term in exactly the same way. There has hardly been any discussion of when and under what conditions civil society came into existence in India, and, in the absence of such a discussion, the term is inevitably used somewhat promiscuously.

It may be said of course that in discussing the relationship between society and politics in India, we do not need to bind ourselves to the conventions of terminology established in the west. Those conventions have changed in the last two hundred years, and contemporary

* Revised and expanded version of *Civil Society and Its Institutions* (The First Fulbright Memorial Lecture), Calcutta: USEFI, 1996.

discussion of the subject in the west may be too narrowly focused on the particularities of western society for its conclusions to be usefully applied in the Indian situation. At the same time, social theorists in India draw freely from the general repository of terms and concepts, with or without acknowledgement, and it is best, while using a term from that repository, to keep in mind the meanings that have usually been associated with it. Moreover, Indian scholars need to explain, at least to themselves, the meanings they attach to the terms they employ so that their discussions with each other may be fruitful. If there is to be a distinctively Indian meaning of the term 'civil society', that too needs to be specified.

One reason for the ambiguity of usage is that the writings of Indian authors echo, consciously or unconsciously, the views of various western authorities who, as I have already indicated, have not all approached the subject from the same angle. A second and related reason lies in the differences of disciplinary perspective among those who speak and write about the subject. 'Civil society', if it is to mean anything at all, must mean some form or aspect of human society, and it should therefore be of interest to sociologists, but so far Indian sociologists have written little on the subject. Political theorists, who are concerned more centrally with the state, have given greater attention to it while examining the relationship, whether of harmony or antagonism, between state and civil society. My own approach to the subject reflects my interest not so much in the state as such as in the institutions of society. It is in short the approach of a sociologist, and while it is not the only possible approach, it has its uses.

In retrospect, it is easy to understand why the initial impulse of looking at civil society came from the political scientists, for in India it arose largely from a disenchantment with the state. This may be seen most clearly in the work of Rajni Kothari (1988a, 1988b), arguably India's most influential political scientist. Those who were young at the time of independence had expected a very great deal from the transfer of power in 1947. Many of them became bitterly disappointed when they saw that no miracle accompanied the change from a colonial to a national state. They watched with dismay as the apparatus of government became corrupt and inefficient, and in some respects even more oppressive than it was under the British.

Some have come to believe that what the government has failed to do should be left in the care of the market. But such a belief is not universally held among social theorists in India, many of whom now regard both state and market with an even measure of suspicion. For them, the real wealth of the nation consists of neither the state nor the market, but the people. In this perspective, bringing civil society into operation simply means creating a more active and a more participatory role for the common people, and especially for the poorest and the lowliest among them. One can easily detect the influence of Gandhian thought in this perspective, although Gandhi himself did not use the concept of civil society explicitly.

Since I have a somewhat different conception of civil society, I would like to indicate very briefly an alternative source of the recent interest in the subject. Here too, the impulse came from a disenchantment with the state, in this case the state that was to create and sustain the world of real socialism in eastern Europe. By the eighties it had become apparent even to left leaning intellectuals in the west that the socialist state had taken a heavy toll of both individuals and institutions. This could no longer be attributed to the 'cult of personality' or the evil propensities of particular individuals: its causes had to be sought in some fundamental failure of society in those countries.

Liberal democracy has survived and prospered in the west because it has respected the autonomy and the plurality of institutions. The socialist state under Stalin not only swallowed up the commanding heights of the economy, but brought virtually all public institutions, such as universities, scientific laboratories, hospitals, publishing houses and newspapers, under its command and control. This caused untold hardship to individuals, and it impoverished and degraded society as a whole. For those who reflected on this experience—as also the experience of Germany under Hitler—civil society was not simply a matter of bringing the people back in, but also of safeguarding the autonomy and plurality of institutions.

I would like to make a quick note here of two common points brought up by the discussion so far. Firstly, most current discussions of civil society rest on a positive evaluation of it. Secondly, underlying that positive evaluation is the tacit assumption of a kind of elective affinity between civil society and democracy. I doubt that there would be many promoters of civil society in India—or anywhere else—if they felt that the interests of democracy might be injured by it. Civil society shows the societal face, as it were, of democracy; its political face, including not only the government but the various organs closely associated with it, has shown so many ugly scars in India recently that it is understandable that many should pin their hopes for democracy on civil society.

The positive evaluation of democracy and of civil society does not extend fully to the state itself. There is undoubtedly an element of ambiguity in the relationship between state and civil society. Although none would wish to promote civil society at the expense of democracy, there are, as we have indicated, at least some in India who might wish to promote it at the expense of the state, not just the present, somewhat unsatisfactory one in the country, but the state as such. Viewed in historical and comparative terms, the state will appear to have acted negatively as well as positively on civil society. Its contribution had been negative, not to say destructive, in the Soviet Union under Stalin and in Germany under Hitler, but in the Scandinavian countries, in the Netherlands and in the United Kingdom, its role in the twentieth century has been on the whole beneficial. I do not believe that the state has had only a negative effect on civil society in India in the last fifty years. It has been ineffective rather than destructive.

Historical Antecedents

Although the idea of civil society has caught the attention of social scientists in India only recently, it has a long, though somewhat discontinuous, history in the west. At the same time, the idea as understood and used by most persons today is a distinctively modern one. This is clearly the case as far as India is concerned. In the sense in which I use the term and the one given to it by most scholars, civil society did not exist, or existed in only the most rudimentary form, in the ancient and medieval worlds. This is not to ignore the fact that the idea of a civil domain as distinct from other domains may be found in pre-modern times, particularly in the west, as, for instance, in the distinction between 'civil' suits and 'criminal' suits, and, more importantly, between civil law and canon law.

A certain line of argument about the nature and limits of civil society was established by Hegel in the early part of the nineteenth century. Hegel's ideas have had some influence in our time, partly because of the attention he received from Marx who retained some of the master's terminology even while opposing his arguments. The term actually used by Hegel permits translation into English as either 'civil society' or 'bourgeois society'. He stressed the importance in it of private property, individual rights and what we now call the market. His observations on civil society are situated within his scheme of the succession of historical epochs in which it constitutes a phase, or, in his language, a 'moment' between the family and the state. This succession is governed by a two-fold dialectic, of altruism and egoism on the one hand, and of the particular and the universal on the other. Civil society in this scheme expresses the moment of universal egoism, following upon that of the particular altruism of the family, and to be followed in turn by the universal altruism of the state.

Marx did not write extensively or systematically on civil society, and his observations on the subject are to be found mainly in his early writings, some of them in the form of notes. While Marx disagreed sharply with Hegel on the nature and significance of the state, his conception of civil society appears to have been in line with that of his predecessor. It is mainly a negative one in which civil society is driven by private economic interests even when they appear in the clothing of universal rights. One does not get a very clear sense here of the differentiated internal structure of what is represented as civil society.

Contemporary Marxists have turned to Gramsci rather than to Marx himself (or Lenin) as their source of insight into civil society. The attraction of Gramsci's approach is that it addresses itself to the complexity of civil society. Society is not a matter only of legal rights guaranteed by the state or of economic interests driven by the market. It is a matter also of ideas, beliefs, values, customs and habits that act on the state and the market and are in turn acted upon by them in complex ways and at different levels. State and market contribute something, but not everything towards the cohesion and the dynamics of societies.

Even sympathetic observers have noted that Gramsci's writings on civil society are not always consistent. The relations between state and civil society are expressed through an imagery whose import often remains obscure. One is left in doubt as to where, if anywhere, the distinction between state and civil society is to be drawn; and, where capitalism is concerned, the reader is not quite sure whether the writer's intention is to clarify or obscure the distinction between the two. The frequent use of military metaphors—earthworks, ditches, ramparts, and so on—serves to cast a lurid glow over both state and civil society (Gramsci 1973: 206–76).

An obvious problem is that much of Gramsci's writing on the

subject has come down to us in the form of sketchy and unfinished notes written in prison, and he had in his own writing warned against reading too much into what an author did not himself present as his finished work. But there is another, and in my judgement a more fundamental, problem. That problem has to do with his inner conviction about the historical destiny of the working class and the unique role of the working class party. I believe, on the other hand, that a concept of civil society that singles out the political party as its preeminent institution is inherently flawed; and historical experience has shown that the effort to build a democratic way of life on the basis of a single party is self-defeating if not self-contradictory. The failure of the Soviet experiment has made many of Gramsci's arguments obsolete, but he continues to have a dedicated following.

Hegel not only had successors, he also had predecessors. An approach to civil society somewhat different from his may be found in the writings of the Scottish moral philosophers of the eighteenth century, most notably Adam Ferguson whose *Essay on the History of Civil Society* was first published in 1767 (Ferguson 1986). Ferguson had himself been greatly influenced by Montesquieu whose *Spirit of the Laws* marks a turning point in the systematic and comparative study of human societies (Montesquieu 1949). It is Montesquieu and the Scottish moral philosophers, rather than Hegel, who are today regarded as the real predecessors of the related disciplines of sociology and social anthropology (Aron 1965; Evans-Pritchard 1951).

Ferguson's conception of civil society had an emphasis which differed from Hegel's: for him, the basic contrast was not between 'civil society' and 'political society', but between 'civil society' and 'natural society'. The Scottish moral philosophers were evolutionists before the biological theory of evolution had arrived on the scene. They used the method of conjectural history (or 'theoretical history') to discover the stages through which human societies had evolved from the most primitive to the most advanced forms. They were among the first, following the lead given by Montesquieu, to treat society rather than the state as a subject for science.

To be sure, those who made society instead of the state the subject of their science did not all write or think about civil society in the present sense, or even in any very definite sense of the term. But they opened up for their successors in the nineteenth and twentieth centuries a vast field for systematic empirical enquiry. They showed that society is made up of many interrelated parts each of which contributes something to the working of the whole. For them, the life of a nation depended not only on such grand institutions as the state and the church, but equally on a multitude of ordinary, unnoticed and even obscure social habits and practices.

The great importance of everyday social practices for the successful working of democracy was brought out with telling effect in the first part of the nineteenth century by Alexis de Tocqueville who may be regarded as the direct successor of Montesquieu. It is true that Tocqueville did not use the concept of civil society in his work. But, for him democracy was not just a political system, it was above all a social system whose success depended on good customs even more than on good laws. By assigning primacy to custom over law, Tocqueville implicitly brought society rather than the state to the centre of attention. Fifty years of experience with a republican constitution has taught us that nothing is easier than to replace bad laws by good ones, and nothing more difficult than to replace old customs by new ones. Our understanding of civil society, no matter how we define it, will have little depth if we confine our attention to the state and its laws, and ignore the customs by which the everyday life of society is regulated.

Here it may be pointed out that one of the meanings that has remained attached to the idea of civil society in the west is that of civility in the sense of refined, or at least restrained manners. This was important for Adam Ferguson who believed that civil society was the end product of a civilizing process through which the passions came to be gradually tempered by reason, leading to a general softening of manners. Tocqueville's definition of customs gives an important place to manners, but it is at the same time more inclusive: 'I here use the word *customs* with the meaning which the ancients attached to the word *mores*; for I apply it not only to manners properly so called—that is to what might be termed *the habits of the heart*—but to various notions and opinions current among men and to the mass of those ideas which constitute their character of mind' (Tocqueville 1956: I, 299, emphasis in original).

Some contemporary authors have stressed the importance of civility as a component of civil society (Shils 1997). There are two important ways in which civility of manners contributes to the democratic way of life. Firstly, democracy requires continuous dialogue between persons and parties with divergent, if not opposed, ideas and interests. That dialogue will have little chance of success unless some moderation and restraint is exercised. Where civility is thrown to the winds, as is happening increasingly in our legislatures and other public institutions, the social fabric of democracy becomes weakened.

There is another, deeper sense in which the softening of manners contributes to civil society and to democracy. The success of democracy requires a certain inner acceptance of equality as the basis of social interchange in the public domain. It is not enough to enact laws that call for equality of status and of opportunity. Those laws will amount to little if there is no change in the habits of the heart characteristic of earlier aristocratic, feudal or hierarchical societies. Democracy cannot cancel out all distinctions of authority and esteem; at the same time, it cannot function effectively in the absence of a certain civility in the treatment of all human beings irrespective of those distinctions. Indians who thunder against inequality in public rarely show much civility in the treatment of their social inferiors.

Framework of Analysis

I have said enough to indicate that many different components have featured in discussions of civil society in the last two hundred years. It will be futile to attempt to reconcile the many points of view that have been expressed in those discussions. Some have represented civil society as a new kind of society, while others have represented it as a new aspect of societies that might yet retain some, though not all, of their old aspects. I am more inclined to the second than to the first point of view.

I will now attempt to provide a clearer focus to the context in which the idea of civil society has to be examined. I ought to say at once that what I am attempting here is not the formulation of an exact or consistent definition of civil society, but the clarification of the issues that might lead to such a definition.

The framework within which the idea of civil society must be examined is provided by the three-fold relationship between (a) state; (b) citizenship; and (c) mediating institutions. Each is important in its own right, but it is only in their mutual association that the three together provide the setting for the operation of civil society. The importance of state and citizenship is obvious, and does not call for any further clarification at this point. The dependence of both state and citizenship on mediating institutions is no less important, although this may not be apparent at first sight.

State

The relationship between state and civil society is at the same time intimate and ambiguous. Civil society has been generally defined in opposition to the state,-as a sphere that is distinct from the state, no matter how closely related to it. Some authors have stressed their distinct spheres of operation while others have stressed their mutual interpenetration. We have already noted Gramsci's ambivalence about the relationship between state and civil society. This ambivalence derives in part from the fact that the differentiation between state and civil society is an emergent property, not equally manifest under all historical conditions. Clearly, the interpenetration of state and civil society was much closer in the USSR under Stalin than it was in the USA under Roosevelt.

It hardly needs to be said that there have been different kinds of states in human history. Among these, only the modern constitutional state is directly relevant to the present discussion. It cannot be too strongly emphasized that the modern constitutional state is a novelty in India where it has had to sail in troubled waters in the last twenty-five years. There have no doubt been wise and benevolent rulers in the past who looked after the welfare of the people and secured a measure of peace and prosperity for them. But there never was in the past anything like the kind of state that India has had since it became a constitutional republic.

Civil society, as I understand it, cannot be sustained without the rule of law, and the ultimate guarantor of the rule of law is the constitutional state. This simply means that there must be an impersonal order that secures for all members of society the equal protection of the laws and equality before the law. In such an order nobody is outside the law, and nobody is above it. The highest public official is, at least in principle, subject to the same law as the lowliest member of society. Where the rule of law is in practice violated habitually by the very public officials who are its designated overseers, the costs have to be borne not only by the constitutional order but by civil society as well.

If the state is to play its part as the guarantor of the rule of law, it must have its own structure of authority. It is in the nature of the modern constitutional state to have its own division of functions and powers. The idea of the separation of powers is a familiar one in modern constitutional theory, and its justification lies in the diversity of functions that the state is required to perform. No state can perform those functions unless it is vested with the appropriate powers, but those powers are in the present case powers of the office rather than the person.

Some separation of powers is essential if the distinction between the office and the person, and the rule of law that requires that distinction, is to be maintained. It is impossible to determine in advance the full range of functions that the state may be called upon to perform. The modern state has everywhere shown a certain expansionist tendency. It expands the range of its functions, and in that way justifies the expansion of its powers. On the other hand, the very idea of civil society presupposes a certain separation of functions between the state and itself. A constitutional state is simply one which sets limits to its own functions and powers.

In the twentieth century, the totalitarian state has squeezed civil society out by appropriating functions—and the corresponding powers—in an increasing range of domains: production, distribution, education, science, culture and so on. The idea of civil society rests on an appreciation of the differentiation of society, not on the denial to the state of the powers and functions appropriate to it. Of course, powers and functions are never exactly balanced among the different domains except in the mind of the philosopher. In the real world, the state may appropriate powers in a certain domain—let us say higher education—and yet perform the required functions very inadequately. Conversely, demands may be made that the state expand its range of functions and simultaneously reduce its powers. In India, those who attack the state for concentrating more and more powers also expect it to provide education and employment to all those who wish to have it.

The constitutional state can work only through an apparatus which is a system of graded authority. This is gall and wormwood to all those who believe that since, in a democracy, the state is of the people, it should be at one with them—particularly the common, ordinary people—and not set itself apart from them. The gradation of authority and the abuse of power are, of course, two different things, but in newly created democracies, they are easily confused, and the functionaries of the state become the natural targets of the hostility towards 'elitism'.

Citizenship

Not only the constitutional state, but citizenship as well is a novelty in India's long historical existence. The two ideas found their most complete expression in the same charter, namely, the Constitution of India, although they had both been in the air for some decades before the adoption of the Constitution in 1950.

We will not appreciate the significance of citizenship as a social, historical and jural category if we fail to recognize its novelty. Traditional Indian society was a society of castes and communities, and not a society of citizens. The significance of citizenship for the present discussion lies simply in this, that without citizenship, civil society is impossible.

The subordination of the individual to the group was a feature of most, if not all, pre-modern societies. The individual as an autonomous legal and moral agent, entitled to respect and responsibility in his own right, is not the starting point of social evolution, but the end-product of a long historical process. That process faces many obstacles in India where the loyalties due to caste and community are not only very strong but often reinforced by the democratic process itself. The rights of citizenship can be respected only in a society in which the autonomy of the individual is valued.

It is obviously impossible to assign an exact date to the birth of the modern concept of citizenship, but the French Revolution of 1789 was an important landmark. As is well known, the Revolution looked back to the world of Roman antiquity for many of its images and metaphors. But the fact is that it reinvented the concept of citizenship by presenting it in a universalistic idiom. The modern concept of citizenship expresses the principle of universality in a manner completely alien to that of classical antiquity. It denies slavery, and it overrides all distinctions of race, caste, creed, sex and place of birth. Universal citizenship is a modern idea, unknown to the ancient and medieval world, certainly in India.

I have elsewhere explained the distinction between equality and universality (Béteille 1994). The idea of 'equal citizenship' is at bottom an expression of the principle of universality. It cannot and indeed does not seek to cancel out all distinctions of wealth, esteem or power. But it does seek to ensure at least three things: (a) that each member of society be treated 'as an end in himself, and never as a means only'; (b) that certain basic rights and capacities be available to all members of society; and (c) that positions of respect and responsibility be open to every member of society irrespective of birth or social antecedent.

While we may treat the Declaration of the Rights of Man and of the Citizen of August 1789 as the starting point of the modern idea of universal citizenship, it cannot be regarded as its terminus. Practice lagged far behind principle in France, the United States and other western countries throughout the nineteenth century and well into the twentieth. Women were denied participation not only in politics but in most other public spheres as well. Positions of respect and responsibility were kept outside their reach not only in practice but, often, also in principle. Napoleon's well-known slogan of 'careers open to talent' applied only to men and not to all members of French society.

In the United States, slavery continued as an established social arrangement well into the second half of the nineteenth century. Even after its abolition, Blacks and other minorities continued to be treated as second-class citizens. Many would say that 'full citizenship for the Negro American' (Parsons 1965) is still an unrealized possibility. Nor is it a matter only of race and gender. It is now obvious that citizenship is made up of diverse components (Marshall 1977), and the progress towards full or substantive citizenship has even under the most propitious circumstances been slow, discontinuous and a prey to unsuspected turns and setbacks (Lockwood 1992: 257–67).

The idea of citizenship was introduced into India, but only as a germ, by the British in the nineteenth century. The main channels for its transmission were the law courts, the institutions of higher education and the press. It is remarkable how quickly it secured a toehold in an unpromising and incongenial environment. Among the principal social obstacles to it were the caste system and the joint family system, especially under the rule of Mitakshara. It cannot be too strongly emphasized that citizenship is not just a universalizing but also an individualizing concept. Throughout the nineteenth century, such appeal as it had was confined almost entirely to the urban intelligentsia. The extent of its diffusion beyond that circle until the middle of the twentieth century is not very easy to assess.

The British introduced the Indian intelligentsia to the idea of citizenship, but denied them its substance. This contradiction was felt acutely by the leaders of the nationalist movement and quickened in them the urge for self-rule which alone would enable them to cease being second-class citizens and become full citizens in their own country. No one has expressed the contradiction more eloquently than Nirad C. Chaudhuri who dedicated his *Autobiography* to the memory of the British empire which, he wrote, 'conferred subjecthood on us but withheld citizenship; to which yet every one of us threw out the challenge: "civis britannicus sum"' (Chaudhuri 1951: v). With the end of empire and the adoption of a new constitution, Indians changed from being subjects into becoming citizens in the formal sense. But historical experience everywhere has shown that the form of citizenship is not the same as its substance.

The political and legal passage from subjecthood to citizenship does not lead automatically to the conversion of a society based on caste to one based on citizenship. For it is not only the hierarchical ranking of castes that stands in the way but also the subordination of the individual to the group. The leaders of the nationalist movement rightly believed that they could not build a new society unless they got rid of the two impediments of colonialism and casteism. The second impediment has proved to be more obdurate than the first.

Speaking in the Constituent Assembly on the eve of India's independence, Pandit Govind Ballabh Pant drew attention to the threat to citizenship from the assertion of group identities. When he said, 'There is the unwholesome and to some extent a degrading habit of thinking always in terms of communities and never in terms of citizens', his remarks were greeted with cheers (Constituent Assembly Debates 1989: 332). At that time it was easy to blame the British for suppressing the claims of citizenship and playing upon group interests in the name of minority rights. But we have been on our own for more than fifty years, and citizenship still remains precariously balanced in the face of caste and community.

Mediating Institutions

A society with only individuals (or citizens) at one end and the nation (or state) at the other would be difficult not only to live in but also to think about. Every society has its own internal arrangements: its groups, classes and communities; its associations, organizations and institutions; and its networks of interpersonal relations, linking the different parts to each other and to the whole. Here I would like to stress only the variety and complexity of these internal arrangements. Some of them are ephemeral and bind only a few persons to each other; others are very extended in scale, have great continuity over time, and are highly visible. Indeed, when the sociologist speaks of society, it is these various arrangements, rather than the individual or the nation, that he has most often in mind.

Reacting strongly against the demand for quotas based on caste and community, the much respected Gandhian, Kaka Kalelkar had argued as Chairman of the first all-India Backward Classes Commission that only the individual and the nation should count in public affairs. He had stated that 'nothing should be allowed to organize itself between these two ends to the detriment of the freedom of the individual and the solidarity of the nation' (Kalelkar 1956: iv). Put in this form, the statement stands as a serious misrepresentation of human society. No society, least of all Indian society, is merely an atomistic aggregate of individuals. Today, what makes the inhabitant of this country an Indian in the formal sense is the fact that he is a citizen of India; but that would amount to little in the absence of the innumerable bonds by which he is tied to particular persons and particular places. A citizen of India may live abroad, adopt the citizenship of another country, and renounce his Indian citizenship; but he might still think and feel that he is an Indian so long as those particular bonds are cherished and sustained.

It is not my argument that mediating social arrangements are a unique feature of what I describe as civil society; they are a universal feature of all human societies everywhere. I have also indicated that they are of many different kinds. Among these, I would like to devote special attention to what I call institutions. An institution is a social arrangement with a distinct identity, a distinct internal structure and culture, and a life-span extending well beyond the lives of its individual members. Mediating institutions are of many different kinds, and only some, and not all, contribute to the health and well-being of civil society.

In the traditional order of Indian society, there were many different kinds of structures and institutions by which the individual was linked with other individuals and with the wider society. This is so well known that it hardly requires reiteration. Nevertheless, I would like to stress the importance of groups with more or less closed and fixed boundaries, pre-eminent among which were village, caste and joint family. What should be noted in particular is that the attachment of the individual to the group was based in each case on the principle of hierarchical subordination.

In pre-modern societies, whether in India or Europe, the individual was firmly embedded in a social matrix: he was not a detached or free-floating monad. The process of modernization, with which the emergence of citizenship and the constitutional state are associated, detaches the individual by loosening, at least to some extent, the bonds of his attachment to that matrix. Here I cannot do better than to quote Tocqueville: 'Aristocracy had made a chain of all the members of the community from the peasant to the king; democracy breaks that chain and severs every link of it' (Toqueville 1956: II, 99). The ideal of hierarchical integration was a commonplace of medieval European thought, and it has been memorably depicted by Jan Huizinga in his classic study, *The Waning of the Middle Ages* (Huizinga 1924).

Among all the societies known to history, it was in the Indian that the work of hierarchical integration found its most complete realization. Now when people look back fondly on the integrated communities of the past, they tend to forget the hierarchy; and when they attack the iniquities of the past, they tend to overlook the integration. The problem we face today is that of constructing and sustaining an integrated society on the basis of equality instead of hierarchy; it was a problem over which Tocqueville agonized in France more than a hundred and fifty years ago. The view that equality and unity are inseparable is a modern myth rather than a conclusion of social science.

Hierarchical integration was maintained in India through the social institutions of kinship, caste and religion. Caste has been represented by generations of sociologists and social anthropologists as the pre-eminent institution of India, and it reached into every aspect of Indian social life. But caste did not stand alone, being related on one side to kinship and on the other to religion. Caste may be viewed as a metaphorical extension of kinship, for all the members of a subcaste are related, at least in their own belief if not demonstrably, by ties of blood and marriage. And, for two thousand years, the rules of caste were the rules of religion, at least among the Hindus. Caste, kinship and religion combined to give a distinct character to all social relations, associations and networks in India.

The mediating institutions that I consider to be congenial, if not indispensable, to the growth of civil society are very different from those based on kinship, caste and religion. They are open and secular institutions. They are open in the sense that membership in them is independent of such considerations as race, caste, creed and gender: selection to positions of respect and responsibility in a university, a research laboratory or a public hospital, to pick only a few examples, is based, at least in principle, on open competition. They are secular in the sense that their internal arrangements are not regulated by religious rules or religious authorities.

New institutions of the kind I am now describing began to emerge gradually under the influence of colonial rule from the middle of the nineteenth century onward, first in the presidency towns of Calcutta, Bombay and Madras; from there they spread their influence elsewhere. They included schools, universities, hospitals, banks, municipal corporations, professional associations, newspapers, publishing houses and others of many different kinds. To be sure, their growth was facilitated by the introduction of a new legal order and new economic opportunities. But their appeal lay no less in the fact that they offered a new ideal of social life and a new model of social association.

The new institutions began to extend their influence, and when the country became independent in 1947, the drive was not for a return to the old social order, but for development and modernization. The building of new, open and secular institutions was an integral part of that drive. It was supported by a new system of education that provided avenues of economic advancement to aspiring individuals mainly from the upper castes. One cannot emphasize too strongly the part played in it by the emerging middle class imbued with a new outlook on life. The history of civil society is inseparable from the history of the middle class, not only in India, but everywhere. To repeat, the term used by Hegel for what we are here describing as civil society was 'bürgerliche Gesellschaft', literally 'bourgeois society'.

It is evident that the new social arrangements—institutions, associations, networks of interpersonal relations—did not displace all the old ones based on kinship, caste and religion even among the most advanced sections of the urban middle class, not to speak of other sections of Indian society. It is in some sense remarkable how quickly the new social arrangements with which I am now concerned made room for themselves in a society whose basic design and social morphology were so greatly at variance with them. Perhaps there was something congenial in the heteromorphic and open-ended character of Hindu civilization that allowed the accretion of new social and cultural components without fully assimilating them. The state also played an important part in encouraging their adoption in the early years of independence in keeping with its commitment to the modernization of Indian society. I have earlier indicated that the state may play either a positive or a negative part in the development of civil society. No two states could be more different in their orientations to civil society than the Republic of India under Nehru and the Peoples' Republic of China under Mao.

The well-being of civil society depends upon the emergence of open and secular institutions, and on their differentiation from each other. Not only should the domains of finance, education, research, communications and so on be differentiated from each other, but within each domain there should be institutions of more than one kind, and preferably several of each kind. Thus, the institutions of administration and of politics should be differentiated from each other, and there should be a plurality of political parties and associations. To revert to a well-worn example, a one-party system, even where it claims to represent the interests of the people as a whole, is not a party system at all.

In civil society, the plurality of institutions goes hand-in-hand with the autonomy of institutions. To be sure, this autonomy is both relative and dynamic. The state has in the present century acted as the most serious threat to the autonomy of the kind of institutions about which I have spoken. This does not mean that no accommodation is possible between the state and the other institutions of society. Mutual accommodation is indeed essential for the health and well-being of both state and civil society.

The long-term evolutionary trend, as I have argued, is towards the differentiation of society. But the long-term trend does not provide guarantees against reverses and setbacks in the short term. There have been examples of institutions moving towards differentiation and autonomy, and then being brought back in line and even swallowed up by the state. In the twentieth century, where the state has most often damaged or destroyed the autonomy of mediating institutions, it has done so almost invariably in the name of the people.

In seeking to be consistent in maintaining the distinction between the state and mediating institutions, I may have given rise to a misunderstanding which I would like to dispel before proceeding further. It will be a serious error not to recognize the fact that the state is itself an institution, homologous at least in certain respects with many of the institutions with which I have just dealt. For many political theorists, the state is not only an institution, it is the pre-eminent institution. The sociologist, by contrast, hesitates to assign pre-eminence to any one of the major institutions of society, although that does not mean that we must assign equal importance, either historically or functionally, to each and every institution.

Civil Society and Religion

In our times, it is not just the state, but also religion that has acted as a threat to civil society. Where church and state have acted in conjunction, as in Iran, they have severely damaged both the autonomy of institutions and the freedom of individuals. Nothing can be more inimical to civil society than the combination of religion and politics. At the same time, the relation between religion and civil society, some what like the one between state and civil society, is a relation of ambivalence rather than of inherent contradiction.

In writing about mediating institutions, I kept the state aside because, obviously, the state cannot mediate between itself and the citizen. I also kept religion aside because I dealt by choice with 'open and *secular*' institutions. Indeed, secular principles define not only the mediating institutions about which I wrote, but also the constitutional state and citizenship as I understand them. The constitutional state is governed not by religious authority or religious regulations, but by man-made laws: the prospects of civil society are at best uncertain in a state whose legitimacy rests on religion. Moreover, citizenship in the sense given to it here is defined independently of religion: a citizen may be of any religion or have no religion at all.

The state as such is not an enemy of civil society; it is only when the state seeks to dominate every sphere of life and to control every institution and every individual that it becomes a threat to civil society. Religion as such is not an enemy of civil society; it is only when it seeks to encompass every aspect of society and to regulate every individual and every institution that religion stifles the growth of civil society. Historically, both church and state have been extremely powerful institutions. Civil society has grown not by destroying them, but by creating and inhabiting spaces outside their direct control.

Those who wrote about civil society in the eighteenth and nineteenth centuries did not generally regard religion as an enemy of civil society. Many of them were religious believers who favoured religious tolerance. This was largely the case with the Scottish moral philosophers of the eighteenth century. Alexis de Tocqueville believed that religion contributed positively to the growth of democratic institutions in America, but he also pointed out that it was most effective where there was a separation of church and state (Tocqueville 1956: I, 308–14).

In the western countries where civil society as we know it had its origins, an important step in its emergence was the separation of church and state. The church gradually relaxed its hold not only over the state but over many of the other institutions of society. The university provides a good example of what I have in mind, although many other examples may be found. From the Middle Ages, when they were founded, till well into the nineteenth century, the universities of Oxford and Cambridge were governed in accordance with religious rules. The members of a college, both senior and junior, had to be Christians, and church service was an important part of its life. This is now no longer the case, although some traces of religious symbolism may still be found, particularly in the older colleges. Many other institutions that have come up in the western countries in the last hundred years have been secular since birth.

Secularization has been viewed by some religious believers as the beginning of the end of religion. But it may also be viewed as part of a long-term process of differentiation which allows religion to retain its pre-eminence within its own domain, but not over every domain. The Indian constitution is a secular constitution only in the sense that it denies religion pre-eminence in every domain, and not in the sense that it denies to religion what is due to it in its own domain. It gives every religion an equal place, and at the same time insulates certain domains from regulation and control by religion.

If civil society is to be based on the acceptance of a plurality of institutions, it would be contrary to its spirit to wage a war against religious institutions. The refusal to tolerate religion can hardly be an answer to religious intolerance. The brutal assault on the church in the Soviet Union and elsewhere in Stalin's time was a denial and not an assertion of the spirit of civil society. And when the tide turned in the eighties, in Poland, the German Democratic Republic and elsewhere, the church played a significant part in the revival of civil society.

Religious tolerance and the respect for religion are fundamental components of the culture of civility to which, as we have seen, some authors have given a prominent place in their conception of civil society. In a country like India, where historical and demographic considerations require the co-existence of communities professing and practising distinct faiths and rites, secular institutions are difficult to sustain, but they are no less indispensable for that reason. Their survival depends upon a culture of civility, and the state alone cannot create or sustain that culture. The culture of civility is a culture of tolerance: militant atheism is no less alien to it than the glorification of holy war.

Secular institutions and the culture of civility often lack the energy and vitality that come from unshakeable religious faith. Where those institutions are weak and infirm and have to work in an incongenial environment, they become easy targets of attack, not only from outside but also from within. In such an environment, they have to make many compromises, if only to survive, and they are then attacked 'from the religious point of view' for making those very compromises and for being venal and corrupt. Proponents of secular ideas and institutions can never offer the promise of an incorrupt and unblemished future society with the same conviction with which religious believers can. The political appeal of such a promise may of course have little to do with the actual conduct of those who make it, and there is little evidence to show that religious institutions as they are, in India or elsewhere, are less corrupt, less venal and less feeble than other institutions.

The real challenge to civil society comes from those religions that advance totalizing claims. These totalizing claims are, of course, not pressed with equal insistence by all religions, or by any religion at all times. On the whole, the religions of the book, the monotheistic religions, have pressed those claims more strongly than the others, but rarely, if ever, with full consistency. But where it comes to advancing totalizing claims, we cannot take any religion, monotheistic or polytheistic, for granted; even the most seemingly accommodating among them might feel that the time has come to take the world in its grasp and give it a firm moral foundation. Religious ideologues learn quickly from each other, not only the lessons of compassion and humility, but also those of bigotry and intolerance. Even so, religious institutions themselves have shown a great capacity to outlive the ebb and flow of the intolerance of religious ideologues.

Civil Society and Communities of Birth

I have spoken of open and secular institutions and, more briefly, of religious institutions, and have stressed their great variety and multiplicity. But those institutions taken together do not exhaust all the space that lies between individual and society. There are also communities that occupy an important place in the wider society and act upon its individual members in a variety of ways.

India has been described as 'the land of the most inviolable organization by birth' (Weber 1958: 3). It is also a land in which the individual has been subordinated to the community to an unusual degree. Communities of birth exist in all societies, but they do not have everywhere the same salience that they have had in India and some other societies. Among communities of birth, I include those based on clan, tribe, caste, sect and also religion. They are all bound together by ties of real or putative kinship. They are very different from secular institutions such as the university, the bank and the political party, and also different from religious institutions such as the temple, the church and the monastery.

I would like to make a brief observation on religious communities, including sects. No doubt religion is a matter of faith, even personal faith. But it is not only a matter of personal faith since it cannot be sustained for long without institutions governed by distinctive rules and practices . Finally, religion is also a matter of membership in a community. A religious community is not necessarily or in principle a community of birth. In fact, the religious sect begins typically on the basis of personal and voluntary acts of subscription. But in course of time, the sect too becomes for all practical purposes a community of birth. Particularly in times of political turmoil, the individual's loyalty to his religion is more often a matter of loyalty to his community of birth than to any particular doctrine or practice.

What is true of the religious community in this respect is even more true of clan, caste and tribe. Although the three are not the same, it is of interest to note that they have been persistently confused with each other in the ethnographic literature on India. Membership in all three is acquired at birth, and one cannot choose at will to be a member of a particular tribe, caste or clan as one can, at least in principle, opt for a religion other than that of one's forebears.

The elementary family is the building block of all the three types of community just referred to. It is a social unit of universal significance, present in one form or another in all human societies. In India, as in many other parts of the world, it does not stand alone, but is embedded in a wider matrix of kinship and marriage. The clan, the caste and the tribe may all be viewed as kinship systems writ large or as metaphorical extension of the family.

Civil society, whether in India or the west, has to accommodate the family. No one has, to my knowledge, recommended the abolition of the family as a condition for the advance of civil society, although the family has been attacked on other grounds. But to what extent can the extensions of kinship, real or metaphorical, be accommodated by civil society as here understood? More generally, what should be the place of communities of birth in a society committed to open and secular institutions?

Where the claims of kinship have a strong social appeal, they are carried over, overtly or covertly, into public domains in which they are not wholly appropriate. They manifest themselves in various ways in the domain of politics. The son, the daughter, and, surprisingly, even the widow are widely acknowledged to have a natural claim to the highest political office in many Asian countries that have resolutely renounced the monarchical principle. This happens even when the claimant has shown little aptitude or inclination for politics in his previous career. It cannot be explained solely by the personal ambitions of the claimant or the coterie which promotes his or her claims; millions of persons, including many who are totally non-partisan, feel that the son, the daughter or the widow has a rightful claim which should not be denied.

In a society where the sentiment of kinship is so strong and its ties are so extensively reckoned, it is difficult to fully insulate any part of the public domain from its claims. It is difficult to say to what extent the working of public institutions such as banks, hospitals or universities is vitiated by benefits being granted or withheld, not in accordance with the rules of those institutions but in conformity with the claims of kinship. But the proper working of those institutions according to their own norms does not require the denial of the claims of kinship, no matter how extensive, in those domains that are appropriate to them. Again, as with religion, so also with kinship: the development of open and secular institutions calls for the differentiation of society, not for the war of one part of society against another. Further, the well-being of civil society in India does not require its kinship system to become an exact replica of the European or the American kinship system.

Caste is of course much more than a kin group in the literal sense of the term. The caste system has in many ways dominated the structure of Indian society for centuries. It has been changing over the last hundred and fifty years, but has by no means disappeared. It has been widely noted that while the ritual aspects of caste have declined greatly in significance, its political aspects have gathered strength (Fuller 1996). Not only are the distinctions of caste still widely manifest, the sentiment of caste has acquired a new lease of life on account of its continuing involvement in electoral politics, and through it, in public life in general. This is a more serious challenge to the growth of civil society in India than the state's hunger for power.

I have already indicated that caste and citizenship are antithetical principles. The normative basis of caste and of the open and secular institutions on whose success the vitality of civil society depends are also at odds with each other. Does this mean that civil society cannot take root in Indian soil unless caste is first uprooted from it? It certainly means that unless the state as well as the other open and secular institutions of society are substantially insulated from caste, the prospects of civil society will remain uncertain.

In part, the claims of caste insinuate themselves into public institutions such as universities, hospitals or banks in the same way in which the claims of kinship do. The scale on which this happens is difficult to estimate even approximately, and it obviously varies a very great deal from one institution to another, and possibly also from one part of the country to another. It has analogues in other parts of the world, including countries such as the USA, the Netherlands and Belgium. It is often viewed as a form of corruption, and is both criticized and accommodated.

But the penetration of caste and community into what are designed to be open and secular institutions may not take place only through the backdoor; they may also enter through the front door, and that too on a fairly extensive scale. The colonial regime had introduced quotas based on caste and community in public service well before independence.[1] Those quotas had on the whole been viewed with disfavour by the leaders of the nationalist movement. When Kaka Kalelkar had declared that nothing should be allowed to stand between the individual and the nation, what he had in mind were not the open and secular institutions discussed earlier, but castes and other communities of birth. He tried to prevent the intrusion of caste into the public domain, but failed. Whether the trend introduced into public life by Mr V.P. Singh's government in 1990 will fade away or gather strength, only time can tell.

Democracy and Civil Society

I began by pointing out that the idea of civil society has in our times become inseparable from that of democracy. It became evident from the beginning of the nineteenth century onward that democracy is not just a form of government, but a whole way of life. This insight was first fully articulated in the work of Alexis de Tocqueville who showed how democracy alters the texture of society, its institutions, its customs and manners, and the very character of interpersonal relations. From this point of view it may be said in a very broad way that civil society represents the societal as against the political aspect of democracy.

Again, as I pointed out at the beginning, in India, the recent interest in civil society has arisen less from a natural curiosity about changes in the inner life of society than from a concern over the problems and prospects of Indian democracy. It has arisen because many persons have begun to feel that democracy is facing a crisis, and that this crisis has been created, or at least intensified by the state. It is in civil society that these persons invest their hope for rescuing democracy from an oppressive state and its uncaring elite. They believe that civil society already exists, only that it is lying dormant among the common people and needs to be awakened so that democracy may be restored to its rightful place. Others believe that creating civil society in India is and has been an uphill task because it involves the care and nurture of new institutions in an inhospitable social and cultural environment.

Much of the confusion over what we should mean by civil society arises from the failure to maintain a clear distinction between two different conceptions of democracy, the constitutionalist and the populist. We started at independence with a constitutionalist conception of democracy, but have since moved some distance in the direction of a populist one. As I have already noted, the Emergency and its aftermath provided a kind of watershed. More and more persons began to represent not only the state as the enemy of democracy but public institutions in general as enemies of the common people. In this environment, those who seek to make the case for civil society from the constitutionalist point of view must learn to sail against the wind.

When India became independent after a long period of colonial rule, there was understandable optimism about the prospects of all-round economic and political development through constitutional means. But India's archaic and ponderous social hierarchy proved far more resistant to modernization than had been anticipated, and modernization itself brought new and unforeseen social problems in its wake. Economic growth was slow, and the fruits of that growth continued to be unequally distributed between individuals and among communities. The politics of parties and elections, far from dissolving the boundaries between castes and communities, deepened the awareness of those boundaries. As more and more laws came to be enacted, their inability to overcome the obduracy of custom became more and more apparent.

By treating the constitution lightly, the Emergency strengthened the appeal of populism. The politics of caste and community, till then viewed as a barely tolerable evil, became legitimized in the name of social justice. Such open and secular institutions as had begun to take their faltering steps in an incongenial environment came under severe attack for being unrepresentative, elitist and against the real interests of the people. Politicians began to undermine the very institutions from which they derived their sustenance, and many intellectuals who were modernized to their fingertips began to attack modernity itself.

Constitutional democracy depends upon respect for rules and procedures and for the gradations of legitimate authority in the state and in other public institutions. Populism represents all established authorities as fortresses against the exploited and the oppressed, and all rules and procedures as instruments of vested interests. It has little regard for the functional requirements of the kind of open and secular institutions about which I have written. It seeks instead to promote democracy through the direct empowerment of the people, and especially of disadvantaged, disesteemed and marginalized communities. Populism is at once emancipationist and antinomian in its orientation; it has little regard for civility and for the rights of the citizen as an individual.

References

Aron, Raymond. 1965. *Main Currents in Sociological Thought*. London: Weidenfeld and Nicholson, vol. 1.

Béteille, André. 1994. 'Equality and Universality', *Cambridge Anthropology*, vol. 17, no. 1, pp. 1–12.

Chaudhuri, Nirad C. 1951. *The Autobiography of an Unknown Indian*. London: Macmillan.

Constituent Assembly Debates. 1989. *Official Report*. New Delhi: Lok Sabha Secretariat, 2nd reprint, Book 1.

Evans-Pritchard, E.E. 1951. *Social Anthropology*. London: Cohen and West.

Ferguson, Adam. 1986. *An Essay on the History of Civil Society*. New Brunswick: Transaction Publishers.

Fuller, C.J. (ed.). 1996. *Caste Today*. Delhi: Oxford University Press.

Gramsci, Antonio. 1973. *Selections from Prison Notebooks*. London: Lawrence and Wishart.

Huizinga, Jan. 1924. *The Waning of the Middle Ages*. London: Edward Arnold.

Kalelkar, Kaka (Chairman). 1956. *Report of the Backward Classes Commission 1955*. New Delhi: Government of India.

Kothari, Rajni. 1988a. *State Against Democracy*. Delhi: Ajanta.

—— 1988b. *Transformation and Survival*. Delhi: Ajanta.

Lockwood, David. 1992. *Solidarity and Schism*. Oxford: Clarendon Press.

Marshall, T.H. 1977. *Class, Citizenship and Development*. Chicago: University of Chicago Press.

Montesquieu, C.L. de S. 1949. *The Spirit of the Laws*. New York: Hafner Press.

Parsons, Talcott, 1965. 'Full Citizenship for the Negro American?', *Daedalus*, vol. 94, no. 4, pp. 1009–54.

Shils, Edward. 1997. *The Virtue of Civility*. Indianapolis: Liberty Fund.

Tocqueville, Alexis de. 1956. *Democracy in America*. New York: Alfred Knopf, 2 vols.

Weber, Max. 1958. *The Religion of India: Hinduism and Buddhism*. New York: The Free Press.

9

India's Heritage of Diversity*

A sociological perspective on the heritage of India must ensure against yielding either to a nostalgia for the past or to a wholly negative attitude towards it. There are extreme examples of both in the available literature, and it is difficult to achieve and maintain a proper balance between the two. At the height of the national movement, many Indian writers felt impelled to reconsider their own heritage and to present a picture of a pristine past in which people lived in peace and harmony with each other, and the community met the basic needs of the individual to everybody's satisfaction. This kind of nostalgia for the past is intellectually sterile, and can serve very little practical purpose in the contemporary world.

At the other extreme is the view that India's past was characterized by ignorance, superstition, oppression, exploitation and disorder, and as such there was nothing of value in it. One can find plentiful evidence of all these from the present and the recent past, and this evidence cannot be easily swept under the carpet. At the same time, it is difficult to believe that a civilization of such wide span and historical depth could have maintained itself for two thousand years and more while negating all fundamental human values. A characteristic response to this is to say that the present and the recent past tell us less about the Indian heritage than about the subversion of it by modernization. This intransigent hostility to modernity leads inevitably to a glorification of the past.

We cannot disregard our heritage without depriving our present identity of its meaning and significance; nor can we opt out of the

* Originally published as 'The Indian Heritage: A Sociological Perspective' in D. Balasubramanian and N. Appaji Rao (eds), *The Indian Human Heritage*, Hyderabad: Universities Press, 1998.

modern world any more than a man can jump out of his skin. The perspective I propose to present builds on the writings of several earlier Indian anthropologists, notably Irawati Karve (1968) and N.K. Bose (1975). These scholars not only made extensive field investigations of contemporary Indian society but also examined the classical texts in order to get a better understanding of the present in the light of the past. Their view of their past was appreciative but critical, and they were acutely aware of the need to be selective in using materials from the past for constructing the future.

The modernization of India that began with British rule has revealed the strengths as well as weaknesses of India's social and cultural heritage. It is important to view objectively and with the maximum possible detachment both the strengths and the weaknesses, although there are no satisfactory measures of either the one or the other that will enable us to draw up an exact balance sheet. Much can be learnt by reflecting not only on the strengths but also on the weaknesses of what has come down to us from the past. There is, no doubt, continuity of both social structure and culture, but our present goals are not identical with the ones by which life had been governed in the past; and it is well to remember that what had been strengths in the past may become weaknesses in the present, and vice versa.

The first striking feature of India's social and cultural heritage is its diversity. It is true that India is a large country with every type of geographical environment and a very numerous population. But even for a country with its extent and population, the diversity is remarkable. There is, first, the great diversity in the biological composition of the population: every type of physical trait, such as height, head form, shape of nose, skin colour and even eye colour, is found in notable proportions in one group or another. At the same time, it is doubtful that any clear relationship can be established between the bio-diversity of India's human population and its social and cultural diversity. And despite the enormous range of physical traits, attempts to establish a racial classification of the population have not met with any notable success.

Many anthropologists have recorded in detail the inexhaustible variety in the habits, practices and customs of the people of India. It was customary among anthropologists of an earlier generation to start with the distribution of material traits, such as food, dress, habitation and the material arts and crafts. Irawati Karve pointed to the 'endless variety in the type of foods eaten and their preparation' (Karve 1968: 1). Some of this variation, she noted, can be easily attributed to variations in the types of food grown under different geographical conditions. But these simple variations were subjected to infinite elaboration through the action of customs, conventions, rituals and other social prescriptions and interdictions whose operation has little or no connection with the known facts of geography.

Karve made an interesting observation while recording variations in forms of dress. After pointing out that in the north women generally wear white whereas colours are much in evidence in the south, she noted: 'In Orissa the north and the south meet somewhere on the coastal plain near Kalingapattanam. In all Kalinga villages, women are dressed in white, in the nearby non-Kalinga villages women have coloured saris' (1968: 4). N.K. Bose devoted much time to the study of traditional crafts such as those of the oilpresser, the potter and the blacksmith (1975: 73–86). He noted that there was an enormous variety of techniques in each case and that differences in technique were jealously maintained by their practitioners from generation to generation even when they lived in the same village or in adjacent villages.

Side by side, there were differences in social relations and social institutions such as those associated with family, marriage, kinship, inheritance, succession and residence. To quote Karve again,

> The variety of family organizations is equally great. Polygamy and polyandry are both found. There are groups which are matrilineal, others which are patrilineal. The taboo on consanguine marriages changes from region to region and from caste to caste. ... The modes of inheritance and succession are also different (1968: 4–5).

Here as well, variation may be noted not only between different regions but also within a single district and sometimes even a single village.

There is finally the inexhaustible multiplicity of religious beliefs and practices. Within Hinduism itself one can pass from the crudest worship of sticks and stones to the most profound speculation about the nature and significance of the universe. But Hinduism is not the only religion of India. In addition to its offshoots, Jainism and Buddhism, other religions such as Islam and Christianity have also made their home in the country. It is well to remember that there are more Muslims in India than in any other country in the world save Indonesia, and that Christianity has existed in some parts of India longer than in many European countries.

Although Islam, Christianity and other religions have an important place in contemporary Indian society, it is Hinduism that has contributed the most towards giving Indian civilization its distinctive form and ethos. It is the oldest among the major religions of the country, and most Indians from ancient to modern times have been Hindus in one sense or another. Although Islam was the politically dominant religion in large parts of the country for several centuries, it did not absorb Hinduism, or efface the basic design of Hindu social structure. Nor did Hinduism, where it was demographically and otherwise dominant, seek to eliminate the beliefs and practices characteristic of other religions. India has been and continues to be a land of many religions and religious sects, each enjoying a measure of autonomy in its own sphere. It is not uncommon to find local communities even in the rural areas in which not only Hindus with various beliefs and practices but also Muslims and Christians pursue and maintain their distinctive styles of life.

The heritage of India has been built out of many components. This becomes evident when we look at its linguistic and religious diversity. New components, whether from within or outside, have been continuously accommodated throughout history. In being accommodated, these components acquired new orientations, but their old identities were not allowed to lapse. N.K. Bose provided an outstanding account of the Hindu method of tribal absorption (1941) which applies by and large to the accommodation of all kinds of social formations, tribal as well as non-tribal, from within and outside the country.

Accommodation without assimilation has been the characteristic of Indian civilization until modern times. This has enabled the co-existence of a large multiplicity not only of beliefs and practices but also of collective identities. Adding new components has not meant discarding old ones, so that new and old components of the most heterogeneous kinds have existed cheek-by-jowl to a far greater extent than in other civilizations. Karve has put it thus: 'The historical process is one of continuous accretion. There does not seem to be a stage where a choice was made between alternatives, a choice involving acceptance of one alternative and a definite, final rejection of the others' (1968: 7). One can say in this light that Indian civilization has not been the outcome of a single, consistent or exclusive ideology; or, that the accommodation of diversity has been its underlying ideology.

The presence of diversity has been more than a matter of mere existence. Here, according to most authorities, a decisive part has been played by the core values of Hinduism in shaping not only Hindu society specifically but Indian society as a whole. Respect for diversity of habits, customs and practices was enjoined not only by Hindu religion but also by Hindu law. There is a maxim of Yagnyavalka that says that 'one should not practise that which, though ordained by the Smriti, is condemned by the people' (Kuppuswami 1991: 44). P.V. Kane's monumental *History of Dharmasastra* gives a vivid account of the extraordinary maze of law, custom and usage by which social life was regulated in the past. *Deshachar* or the customs of the locality and *lokachar* or the customs of the community generally prevailed over what was prescribed by the *shastras*.

N.K. Bose examined in detail the implications for the structure of society of the primacy of custom and usage over codified law. Society came to be divided into innumerable tribes, castes, subcastes, clans, sects and communities each of which sought jealously to maintain its own style of life and its own code of conduct. The classical and medieval authorities sought again and again to fit the multitude of actually existing groups into the four-fold scheme of *varnas*, but their efforts were never wholly successful. At all times there were groups that existed on the margins of the four-fold division, or in its interstices, or beyond the pale. The establishment of Muslim rule over large parts of the country added to the inventory of groups and at the same time made it even more difficult to fit them into the scheme of *varnas*.

The polymorphous structure of Hindu society and its pluralist, not to say polytheist, cultural tradition provide congenial conditions for the growth of democracy. Democracy favours a diversity of ends and is averse to a single plan of life for everyone; it supports a plurality of parties and interest groups and opposes the control of society and politics by one single group or type of group. In short, the building of democratic institutions in modern India is likely to benefit from its long tradition of diversity and accommodation in social and cultural life.

Having taken note of the remarkable accommodation of diversity in traditional India, it is now necessary to ask how this diversity was held together and organized. To put it in a nutshell, its organization was hierarchical and not democratic. Much has been said about democracy in ancient India, but little of it will stand up to careful scientific scrutiny. The Indian village has been described time and again as a 'little republic', but the plain fact is that such unity as it had in the past was a hierarchical unity in which the upper castes owned or controlled the land and the untouchables provided servile or semi-servile labour, with all kinds of grades or ranks in between (Béteille 1980).

Most modern authorities would acknowledge that India's plural society had a hierarchical structure. Some would lay stress on the plurality and others on the hierarchy, but it is important to keep both in mind. Traditional India has been widely regarded as the prototype of a hierarchical society (Dumont 1966, Béteille 1987), and the marks of hierarchy are readily visible in its contemporary structure. While styles of life of the widest variety were acknowledged and accommodated, they were not all equally esteemed. An elaborate ritual idiom served to express social distinctions between superiors and inferiors. Not only was each group expected to persevere in its own style of life, but there were sanctions against the adoption by groups of inferior rank of the symbols of status allowed to their superiors. The law of the *Dharmashastra* noted in detail the privileges and disabilities of groups in keeping with the positions they occupied in society.

From whichever angle we view the case, the modern principle of equality was largely absent in traditional Indian society. True enough, equality was acknowledged on the metaphysical plane, but it had hardly any place on the plane of everyday social and political existence. Now law and politics have both changed. They presuppose a certain basic equality among persons; but the practice of inequality remains deeply embedded in every sphere of Indian society.

Just as the accommodation of diversity did not go with equality in the traditional order, it also did not go with individual freedom. Now it is a characteristic of hierarchical societies in general that collective identities prevail over individual identities, and this characteristic was developed in its fullest form in traditional Indian society (Tocqueville 1956, Béteille 1987). Speaking of village, caste and joint family as the fundamental institutions of traditional Indian society, Nehru had observed, 'In all these three it is the group that counts: the individual has a secondary place' (Nehru 1961: 248). Individual freedom could of course be asserted by renouncing society and adopting the way of the *sannyasi*; but even here, *sannyasis* in course of time became organized into groups of various kinds.

Thus, while a great variety of occupational techniques, marriage practices and ritual procedures were present in society as a whole, no individual could choose from among these according to his own inclination or convenience. The actions of the individual were severely constrained by the rules and practices of the group into which he was born. India has been described as 'a land of ... the most inviolable organization by birth' (Weber 1958: 3), and here too the spirit of the old social order was antithetical to the spirit of democracy.

It has been noted over and over again that India's continuity as a civilization was social and cultural rather than political: order and stability were maintained not by means of the state but through a peculiar balance of social morphology and cultural values (Baechler 1988). In this view, the state was weak and transient whereas culture and society were cohesive and enduring. Today it is not altogether clear how effectively order and stability were in fact maintained in past times. The authorities prescribed rules of conduct of such complexity that it is doubtful that any real society could ever be regulated by them. The classical authorities convey a strong sense of living in times of great disorder together with their obsessive preoccupation with rules. Perhaps this pervasive sense of disorder and the urge to prescribe the most detailed rules of conduct were two sides of the same coin.

What is clear is that the old principles by which society had been governed for two thousand years and more are no longer adequate for maintaining either order or stability under modern conditions. Whatever may have been the degree of disorder and instability at particular times and particular places, both inequality of status and the subordination of the individual to the group were, generally speaking, morally acceptable principles in the past. Such is no longer the case. The challenge today is to maintain the diversity and the spirit of accommodation inherited from the past while repudiating hierarchy and creating more spaces for individual freedom.

Today Indian society is characterized not only by diversity but also by conflicts of various sorts. Among these I will point only to the conflict of norms and values. By values I mean the generalized ends that are culturally prescribed or at least considered desirable; by norms I mean the regulatory rules by which conduct is governed in society. Here, there are pervasive conflicts between the norms and values inherited from the past and those regarded as appropriate to the modern world. The normative order of classical India, its design so to say, may be found in the *Dharmashastra*, and in particular in the *Manusmriti*; the normative order of modern India is encoded in its Constitution. There is a striking discordance between the two.

The generalized ends considered desirable in the past have not entirely lost their salience, but new ends have now come into view. Today equality in social life has acquired a certain appeal among persons in many walks of life; but the commitment to hierarchy that marked the traditional order is still widely manifest beneath the surface. Recognition of the autonomy of the individual and the respect due to him or her is now an important value; it is at odds with the strong sense of obligation to the group of which one is a member by birth.

Diversity on the plane of values or generalized ends is to be expected in any large society undergoing a major transformation, and its tolerance is healthy upto a point. But how far can a modern society accommodate a plurality of norms or regulatory rules that are not only diverse but unclear, ambiguous and mutually inconsistent? Whereas the diversity of generalized ends is diffused through society as a whole, the contradictions among the regulatory rules manifest themselves most clearly in particular institutional domains. There is widespread anxiety today over the many problems with which public institutions are beset: misuse of funds, lack of discipline, absenteeism, work stoppages, strikes, and so on. All of these are related in one way or another to the failure of regulatory rules. Allegations about the violation of rules have become endemic, and they lead to the creation of new rules which are in turn violated.

I would like to conclude by drawing attention to two striking features of contemporary Indian society that manifest themselves in all public institutions from the state downwards. The first is the drive to create rules of every kind and to the last detail; and the second is the wide disregard of those very rules. My view is that the proliferation of rules and the disregard of rules are two sides of the same coin; and, further, that these two complementary tendencies are both very deeply rooted in India's traditional culture.

Citizens the world over complain about the obstacles created by the multiplicity of rules they have to face in their dealings with any branch of the government, but the problem is particularly acute in India. In our government offices, rules are used as weapons of offence and defence, and every official and his clerk is equipped with an inexhaustible armoury of them. Part of this is the wilful display of authority by the man sitting on an official chair, but there is more to it than that. In the Indian case the rules themselves are numerous, complex and ambiguous; this car be checked by looking at rules in comparable systems elsewhere. Even when an official wishes to be helpful or expeditious, he is kept in check by the jungle of rules endemic to our way of administration.

I would like to stress that I am dealing with a tendency that is deeply rooted in our culture, and not simply with the malfunctioning of governmental bureaucracy. The jungle of rules is all-pervasive and we can examine how it works in universities, hospitals and many other institutions that have no direct connection with the government. I shall take the example of universities since I have direct personal knowledge of their functioning. Nowhere in the world is the work of universities obstructed by so many rules; and nowhere in the world are the rules relating to academic work so extensively violated. There are many thoughtful and well-intentioned scholars who are aware of this and disturbed by it; but they seem unable to do very much about it. Committees set up to streamline procedures invariably create new rules, and then Karve's law comes into operation: the addition of new rules does not lead to the elimination of old ones; those are simply put into cold storage, to be taken out when required to trip up an unwary newcomer who tries to put some dynamism into the system.

I have come to the conclusion that we have an orientation towards rules that is largely our own and that is strikingly different from the orientations characteristic of other cultures. Bankimchandra, the great nineteenth century Bengali writer, was troubled by the tendency of some of his contemporaries to quote prescriptions from the *shastras* to support one or another reform they wished to promote. He found those prescriptions to be prolix, ambiguous and self-contradictory. He wrote,

> Indeed, it is not possible for any society to be fully regulated by all the prescriptions to be found in the *shastras* of Manu and the others. It is doubtful if ever, at any time, those prescriptions were fully operative in any society. Many of them are inoperable. Many, though operable, involve such hardships to man that they would drop out on their own. Many are mutually contradictory. If any society is ever destined to keep all these prescriptions in operation, such a society must indeed have an evil destiny (Bankimchandra 1975: 316).

Those who are frustrated by the jungle of rules in offices in modern India may secure some consolation from Bankim's reflections on the past.

How do people get things done in the face of this plethora of obsolete, unclear and inconsistent rules? They improvise, activise personal networks, and go about their business without paying too much attention to the rules. This probably is how they worked the system in the past, and this is how they try to work it today. But people lived largely in small, face-to-face communities in the past. They now operate in a world that is organized in a very different way and on a very different scale. Is it possible to act effectively in the modern world without a radical change of orientation towards the regulatory rules of society?

References

Baechler, Jean. 1988. *La solution indienne*. Paris: PUF.

Bankimchandra. 1975. *Bankim Rachanabali* (in Bengali). Calcutta: Sahitya Samsad, vol. 2.

Béteille, André. 1980. 'The Indian Village: Past and Present' in E.J. Hobsbawm, K.N. Raj and I. Sachs (eds), *The Peasant in History: Essays in Honour of Daniel Thorner*. Calcutta: Oxford University Press.

—— 1987. *The Idea of Natural Inequality and Other Essays*. Delhi: Oxford University Press, 2nd edn.

Bose, N.K. 1941. 'The Hindu Method of Tribal Absorption', *Science and Culture*, vol. VII, pp. 188–94.

—— 1975. *The Structure of Hindu Society* (translated from the Bengali with an introduction and notes by André Béteille). New Delhi: Orient Longman.

Dumont, Louis. 1966. *Homo Hierarchicus*. Paris: Gallimard.

Karve, Irawati. 1968. *Hindu Society: An Interpretation*. Poona: Deshmukh Prakashan, 2nd edn.

Kuppuswami, Alladi (ed.). 1991. *Mayne's Treatise on Hindu Law and Usage*. New Delhi: Bharat Law House, 13th edn.

Nehru, Jawaharlal. 1961. *The Discovery of India*. Bombay: Asia Publishing House.

Tocqueville, Alexis de. 1956. *Democracy in America*. New York: Alfred Knopf, 2 vols.

Weber, Max. 1958. *The Religion of India: Hinduism and Buddhism*. New York: The Free Press.

10

The Conflict of Norms and Values*

Norms, Values, and Interests

Conflict and change are universal features of contemporary societies and may be considered normal and, within limits, even conducive to their well-being. But the limits are easily transgressed, and hence their members are perennially beset by anxieties about total stagnation on the one hand and endemic disorder on the other. Fifty years ago, at the time of independence in India, the anxiety was about the stagnation engendered by an atrophied traditional order. Today, as all the tensions associated with a major social transition become manifest, it is disorder that appears to be the larger threat, although the two kinds of anxiety might be experienced simultaneously.

The turbulence that is endemic in contemporary India is often attributed to the decline of moral values or their displacement by the pursuit of narrow personal or sectional interests. There is a constant refrain that values have gone out of politics, civic life, the professions and education. These are represented as being driven increasingly by the desire for individual gain as against social well-being.

When people who are placed differently in society strive for the same scarce objects, conflicts of interest are bound to occur, and they tend to overshadow all other conflicts. The focus of this chapter will not be on the conflict of interests but on the conflict over values and norms: over what people consider to be right, proper and desirable, and what they regard as legally and morally binding. The issue of contending norms and values is not the same thing as that of conflicting interests,

* Originally published as 'The Conflict of Norms and Values in Contemporary Indian Society' in Peter L. Berger (ed.), *The Limits of Social Cohesion*, Boulder: Westview Press, 1998.

but it is difficult to convey a sense of the dynamics of the former without taking some account of the latter.

Though I shall be concerned with the normative order in the broad sense, it will be useful to keep in mind the distinction within that order between values and norms. Here I will follow the convention of terminology established by Parsons and his associates (Parsons and Shils 1951). As Parsons has put it, 'On the normative side, we can distinguish between *norms* and *values*. Values—in the pattern sense—we regard as the primary connecting element between the social and cultural systems. Norms, however, are primarily social.' For us, as for Parsons, 'the structural focus of norms is the legal system', although this too has to be conceived in a broad sense (Parsons 1966: 18).

Following Parsons, Smelser (1962: 24) has described values as the 'generalized ends' characteristic of a culture, and norms as the 'regulatory rules' prevalent in the corresponding society. As we shall see, one of the reasons for the persistent failure of regulatory rules in contemporary public institutions in India is that they are often at odds with certain generalized ends that are deeply embedded in India's traditional culture.

The diversity of norms and values is related both to the conflict of interests and to the social morphology. Society is not a simple aggregate of individuals but a differentiated structure of groups, classes and categories. The ideas and values of the individual are shaped in part by his location within this differentiated structure. Even where uniform rules are established, these are refracted by the social morphology so that they are perceived and applied differently by the different sections of society.

Societies differ greatly in their scale and complexity. India has a population of around 950 million, divided by language, region, religion, sect, caste, tribe, wealth, occupation, education and income. It is also a nation-state with a formal legal and administrative structure designed to maintain some measure of unity without doing violence to the distinctive lifestyles cherished by its major religious and cultural groups. Indians believe, rightly or wrongly, that the tolerance of diversity was a core value within the Indian tradition, which has for that reason a great deal to contribute to the growth of a pluralist democracy.

The tolerance of diversity can accommodate the conflict over norms and values only up to a point. Those responsible for managing the affairs of state in India view such conflicts as clear signals of disorder and impending disintegration. That is not the point of view from which this chapter is written. There is no way in which change can come about without the displacement of some norms and values by others. Nor do all conflicts over norms and values end by tearing apart the fabric of society; indeed, the suppression of such conflict may as easily lead to that outcome. It is important to acknowledge their presence and even their necessity, and to create and sustain institutions to negotiate them. This cannot be done by wishing present conflicts out of existence, or hoping for a future in which no conflicts will arise.

Indian Civilization: Design and Morphology

India is a society with a long past, and many different elements have contributed to its moral and intellectual tradition. It would be fair to say, though, that the organizing principles of its social life came mainly from Hinduism; and the majority of its population, from ancient to modern times, has been, in one sense or another, Hindu.

Hinduism is a religion of many gods and goddesses, each having many different forms. Further, as the noted anthropologist and writer Irawati Karve (1968) observed, the Hindu moral and intellectual climate absorbed new elements of belief and practice while allowing old ones to remain, without too much anxiety about consistency. The accommodation of apparently inconsistent beliefs has been a notable feature of Hindu civilization through the ages.

Though the Muslims dominated large parts of India politically for centuries, they did not destroy the basic design of Hindu society; rather, they adapted themselves to it (Bose 1975). Islam is a religion of equality, Hinduism of hierarchy. Islam softened to some extent the hierarchical basis of Indian social structure by weakening at least a little the legitimacy of the Hindu order of *varnas*. But Muslims came to accept ascribed and invidious social distinctions more or less as the Hindus did; the same holds true by and large for Christians.

Diversity in ideas, beliefs, and practices was encouraged by the system of values, and the tolerance of diversity had an ethical basis in Hinduism. *Dharma*, commonly translated as 'religion' but better regarded as 'right conduct', is classified into *varnashramadharma*, or rules appropriate to particular stations and stages in life, and *sadharanadharma*, or rules common to all; far more stress is given to the former than to the latter (Kane 1974: 3). The classical texts provide little authority for one single and uniform normative standard for all sections of society.

Modern Indians sometimes say that the acceptance of diversity as a core value in Indian civilization gives Indians a special advantage in building a democratic society. However, tolerance of diversity should not be mistaken for individual freedom. Although society as a whole tolerated the widest range of practices among its multifarious groups, the individual had very little freedom to choose his own life plan for himself in work, worship or even leisure. Classical law stressed duties more than rights (Kane 1974, Karve 1968), and one's most important duty was to uphold the way of life of the group into which one was born.

What was important in the social ethic was not individual choice but the immemorial tradition by which the life of each particular group was in principle governed. Not that ideas, beliefs and practices never changed—they changed slowly and imperceptibly, and not generally through the consciously designed actions of the individual. Either the group as a whole or, more commonly, a section of it would adopt a new way of life, always claiming that it was its traditional way of life from which its members had deviated in recent times through some accident or misfortune.

Just as the tolerance of diversity did not go with individual autonomy, it also did not go with equality. The diverse ways of life were all considered legitimate in their respective spheres; but they were not all equally esteemed. The various groups that were their bearers had their assigned places in society, but some were at or near its sacred centre, and others on the periphery or even beyond it.

The ideological justification of hierarchy was expressed symbolically through the opposition of purity and pollution. These ideas were a central part of the Hindu tradition, but other religious groups, such as Muslims and Christians, did not escape their influence. The two poles of the social hierarchy were represented by the Brahmins who were the bearers of the highest purity, and the Untouchables, among whom all forms of pollution were concentrated. But even in the traditional order, there was more to social disparity than its expression in the ritual idiom of purity and pollution. It was maintained and perpetuated through extreme inequalities in the distribution of economic and political power, that is, in the control over things and persons. That distribution does not change automatically with a change in religious beliefs and practices, and Indian society today continues to be marked by large inequalities in the material conditions of existence.

An account of the conflicts in contemporary Indian society has to begin with the transformations in it during the past hundred and fifty years, and particularly since independence. What is most striking from the present point of view is the change from a hierarchical normative order to one based on the principle of equality: equality before the law, the equal protection of the laws and equality of status and of opportunity.

Traditional Hindu society was governed for 2000 years by the law of the *Dharmashastras*, whose influence was pervasive and far-reaching. The *Dharmashastras* in general and the *Manusmriti* in particular provide the most complete and elaborate design for a hierarchical social order known to human history. In 1950 India adopted a new constitution in which provisions for equality are given a prominent place. No two charters for a social order could be more strikingly different than these. It is no accident that Dr B.R. Ambedkar, widely regarded as the father of the Indian constitution, publicly burned the *Manusmriti*, which he viewed as the embodiment of injustice and oppression.

The whole life of a society does not change with the adoption of a radically new constitution. New laws may be enacted, but many old customs and conventions remain. In India these are often at variance, and it cannot be assumed that the law is always more binding than custom and convention. Relations based on kinship, caste and community have not remained exactly as they were, but they have not changed beyond recognition. Old identities and invidious distinctions based on them continue to be prominent features of the social landscape.

The design of traditional Indian society was most fully embodied in the structure of Hindu society, but it has left its mark on Indian society as a whole. Its distinctive morphological feature is the caste system. Caste may be understood either as *varna*, representing the conceptual design of Hindu society, or as *jati*, representing the actual social divisions operating in everyday life. *Varna* and *jati* never fitted together exactly (Srinivas 1962: 63–9), and today *varna* has become anachronistic (Béteille 1996), whereas *jati* continues to be important. Only Hindus had *varnas* in the proper sense of the term, whereas *jatis* existed and continue to exist among Muslims, Christians and others (Ansari 1959, Ahmad 1973, Caplan 1980, Godwin 1972).

The conceptual scheme of *varnas* divided Hindu society into the four ranked orders of Brahmin, Kshatriya, Vaishya, and Shudra. These divisions were exclusive and in principle exhaustive. The classical texts declared: 'Brahmin, Kshatriya, Vaishya, and Shudra, these are the four *varnas*, and there is no fifth.' In fact there were many groups whose status was interstitial, marginal, or beyond the pale: 'sectarian' communities, 'aboriginal' tribes, 'exterior' castes and others. All of these were in some sense regarded as *jatis*, similar in their constitution to those that constituted the basic building blocks of traditional Hindu society.

The system of *jatis* lacked the neatness and symmetry of the order of *varnas*. The *varnas* were only four in number, but the *jatis* were innumerable. Moreover, while all Hindus acknowledged the same immutable order of *varnas*, in the same hierarchy of rank, each region had its distinctive complement of *jatis*, although the pattern of differentiation and ranking was broadly the same everywhere. It is clear from the historical record that old *jatis* disappeared and new ones emerged, either by fission or by the absorption of immigrant or aboriginal groups. While the *jatis* were ranked everywhere, the order of ranking was nowhere strictly linear; there were competing claims to superior status, particularly at the middle levels, and *jatis* regularly rose and fell in rank in the course of time.

Over the centuries many tribal groups were absorbed into Hindu society (Bose 1975). In the course of absorption, the tribe discarded many of its practices, including religious and linguistic practices, but still retained the sense of its immutable identity. Thus when a tribe became a caste it was in some sense still the same group, although in a different dress, and it found a niche for itself within the local system of *jatis*. In like manner, conversion to Islam—or to Sikhism or Christianity—might lead to a change of religion, but not necessarily a change of caste. Sometimes the same caste, such as Ahir, Jat or Rajput, might be found among Hindus, Muslims and Sikhs, occupying roughly the same rank in each of the three religious divisions (Smith 1996: 465).

Although the framework of *varnas* has today lost much of its coherence and legitimacy, the *jatis*, which were the real building blocks of society, continue to be active among Hindus, Muslims, Sikhs, Christians and others. The divisions of caste are intersected by other divisions based on language and religion. The hierarchical principle, or even the principle of social gradation in a broader sense, does not apply to all of them. In some contexts, people might refer to Bengali and Tamil speakers as *jatis*, but that does not mean that they regard them as being mutually ranked; the same is to some extent true of the major religious divisions. But there are conditions under which all of these groups might compete for the same scarce resources. They then act in the manner of the ethnic groups familiar in sociological literature (Béteille 1996; Schermerhorn 1978).

Finally, all these divisions, based on language, religion, sect, caste and tribe, are intersected by other divisions based on the distribution of wealth, income, occupation and education, or divisions corresponding to class in the broad sense. Making the confusion worse, it is quite common in contemporary India to represent the divisions of caste and community in the language of class, in both law and politics.

Positive Discrimination

Attitudes to hierarchy began to change among the Indian intelligentsia from the middle of the nineteenth century onward (Ganguli 1975). This was a slow and gradual process that encountered many unsuspected obstacles, and it has not by any means reached its terminus. British rule acted as an important catalyst, but Indians began on their own to look into their cultural traditions for support for the ideal of equality. With the approach of independence, the tide turned, and caste came to be widely regarded as the main source of inequity and divisiveness in Hindu society.

Nehru (1961: 521) wrote on the eve of independence: 'The spirit of the age is in favour of equality, though practice denies it almost everywhere,' adding that 'The spirit of the age will triumph.' This contradiction between what Nehru saw as the spirit of the age and social practices based on other presuppositions continues to be one of the major sources of conflict in contemporary Indian society. The spirit of the age has not triumphed, at least not in the sense or to the extent that Nehru wished and hoped; nor is it possible to exorcise that spirit today.

The Constitution of India is one of the lengthiest documents of its kind—and it has incorporated some eighty amendments in its brief existence. The length and the number of amendments are good indicators of the ambiguity, uncertainty and conflict over norms in contemporary Indian society. There are strong provisions for equality in the Constitution, although some of then. have required amendment. An Indian jurist has said of the guarantee of equality that 'it must be appreciated that the scope of the guarantee in the Constitution of India extends far beyond either, or both, the English and the United States guarantees taken together' (Tripathi 1972: 47). What has to be added about these guarantees is that their number and variety have themselves become sources of debate and dissensus, for the idea of equality is seen to have diverse components not always easy to harmonize with one another.

The principal provisions for equality in the Constitution are contained in Part III on Fundamental Rights and Part IV on Directive Principles of State Policy. It must be noted first that the provisions in Part III are enforceable by courts of law, whereas those in Part IV are not, even though the latter have acquired increasing strength in recent years, contributing something to the amendments made in the former (Sivaramayya 1984). The provisions in Part III are related to equality before the law (Art. 14), prohibition of discrimination on grounds of religion, race, caste, sex or place of birth (Art. 15), and equality of opportunity in public employment (Art. 16). Here equality is viewed as a right whose bearers are individual citizens. The provisions in Part IV are related to the distribution of material resources (Art. 39) and the promotion of the interests of the Scheduled Castes, the Scheduled Tribes, and other weaker sections of society (Art. 46). Here equality is viewed as a policy that is addressed to the disparities between classes and castes. It will be seen that these provisions contain a number of tensions, firstly, between different conceptions of equality, and secondly, between the rights of individuals and the claims of communities (Béteille 1987a).

The leaders of independent India saw of course that a new constitution could not by itself secure substantive equality. Many of the old disparities between groups remained, and new inequalities between individuals were emerging. Efforts were set in motion to remove or reduce these inequalities through legislation, through democratic politics at the national, regional and local levels, and through economic planning. I will now focus on the programme of positive discrimination in order to bring to light some of the tensions inherent in the pursuit of equality in contemporary India.

India has one of the oldest and most comprehensive programmes of positive discrimination. It has been a source of great social dissension and political strife, leading to the fall of the national government in 1990. The courts have spoken on it in more than one voice, giving judgements that are or appear contradictory (Galanter 1984). The point to note here is that the programme has been both supported and opposed in the name of equality.

The broad basis of positive discrimination is the principle of redress: it seeks to redress the bias of past generations in the direction of greater equality. I have given some account of that bias in the past and also indicated its effects on the present distribution of life chances between the different sections of Indian society. The disadvantaged among these are broadly described as the Backward Classes, and positive discrimination has sought to make various special provisions in their favour with a view to securing greater equality overall.

To understand the conflicts brought to the fore by positive discrimination, we need to have some idea of the benefits offered by it, and also of its intended beneficiaries. The intended beneficiaries are designated as the Backward Classes; they are not in fact classes in the accepted sociological sense but rather groups of tribes, castes and other communities (Béteille 1991). The intended benefits cover a very wide range, but the most important and also the most contentious are reserved positions in political bodies, public employment and education; hence positive discrimination has come to be widely known in India as the policy of reservations or quotas.

The Backward Classes are a very large and heterogeneous category, which may be divided into three broad sections: the Scheduled Tribes, the Scheduled Castes, and the Other Backward Classes. The former two share certain features in common, and the constitutional provisions for their betterment are more clear and specific than for the third. The Scheduled Tribes comprise 7.75 per cent and the Scheduled Castes 15.75 per cent of the population of the country; together, they number over 200 million persons. The traditional hierarchical order imposed numerous hardships on them, from many of which they continue to suffer, the former on account of isolation and the latter because of segre- gation. If equality of opportunity depends not merely on the absence of disabilities but also on the presence of abilities, positive discrimination may be said to aim at creating some of those abilities.

The Constitution requires seats in the lower houses of Parliament and the state legislatures to be reserved for the Scheduled Castes and Scheduled Tribes (Arts. 330, 332) roughly in proportion to their strength in the population; this is political reservation. In addition, Article 335 states, 'The claims of the members of the Scheduled Castes and the Scheduled Tribes shall be taken into consideration, consistently with the maintenance of efficiency in administration, in the making of appointments to services and posts in connection with the affairs of the Union or of a State'; this is job reservation. The provisions for political reservation and for job reservation are somewhat differently phrased, although the various branches of the government have increasingly treated them alike. Finally, there is reservation in education: seats are reserved in educational institutions, including medical and engineering colleges, for students belonging to the Scheduled Castes and the Scheduled Tribes.

The makers of the Constitution were well aware that enlarging the special provisions, whether relating to benefits or to beneficiaries, beyond a certain point might subvert the principle of equal opportunity for which there was general endorsement in the Constituent Assembly. The principle of special opportunities for some, even when designed for reducing social disparities, does not rest easily with that of equal opportunities for all and can be accommodated by it to only a certain extent. The chairman of the Drafting Committee, B.R. Ambedkar, had observed that 'we have to safeguard two things, namely, the principle of equality of opportunity and, at the same time, satisfy the demand of communities which have not had so far representation in the State' (Constituent Assembly 1948: vii, 702). While arguing for some special provisions, he wanted to ensure that they did not 'eat up' the general provision of equality of opportunity for all. Hence the provisions for reservation in the Constitution apply specifically only to the Scheduled Castes and Scheduled Tribes, leaving aside the token representation granted to the very small Anglo-Indian community.

At the same time it was felt in the Constituent Assembly that some measures for social and economic betterment should be adopted also for other disadvantaged groups in addition to the Scheduled Castes and the Scheduled Tribes. Article 340 provided for the appointment of a commission to 'investigate the conditions of socially and educationally backward classes' and to make recommendations relating to them. In fact, reservations in employment and education for these Other Backward Classes had already been introduced by the colonial administration and were in operation in some states when the new Constitution was adopted. Those provisions, which were not uniform in their application, appeared somewhat ambiguous in light of the Constitution (Béteille 1991). The president appointed a commission (the Kalelkar Commission) in 1953, but its recommendations, submitted two years later, could not be implemented because of sharp disagreements among its members. A new commission (the Mandal Commission) was appointed in 1978, and it submitted its report in 1980 recommending extensive reservations in education and employment for the Other Backward Classes over and above those in force for the Scheduled Tribes and the Scheduled Castes. When the union government sought to implement them in part in 1990 there were massive protests, and the government fell.

The Other Backward Classes are socially, economically, and politically even more diverse than either of the two other divisions. Again they are not classes, but an assortment of 3743 castes and communities. Their exact strength in the population is difficult to determine, but they are believed to comprise no less than 50 per cent of the population. Some of them occupy lowly positions, not much above the Scheduled Castes in the social scale; others occupy positions of political dominance, despite their low status in the traditional ritual hierarchy. Their individual members vary enormously in income, occupation and education, much more than do the members of the Scheduled Castes and Tribes. As the law stands now, there is reservation of up to 27 per cent of jobs in the government for them, although that limit has been exceeded in a couple of states. There is also reservation in education for them in some, though not all states, but no reservation of seats in either Parliament or the state legislatures.

The nationwide political turmoil over job reservations for the Other Backward Classes revealed dramatically the conflict between equality as a right and as a policy, between formal and substantive equality. Well before independence, the colonial administration had introduced quotas in education and employment in some parts of the country, which the Congress Party had then viewed as politically divisive rather than as steps toward greater social equality. Moreover, the colonial administration was not hampered in the pursuit of its policies by a constitution guaranteeing equality of opportunity in public employment as a fundamental right. The Constitution has had to incorporate, through amendments, enabling provisions to permit some reservation in education and employment, despite the antidiscrimination and the equal opportunities clauses. How these provisions are balanced depends to some extent on day-to-day political pressures. The Supreme Court initially urged restraint in the use of quotas; a landmark judgement in 1962 struck down the rather generous provisions for quotas in favour of the Other Backward Classes in the then state of Mysore in South India as 'a fraud on the Constitution'. Later judgements have been more accommodating on the ground that Fundamental Rights cannot be interpreted in isolation from the Directive Principles of State Policy (Sivaramayya 1984).

The report of the second Backward Classes Commission, which became the charter of the proponents of job quotas for the Other Backward Classes, maintained that the 'real acid test' of equality was equality of result rather than the purely formal principle of equality of opportunity (Government of India 1981: 22). The progress of equality, in the commission's view, had to show in the extent to which all castes were equally represented in positions of respect and responsibility in public institutions; it was forcefully pointed out that they were in fact less than adequately represented. Opponents of job quotas argue, in their turn, that it is a gross violation of the principle of equality when more qualified candidates from the upper castes have to make room for less qualified ones from the lower castes, particularly when the benefits of quotas go, as they frequently do, to the most advantaged and not the least advantaged members of the lower castes. Moreover, it can be questioned whether bureaucracies should be required to meet the test of representativeness in the same way as legislatures.

A second and closely related conflict of norms has to do with the claims of collectivities as against the rights of individuals. The framers of the Constitution of India sought to base the constitution on equality and individual rights, but both inequality and collective identities have survived as obdurate facts in independent India. In the Constituent Assembly, there were some, mainly Gandhians, who wanted the village to be the basic unit in the new social scheme in view of what they claimed had been its central place in the traditional order. Dr Ambedkar, who was a tireless advocate of the special claims of the Scheduled Castes, opposed their argument, and said, 'I am glad that the draft Constitution has discarded the village and adopted the individual as its unit' (Constituent Assembly 1948: vii, 39). Caste was thrown out by the front door, but it has, in the name of equality and social justice, re-entered through the back door (Béteille 1987b, 1991).

At the time of independence it was hoped that democracy would undermine the structure of caste in the course of creating a more liberal and equal society through the operation of the political process. But caste has been given a new lease of life by the democratic process to which it has provided an easy basis for the mobilization of support (Srinivas 1962). In India caste politics operates somewhat in the manner of ethnic-group politics in the United States, but on an enormously expanded scale and in a much more pervasive way (Kothari 1969). The traditional ritual basis of caste is certainly being eroded, but nobody can ignore its active role in contemporary Indian politics. It is true that politics is altering caste, but caste too is changing the face of democracy in the country.

What was expected from democracy was also expected from economic development. The general belief among Indian intellectuals was that caste was the social basis of a stagnant, backward, feudal or semifeudal economic system and that it would wither away with the advance of a vibrant economy. There has been some economic development in India, but not a very great deal of it. The question that troubles many today is how the fruits of this development are or ought to be distributed. It appears that increasing numbers of people would like to assess this distribution by taking not just individuals or households but also castes and communities as the units in their reckoning. This leads not to a weakening but a strengthening of the consciousness of caste, at least in the short run.

Writing about affirmative action in the United States, the American jurist Owen M. Fiss (1977: 474) distinguished between the 'antidiscrimination' principle and the 'group-disadvantaging' principle in the pursuit of equality. Fiss pointed to the strong bias in the United States in favour of the antidiscrimination principle, but in India we see a marked tendency, in politics as well as in law, to invoke the group-disadvantaging principle. In the report of the important Backward Classes Commission for the state of Karnataka, the chairman, L.G. Havanur, argued that in India, equality between castes had to be achieved first before much could be done about equality between individuals. He offered an interpretation of the constitution that is perhaps more surprising than convincing: 'Hence the Constitution suggests *recognition of castes for their equalisation*' (Karnataka Backward Classes Commission 1975: 36, italics in original).

Havanur appears to have taken it for granted that wherever the constitution pointed to 'socially and educationally backward classes' or even to the 'weaker sections of society', it had castes and communities in mind. That view might be accepted by some Indians, including some Indian judges, but by no means by all. Kaka Kalelkar, the chairman of the first all-India Backward Classes Commission, found himself unable to recommend the adoption of caste as the unit in determining the composition of the Other Backward Classes. In forwarding his report to the president, he expressed his misgivings about the continuing use of caste for such purposes: 'In a democracy, it is always the individual (not even the family) which is the unit. Democracy thrives best when, on the one hand we recognise and respect the personality of the individual and on the other we consider the well-being of the totality comprising the nation' (Government of India 1955: xiv). Kalelkar was expressing a sentiment that is perhaps shared as widely as that of Havanur. Indeed, the modern educated Indian is deeply divided within himself about what is due to the individual and what is due to caste.

Secularism

It is not uncommon to find both supporters and opponents of caste-based quotas who say that they would like to see an end to caste. The supporters say that caste can never be eradicated so long as such massive disparities remain in society; they maintain that the reduction of these disparities through positive discrimination is bound to lead to the weakening of caste in the long run. The opponents say that the policy of reservation as it is practised in India can lead only to the reinforcement of the consciousness of caste and is therefore an obstacle to its natural decline.

In considering the persistence of collective identities in India, we have to consider not only caste but also religion. A person may be reluctant to admit to loyalty to his caste, but it is far less common for him to deny loyalty to his religion. Today religion, like caste, not only unites but also divides people. Like caste, religion is a matter of social identity; but, to a large extent unlike caste, it is also a matter of faith and doctrine. People justify their loyalty to their religious community not only in terms of their birth or by invoking 'immemorial tradition', but also on grounds of doctrine and faith.

The spectre of 'communalism' hung over the subcontinent when India became independent in 1947. The country was partitioned in order to achieve some sort of solution to the communal problem, but the spectre has not been laid to rest. The Indian case at the time of the partition was that Pakistan might become a country for the Muslims, but India would remain a home for Hindus, Muslims, Christians and others. Pakistan has become an Islamic state, but India has, at least so far, rejected the idea of being a Hindu state. As indicated earlier, there are in fact more Muslims in India than in Pakistan. Hindus and Muslims have lived together on the subcontinent, in amity and strife, for centuries, but their co-existence within a modern nation-state has brought new normative issues to the fore, related to secularism and the rights of religious minorities.

The Indian state is based on a constitution whose secular character has been reaffirmed by an amendment to its Preamble. It is at the same time mindful of the claims of religion. Hence it grants 'the right to profess, practice and propagate religion' (Art. 25) as a fundamental right. How does one simultaneously promote 'secularism' and also protect the right to propagate religion?

Many observers from both within and outside the country have commented on the strong and pervasive hold of religion on the people of India. Europeans in the nineteenth and early twentieth centuries generally took this to be an index of their enslavement to superstition, although a few also regarded it as a sign of their superior spiritual quality. In all long-established agrarian civilizations, religion permeates every area of life: family, kinship, work and leisure, and this was perhaps more true of Hinduism than of the other world religions. While religion maintained a strong hold over everyday life, a slow, diffuse current of secularization had set in among Indians by the end of the nineteenth century. More than thirty years ago, M.N. Srinivas drew attention to the inroads being made by secularization, noting at the same time the presence of countercurrents and the uneven spread of the process among the different sections of Indian society. 'Hindus were more affected by the secularization process than any other religious group'; and, further, 'Different sections among the Hindus are affected in different degrees by it ... ' (Srinivas 1966: 119).

We have to distinguish between secularization as an outcome of diffuse technological, economic and other forces operating in society and secularism as a conscious ideology or design for living. It is the ideology of secularism rather than the broad process of secularization that has to be the issue in a discussion of the conflict of norms. The members of the Constituent Assembly by and large took for granted the desirability of having a secular constitution for India; in a sense they had little choice, having committed themselves to the principle that there should be no discrimination among citizens on grounds of religion. In the first two or three decades following independence, there was a general consensus among the intelligentsia that the growth of secular ideas and institutions was both necessary and desirable for the modernization of Indian society. That consensus appears less secure than before, and questions are increasingly raised about the content of secularism as an ideology (Béteille 1994). One of India's more popular intellectuals has even published an 'Anti-Secularist Manifesto' (Nandy 1985).

A major source of disagreement, and hence of potential conflict, has to do with the role of the state in the promotion of secularism. It will be useful here to make a distinction, however crudely, between a secular society and a secular state. I will illustrate the distinction by contrasting the United Kingdom with India. In Britain, secularization as a general social process has gone far, and society has acquired a more secular character than in India where religious beliefs and practices have a much stronger hold over the people. Yet Britain is not a secular state, since it has an established church whose bishops are, by virtue of their office, members of the House of Lords. India is, by contrast, a secular state, without any established church and without any religious representation in the organs of government.

How far can a secular state go in promoting the secularization of life in a society that is deeply permeated by religious beliefs and practices? Is it legitimate for a ruling elite, no matter how well intentioned, to impose its values on a population whose members mostly subscribe to values that are widely different from its own? Can the state seriously promote secularism without interfering with the religious life of the people? Indeed, can it do so without violating the freedom of religion guaranteed by the constitution itself? (Madan 1987) The British had learned to be cautious about tampering with the religious customs of their Indian subjects after making some false moves. Should not a sovereign independent state act toward its citizens with greater responsibility, if not greater courage? Srinivas (1966) drew attention to precisely this enhanced sense of moral responsibility when he suggested that the abolition of untouchability, in whose practice traditional ritual beliefs and attitudes were deeply implicated, could become a state act only after independence and not before it.

The ship of state has to steer a perilous course in India between the norm of secularism and the norm of religious pluralism. It is becoming increasingly clear that there are two distinct, if not mutually conflicting, ways of viewing secularism. In the first view, secularism means disengagement from religion—not this or that particular religion, but religion as such; this appears to be the generally accepted idea of secularism in the west, and it is not without some adherents among Indians. But there is a second view, believed to be more in conformity with the Indian tradition, which regards secularism as the equal tolerance, if not the equal encouragement, of all religions; here the emphasis is on equality and fairness.

These two views of secularism have co-existed among Indians for some time. Not many appear to have been greatly troubled by their discordance; or, if they were troubled, they perhaps felt that, being Indians, they would somehow manage to square the circle. At any rate, these issues were not widely debated and they did not appear to be seriously divisive. For a variety of reasons, having much to do with developments in Indian politics, the divisions have now come to the fore, without any clear resolution in sight.

In order to understand India's peculiar predicament over secularism, we have to keep in mind not only its composite cultural tradition but also its present demography. The presence of large and populous religious minorities makes it difficult to conceive of a stable social arrangement without some degree of religious tolerance as well as some disengagement of religion from public affairs. Secularism, in one form or another, has become India's destiny, however hard it may be for its present leaders to cope with that destiny.

State-sponsored secularism is exposed to attack from various sides. Where it seeks to neutralize religious excesses, it will be attacked by believers for undermining morality. Where it seeks to promote or even protect a religious community under stress, it will be accused by one set of believers of bias in favour of another. In recent years it is the second kind of allegation that has been the most frequently made, since governments have been far too insecure to wish to alienate any section of voters by appearing to undermine their faith.

Successive governments have in fact been involved in the internal affairs of religious communities and in the administration and maintenance of places of worship and other kinds of religious establishments. Their involvement has originated from a mixture of motives, among which the real or expected gains of politics and patronage have always been present. The publicly expressed view of all the major political parties is that religion and politics should be kept apart in the interest of both, and such would appear to be the spirit behind the Constitution of India. But that is more easily said than done in a society in which the temptations of mobilizing political support by appealing to religious sentiment can be resisted only by saints.

Religious establishments in India vary greatly in their wealth. Some are enormously wealthy while others are too poor to be able to manage on their own. It is not altogether unreasonable for a government to wish to keep an eye on the financial affairs of the former and to provide some financial cushion to the latter. This brings forth allegations of interference on the one hand and favouritism on the other. Religious institutions themselves have not been innocent of complicity in these developments. They would like to be free from government interference, but they would not like to miss too many opportunities for securing government funding. In this they seem to have taken their cue from many public institutions, including universities, which are forever approaching the government for more money and forever reproaching it for violating their autonomy. Where a religious institution is large and wealthy, internal disputes are endemic, and one or another branch of the government has to play the part of arbitrator.

The interface between religion and the state brings in not only the administration but also the law. When the British sought to reform the legal system in the nineteenth century, they were confronted by a bewildering variety of laws. They introduced some uniformity in the law of criminal procedure but proceeded cautiously with civil law. Thomas Macaulay, who came to India as the Law Member of the Supreme Council, wrote: 'Our principle is simply this; uniformity where you can have it; diversity where you must have it; but in all cases certainty' (Stokes 1959: 219–20). Between Macaulay and the independence of India, much legal reform took place, but the personal laws of Indians, governed largely by religious tradition, still retained an enormous diversity when the constitution was being written.

Article 44 of the constitution says, 'The state shall endeavour to secure for all citizens a uniform civil code throughout the territory of India.' It is true that this is only a directive principle of state policy and not a law enforceable by the courts, but it has recently acquired great political significance in an unexpected way. Today it is not so much the parties of secularism as the proponents of Hindutva (or the cultural hegemony of Hinduism) that have begun to press for a uniform civil code. This has caught the secularists, both within and outside the government, off guard.

The principal focus of contention today is found in the marriage laws, including the laws relating to the maintenance of divorced women. As is well known, polygamy was allowed by both Hindu and Islamic law, with no restriction as to numbers among Hindus in contrast with Muslims. The Hindu laws relating to marriage, succession, adoption and guardianship were substantially reformed, with some opposition from orthodox Hindus, in 1955 and 1956. Today polygamy is no longer permitted to Hindus, but it still prevails among Muslims, whose personal laws in India, as elsewhere, have been more resistant to change than those of the Hindus. The party of Hindutva has now begun to accuse the 'self-styled secularists' of double standards: acting imperiously in regard to Hindu polygamy, but being coy about Muslim polygamy.

Secularists now find themselves on the horns of a dilemma, between two conflicting norms: the norm of religious tolerance and the norm of equality between men and women. There is an active and articulate women's movement in India, though confined largely to urban, westernized, middle- and upper-middle-class women. They are genuinely liberal and secular, perhaps more so than their menfolk, and their anguish is not difficult to comprehend. Their devotion to the cause of equality is sincere, even passionate; at the same time, they have a generous attitude toward the minorities and would not like to see changes imposed on their personal laws by militant Hindus determined to humiliate the Muslims.

The divisions over secularism bring to the fore the complex interplay of ideas and interests in society. People do have basic and fundamental differences over the meaning of tolerance and the meaning of equality, and over how far religious tolerance can go in accommodating gender inequality. But adherence to a particular position is an expression not merely of inner faith in a particular doctrine but also of loyalty to the community of one's birth. Such loyalty can gather strength even when the faith is growing weaker. Among both Hindus and Muslims, the most intransigent positions are often adopted by persons who have very little to do with the religious life.

Civil Society and Its Institutions

India has a democratic constitution that stresses equality, liberty and the rule of law within a secular framework. But does it have a civil society appropriate to the proper and effective functioning of such a constitution? In this penultimate section, I shall discuss the problem of creating and sustaining a civil society in the light of the conflicts over norms, values and interests on which I have dwelt in the preceding sections.

The concept of civil society is both ambiguous and appealing. I do not wish to propose a definition here, but there are three components that are essential to our understanding of it: state, citizenship, and mediating institutions. It is true that state and civil society are often opposed, but it is difficult to give an adequate account of civil society without keeping the state in mind. Of course what one keeps in mind is not the state as such but the modern constitutional state of the kind that Indians have sought to design for themselves, as I described earlier.

'Citizenship' is a deceptively simple concept. In the contemporary world it is often assumed to be a universal idea, but it is in fact the end product of a long historical evolution. Part II of the Constitution of India is entitled 'Citizenship', but one does not create citizens as autonomous moral and political agents simply by recording their existence in a constitution. Theodore Zeldin (1977: 3), the historian of modern France, has described how, as late as 1864, the peasants in a remote rural district in that country still did not think of themselves as Frenchmen; indeed, if the evidence is to be trusted, they did not even know clearly whether they were Frenchmen, Englishmen or Russians. They thought of themselves as peasants or artisans, as members of a family, a kin group or a parish rather than as citizens of the republic of France.

The plain fact is that in no country in the world is the peasant converted into a citizen overnight. In the remoter rural districts of France, the conversion had not gone very far nearly a hundred years after the French Revolution. The Indian constitution is not even fifty years old and it would hardly be realistic to expect that all Indians—rural and urban, peasant and professional, illiterate and educated—will think of themselves as citizens of India.

For centuries the typical Indian had thought of himself as a member of a particular kin group, village, caste, sect and religious community rather than as a member of a larger society or civilization. For the most part, he had little awareness of what lay beyond his immediate geographical and social horizons. To be sure, there were fairs and pilgrimages, and the depredations of conquering armies that exposed him to the external world. But these were too fitful and intermittent to enable him to incorporate his links with that world as a significant component of his social identity. Being a citizen means adding a new component to one's identity, but that cannot be done without some rearrangement, even displacement, of the old components.

The trajectory from the first formation of the idea of universal citizenship to the attainment of full citizenship is a long, unfinished one. The subject has been examined in great detail by sociologists in Britain, beginning with the work of T.H. Marshall (1977). There it is shown how the content of citizenship became progressively enriched with the creation of first civil, then political, and finally social rights. Marshall's successors have shown how full citizenship still remains a vague and distant goal; and we know today that the entitlements of citizenship may be not only expanded but also abridged.

As I have suggested, the realization of citizenship calls for some degree of social rearrangement. There are many structures that stand between the individual and the wider society of which he is a part. These mediating structures vary enormously from one type of society to another, and they also change in the course of the evolution of each type. Some of them are actual or potential obstacles to the development of civil society; others are necessary and desirable for its sustenance and well-being.

An extreme position, adopted by some secular nationalists, is that if India is to prosper, nothing should be allowed to stand between the individual as citizen and the nation or the state. Such a position is clearly untenable. What makes the inhabitant of this country an Indian today is the fact that he is a citizen of India; but that would amount to little in the absence of the innumerable bonds by which he is tied to particular persons and particular places. Imagine a world of only 950 million Indians and then India, with nothing in between. There would be nothing in it to protect the individual from the arbitrary powers of the state. Also, it would have very little to offer to its members by way of variety, richness, meaning and purpose in life.

The conception of civil society presented here is one that accommodates a variety of institutions operating at different levels between the individual and the nation. They help to connect individuals to each other and to the wider society. Two features of these institutions deserve special comment: they should be of different kinds, and each, within its own sphere, should enjoy a measure of autonomy in relation to the others and to the state. Civil society, in this conception, is pluralistic in principle; it resists absorption by the state as well as by religion.

By an institution I mean something more than the kinds of informal networks of interpersonal relations that emerge and dissolve continuously in every society. I also mean something more by it than the kind of voluntary association that is merely a registered body without any active or continuous social existence. A temple or a monastery is an institution; municipal corporations and universities are institutions. The Bombay Stock Exchange is an institution; an established newspaper with its own traditions, such as *The Times of India*, is an institution. Not all voluntary associations are institutions; but a voluntary association might develop into one after it acquires a definite organizational form and a distinct tradition.

The institutions I have enumerated, more or less at random, cover a very wide range. They include traditional religious institutions because I believe that those should not be placed outside the pale of civil society. However, in countries like India, the real test of the success of civil society will be in the performance of open and secular institutions rather than the rigid and hierarchical ones characteristic of the past. Does Indian society have the resources for creating and sustaining such new institutions?

A variety of new institutions—colleges, hospitals, banks and so on—began to emerge in India from the middle of the nineteenth century onward under the stimulus of colonial rule. Recruitment to these was on a different basis from recruitment to their traditional counterparts; they were open, at least in principle, to all castes and creeds. Their internal structure and functioning were also different, being governed by secular rather than religious principles. These new institutions did not all at once efface the basic design of traditional Indian society, but they opened up new spaces within it.

In retrospect, it seems remarkable how quickly these new institutions made room for themselves in a society whose basic design and social morphology were so greatly at variance with them. Perhaps there was something congenial in the polymorphous character of Hindu civilization that allowed the accretion of new social and cultural components without fully assimilating them. Moreover, these new institutions were backed by a new type of education and a new occupational system that provided avenues of economic advancement to aspiring individuals from the upper castes. A key role was played in these developments by an emerging middle class imbued with a new outlook on life.

Modern institutions, as I have noted, are open institutions, meaning that membership in them is open to all, irrespective of caste, creed and gender. This is in principle true of all public institutions in India. But while they are open in principle, the facts clearly show that recruitment to positions of respect and responsibility in them is generally from a rather restricted social base. The consequences of past inequalities between families manifest themselves in the present distribution of persons in even the most open institutions, to a greater or lesser extent, in all societies. It is this that the policy of positive discrimination seeks to correct in India, and in doing so it has reintroduced caste and community as criteria of recruitment to public institutions.

The idea is to make all public institutions—the civil service, universities, medical schools, engineering institutes—representative of the different castes and communities in society, to make each one of them look a little like India. Even where people agree that this should be ideally so, there are disagreements about acceptable ways of bringing it about. Massive political pressure to achieve social justice through equal representation is changing more than the social composition of public institutions; it is changing their internal relations and the focus of their activity. The divisions of caste and community have been carried over into them, and those divisions affect not only the efficiency of work but also the trust and goodwill that are essential to the smooth functioning of every institution.

I have indicated one kind of pressure that modern institutions have to withstand in India. There are other kinds of pressure, actual as well as potential, that cannot be discounted, but here only a passing remark will be made about secularism. I have said that the institutions distinctive of civil society, those on which its well-being largely depends, are both open and secular in nature. The modern institutions to which I have been referring are secular in principle; they are also by and large secular in practice to the extent that their activities are not regulated by religious rules or religious authorities. The peculiar character of Hinduism probably accounts for this relative immunity. It has neither the kind of unified doctrine nor the kind of centralized authority through which religious regulation can be easily imposed on secular institutions. But by the same token, they are open to penetration by diffuse religious values whose long-term effects it is difficult to determine.

The movement away from hierarchy in India is irreversible, even though no clear destination appears in sight. There is no reason to believe that the decline of hierarchy will necessarily be accompanied by a reduction of inequality in the distribution of income. The experience of western countries in the nineteenth century seems to have been that the decline of a hierarchical order was accompanied, at least for some time, by an increase rather than a decrease in income inequality (Kuznets 1955: 489). Though there is nothing inevitable about this, it needs to be pointed out that government policies for reducing the inequalities of income have so far met with little success.

Politically, the decline of hierarchy does not result necessarily in the consolidation of constitutional democracy; it can lead as well to the ascendancy of populism. It is only the former and not the latter that requires the institutions of civil society for its sustenance. Populism demands an unmediated relationship between a charismatic leader and the people. It does not need mediating institutions; indeed, they are an encumbrance for both leader and people in a populist regime. The real acid test of nation building in India will lie in the capacity of its new mediating institutions to maintain their open and secular character and to extend their influence.

Conclusion: Considerations for Policy

The normative structure of a society is designed to regulate conflicts of interest between the groups, classes and categories that are its constituent parts. But what is to regulate the conflicts that inhere in the normative structure itself? I have noted that the values prevalent in contemporary Indian society, or the ends that are considered socially desirable, are often at variance with each other. There is the commitment to equality that is a part of the modern scheme of things; but the commitment to hierarchy that marked the traditional order is still widely manifest beneath the surface. Recognition of the autonomy of the individual and the respect due to him is now an important value; but it is at odds with the strong sense of obligation to the group of which one is a member by birth.

The courts of law are pre-eminent among the institutions responsible for interpreting and harmonizing the various regulatory rules by which the other institutions of society are governed. Judicial institutions in India, and in particular the Supreme Court and the high courts, have on the whole maintained a high reputation for rectitude and fair-mindedness throughout the period since independence. It will be safe to say that today the judiciary enjoys a greater measure of public confidence than either the legislative or the executive branches of the state. So the first condition for ensuring that the conflict of norms does not go beyond reasonable limits is the maintenance of the integrity and the autonomy of the courts.

The judiciary has in recent years taken an increasingly active role in an effort to set right the endemic violation of rules, particularly by those holding high public office. This has led to discussions in the press and elsewhere on the possibilities and the limits of judicial activism in a constitutional democracy (Béteille 1996, Baxi 1996). In a thoughtful public lecture, the Chief Justice of India has drawn attention to the unusual nature of legislative and executive failures that has led the courts to take a more active role. But he has also sounded a wise note of caution: 'However, by virtue of the fact that the present situation is a corrective measure, the phenomenon of judicial activism in its aggressive role will have to be a temporary one' (Ahmadi 1996).

A new development that has led the courts to take a more active role, as the Chief Justice pointed out in his lecture, is public-interest litigation, which is quite extensive in India. It is now a factor that the state must take into account in ensuring against gross violations of its own norms by its official agents. But such litigation can also put unbearable strains on the courts, which are already overburdened with an enormous backlog of pending cases. Those active in public interest litigation represent diverse interests and act from a variety of intentions. They have had some success in restraining the arbitrary exercise of power by corrupt officials, but the real test of their success will lie in their ability to create the kind of public opinion through which citizens at large become aware of their own rights.

The formation of responsible public opinion is a laborious and demanding task that cannot be left solely to public interest litigation or even to a judiciary with a sympathetic concern for it. Public opinion in India is fragmented, uncertain, and volatile, with a tendency to swing from one extreme to another. The courts address themselves directly to regulatory rules, and only indirectly, and that too not invariably, to the generalized ends that those rules seek to express. Many of the regulatory rules are relatively new and some are against the grain of tradition. New rules cannot be binding unless they are made meaningful through a process of active and continuing education in the widest sense of the term.

Education for meaningful and effective participation in a democratic society and polity is by its nature a many-sided and diffuse process. A variety of agencies, organizations and institutions contribute to it. Their contributions are not all of the same kind, and they are not all consciously directed to the same end. After all, it is in the nature of democracy that such institutions as newspapers, publishing houses and even schools should express and articulate different, if not contradictory, points of view. At the same time, their continuing activity is essential to the widest diffusion of the values on which an open and secular society is sustained.

India has one of the oldest intellectual traditions in the world, with many remarkable achievements to its credit, but it was among the most elitist known to human history, in its social base and in the types of knowledge it favoured. Major changes were initiated in the content and organization of intellectual activity in India in the early part of the nineteenth century (Shils 1961). A new educational system, with new types of schools, colleges and universities, was introduced by the British and on the whole well received by the traditional intellectual elite. What is remarkable in retrospect is the *social* continuity maintained throughout the nineteenth century, particularly among the Hindus, between the traditional literati and the new educated class, despite important changes in the content and institutional setting of education. The new middle class became the bearer of new social values, and it placed the greatest emphasis on the education it received in the new institutions of learning. This class is growing in number, but it still comprises a small proportion of the total population.

Following a process of slow but steady growth in education for a hundred years, there was a spurt after independence. The growth of education has been highly uneven in independent India, and this has been a source of increasing anxiety among planners and policymakers (Karlekar 1983; Tilak 1987). With some simplification, it may be said that secondary education has grown at the expense of primary education, and higher education at the expense of secondary education. There are several reasons behind this. Firstly, it takes far greater material and manpower resources to develop a good system of universal elementary education than to establish a small number of universities and centres of advanced study and research. Secondly, the effects of a good system of elementary education show only indirectly and in the long run, whereas universities and research institutes can show some spectacular results in the form of PhDs and research publications in a much shorter time. But perhaps the really decisive factor has been the conservative bias in Indian planning and in Indian society and culture in favour of established castes and classes.

The neglect of elementary education has been perhaps the single most important factor behind the poor record of development planning in India. It has affected economic and political life in general, and it is now beginning to affect higher education itself. The quantitative expansion of colleges and universities continues apace, but they are already under severe strain on account of the woefully inadequate early education of the students and even the teachers they are now compelled under pressure to admit and promote.

When the first census was taken in independent India in 1951 shortly after the new constitution was adopted, the literacy rate was very low, below 20 per cent for the general population and much lower in some states where female literacy was abysmally low. The constitution had, under Article 45, already declared as a directive principle of state policy that 'The State shall endeavour to provide, within a period of ten years from the commencement of this Constitution, for free and compulsory education for all children until they complete the age of fourteen years.' The magnitude of the economic as well as political consequences of the state's failure to redeem this pledge has now become plainly manifest.

The literacy rate began to climb very slowly in the first three decades of independence, and then began to pick up. By 1991, the state of Kerala in south India had effectively achieved full literacy. The case of Kerala came to be viewed as exemplary because the same state had, among other things, shown impressive results in population control, and the connection between low fertility and literacy, particularly female literacy, has now come to be generally accepted (Sen 1994). The government has begun to show greater determination to eradicate illiteracy by committing substantial resources to its National Literacy Mission.

Total literacy is only the first step in the creation of responsible citizenship. Sustaining a credible system of elementary education demands far greater resources in time and money than eradicating illiteracy once and for all. Primary and secondary schools have no doubt increased in number since independence, but they have also become much more differentiated in terms of the quality of education they provide. The good schools have superior facilities, but they are very expensive and outside the reach of the majority; the majority of primary and even secondary schools are inexpensive, but in many of them there are hardly any facilities at all. The expensive schools are privately funded, and managed by and serve the metropolitan middle and upper middle classes. The rest depend on government funding, which comes in dribs and drabs and is frequently mismanaged and misappropriated.

Fitful and inadequate schooling does not lead to responsible citizenship. It relaxes the grip of traditional values but does not put anything coherent in their place. Some of the wilful disregard for norms witnessed among the urban youth is a result of the failure of schooling in India. A deeper and wider awareness of this certainly helps to clear the atmosphere but does not by itself generate the vast resources required to make available even good quality primary education to all. Private funding will be provided only selectively, and the gap between a few expensive private schools and those accessible to all will remain, but there is no reason why it cannot be narrowed instead of being widened.

Since I attach so much importance to good quality education in the making of civil society, I must in conclusion point to the limits within which it can be expected to work. The effects of good schooling are diffuse, and not specific. Moreover, in a pluralist society, there is no way in which the values imparted by schools can be propelled in a given direction. A technically efficient system of schools, which India seems to need most at present, does not guarantee schooling in liberal and secular ideas. It will be a miracle if the multiplicity of schools through the length and breadth of the country all inculcate a uniform set of values. The same is to some extent true for the press, which is also made up of many diverse strands. Not all newspapers in India propagate the liberal and secular ideology of the constitution; there are some that propagate ideas that are openly violative of its spirit if not its letter.

It is difficult to determine what can be done to regulate the propagation of values contrary to the norms of the constitution in the school, by the press or elsewhere. Here again the courts have a crucial, though delicate, role. They must act when norms are clearly violated; but they cannot snuff out every form of dissent or anticipate the violation of norms in every dissenting idea.

References

Ahmad, Imtiaz (ed.). 1973. *Caste and Social Stratification Among the Muslims.* New Delhi: Manohar.

Ahmadi, A.M. 1996. 'Judicial Activism—I', *The Times of India*, Delhi, 27 February 1996.

Ansari, Ghaus. 1959. *Muslim Caste in Uttar Pradesh.* Lucknow: Ethnographic and Folk Culture Society.

Baxi, Upendra. 1996. *On Judicial Activism, Legal Education, and Research in Globalizing India.* New Delhi: Capital Foundation Society.

Béteille, André. 1986. 'The Concept of Tribe with Special Reference to India', *Europen Journal of Sociology*, vol. 27, pp. 297–318.

—— 1987a. 'Equality as a Right and as a Policy', *LSE Quarterly*, vol. 1, no. 1 pp. 75–98.

—— 1987b. *The Idea of Natural Inequality and Other Essays.* Delhi: Oxford University Press.

—— 1991. *Society and Politics in India: Essays in a Comparative Perspective.* London: Athlone Press.

—— 1994. 'Secularism and the Intellectuals', *Economic and Political Weekly*, vol. 24, no. 10, pp. 559–66, see chapter 4, this volume.

—— 1995. 'Judicial Activism', *The Times of India*, Delhi, 11 December 1995.

—— 1996. 'Caste in Contemporary India' in C.J. Fuller (ed.), *Caste Today.* Delhi: Oxford University Press.

Bose, N.K. 1975 [1949]. *The Structure of Hindu Society* (translated from the Bengali, with an introduction and notes by André Béteille). Delhi: Orient Longman.

Caplan, L. 1980. 'Caste and Castelessness Among South Indian Christians', *Contributions to Indian Sociology*, vol. 14, no. 2, pp. 213–38.

Constituent Assembly. 1948. *Constituent Assembly Debates: Official Report*. New Delhi: Government of India, vol. 7.

Dumont, Louis. 1966. *Homo Hierarchicus: Essai sur le système des castes*. Paris: Gallimard.

—— 1970. *Religion, Politics, and History in India*. Paris: Mouton.

Fiss, O.M. 1977. 'Groups and the Equal Protection Clause' in M. Cohen, T. Nagel, and T. Scanlon (eds), *Equality and Preferential Treatment*. Princeton: Princeton University Press, pp. 84–154.

Galanter, Mark. 1984. *Competing Equalities*. Delhi: Oxford University Press.

Ganguli, B.N. 1975. *Concept of Equality: The Nineteenth Century Indian Debate*. Simla: Indian Institute of Advanced Study.

Godwin, C.J. 1972. *Change and Continuity: A Study of Two Christian Village Communities in Suburban Bombay*. Bombay: Tata McGraw Hill.

Government of India. 1955. *Report of the Backward Classes Commission*. New Delhi: Controller of Publications, vol. 1.

—— 1981. *Report of the Backward Classes Commission*. New Delhi: Controller of Publications, part 1.

Kane, P.V. 1974. *History of Dharmashastra*. Poona: Bhandarkar Oriental Research Institute, 2nd edn, vol. 2, part 1.

Karlekar, Malavika. 1983. 'Education and Inequality' in André Béteille (ed.), *Equality and Inequality*. Delhi: Oxford University Press, pp. 182–242.

Karnataka Backward Classes Commission. 1975. *Report*. Bangalore: Government of Karnataka.

Karve, Irawati. 1968. *Hindu Society: An Interpretation*. Poona: Deshmukh Prakashan, 2nd edn.

Kothari, Rajni (ed.). 1969. *Caste in Indian Politics*. Delhi: Orient Longman.

Kuznets, S. 1955. 'Economic Growth and Income Inequality', *American Economic Review*, vol. 45, no. 1, pp. 257–287.

Madan, T.N. 1987. 'Secularism in Its Place', *Journal of Asian Studies*, vol. 46, no. 4, pp. 747–59.

Maine, Henry Sumner. 1931 [1861]. *Ancient Law*. London: Oxford University Press.

Marshall, T.H. 1977. *Class, Citizenship, and Social Development*. Chicago: University of Chicago Press.

Nandy, Ashis. 1985. 'An Anti-Secularist Manifesto', *Seminar*, no. 314, pp. 14–24.

Nehru, Jawaharlal. 1961 [1946]. *The Discovery of India*. Bombay: Asia Publishing House.

Parsons, Talcott. 1966. *Societies: Evolutionary and Comparative Perspectives*. Englewood Cliffs, N.J.: Prentice-Hall.

Parsons, Talcott and Edward A. Shils (eds). 1951. *Towards a General Theory of Action*. Cambridge, Mass.: Harvard University Press.

Schermerhorn, R.A. 1978. *Ethnic Plurality in India*. Tucson: University of Arizona Press.

Sen, Amartya. 1994. 'Population: Delusion and Reality', *New York Review of Books*, 22 September 1994, pp. 62–71.

Shils, Edward A. 1961. *The Intellectual Between Tradition and Modernity: The Indian Situation*. The Hague: Mouton.

Sivaramayya, B. 1984. *Inequalities and the Law*. Lucknow: Eastern Book Company.

Smelser, Neil J. 1962. *Theory of Collective Behaviour*. New York: The Free Press.

Smith, R.S. 1996. *Rule by Records*. Delhi: Oxford University Press.

Srinivas, M.N. 1962. *Caste in Modern India and Other Essays*. Bombay: Asia Publishing House.

—— 1966. *Social Change in Modern India*. Berkeley: University of California Press.

Stokes, Eric. 1959. *The English Utilitarians and India*. Oxford: Clarendon Press.

Tilak, J.B.G. 1987. *Economics of Inequality in Education*. London: Sage.

Tripathi, P.K. 1972. *Some Insights into Fundamental Rights*. Bombay: University of Bombay.

Zeldin, Theodore. 1977. *France: 1848–1945*. Oxford: Clarendon Press, vol. 2.

11

Governance*

The governance of a society of the scale and complexity of India's is a very large endeavour in which the services of the union and the state governments have an important role to play. The significance of this role is acknowledged in the constitution of which a separate part is devoted to these services. At the same time, the governance of India is too demanding a task to be undertaken single-handed by the Indian Administrative Service or even the administrative executive taken as a whole.

What is needed above all in assessing the role of the IAS is a sense of measure and balance. That sense is easily lost in the kind of troubled time through which we are now passing. Sometimes too much is expected of the administrative executive, not only in the administration of the country but also in its development and transformation, and there were those in the service who used to believe that it could lift the country out of the morass of poverty, illiteracy and oppression by its sole unaided effort. A reaction was bound to set in, and there are many now, including some in the IAS itself, who say that it has little or nothing of value to contribute; or, even, that its contribution is and has been a negative one. Today, it is important to avoid the extremes of euphoria and disillusion while taking a fresh look at the future prospects of the service in the light of its past experience.

The present overview is written in the belief that the IAS has an important role in the governance of India, but that there are limits to its role that need to be clearly identified and kept in mind; and that, further, its effectiveness will depend upon the confidence and the restraint

* Originally published as 'Experience of Governance: A Sociological Overview' in R.K. Dar (ed.), *Governance and the IAS*, New Delhi: Tata McGraw Hill, 1999.

with which it is able to act within the limits of its competence. This is true of any modern profession based on technical qualifications, but the truth is easily lost to sight in the case of the higher civil servants whose technical qualifications are not as easily manifest as in many other cases. Members of the administrative executive have certain things in common with those of the political executive with whom their work is closely intertwined. But they also have many things in common with lawyers, accountants, engineers and members of other modern professions. I make this point at the outset since I regard the technical requirements of modern administration to be of the greatest importance.

The old Indian Civil Service, of which the IAS became the successor after independence, was known as 'the heaven-born'. The IAS took over some of the aura of its predecessor, but the conditions of its operation, particularly the relations between the political and the administrative executives, have changed. The role of the civil servant has become more specialized, which means that it has become more restricted in some respects and more demanding in others. Before the onset of democracy, the district officer was often viewed as the final arbiter of the destinies of those in their care, in a sense their *ma-baap* (surrogate parents). This attitude towards the high official still survives, particularly in the districts where every IAS officer cuts his teeth. It is unhealthy for the official to present himself or to be represented as a patron, for a modern civil service is a bureaucratic and not a patrimonial system of administration.

The successful entrant into the IAS is likely to agree that patronage is not a desirable element in the civil service. This is not to say that in the fullness of time he will not himself become entangled in networks of patronage. Why has it proved so difficult to keep administration insulated from the small and large demands of patronage? Part of the answer lies in the turn taken by democratic politics in India. But there are deeper causes, embedded in the structure of Indian society. This is a society in which the claims of kinship, caste and community are strong, not to say irresistible, and ties of patronage often emerge as concessions to those claims. The general tendency in Indian society is for life to be regulated by persons rather than rules, and today the civil servant has to work against this tendency if he is to be true to his vocation. So the question is not simply what the civil service or the administrative executive can be expected to *do*, but also what one can expect it to *be*.

I would like to emphasize that even the idea, let alone the reality, of a civil service free from the entanglements of patronage is a relatively new one, not only in India but in the world as a whole. It hardly goes further back in time than the nineteenth century. In England until the middle of the last century, it would be unusual for someone to think that he could make a successful career in the civil service without recourse to patronage. That began to change after 1858, and a new breed of civil servants, nicknamed the *competition wallahs* in India came into existence (Trevelyan 1864). Patronage did not disappear altogether or all at once, but its legitimacy began to be undermined, and a new conception of the civil service came to be gradually established. The question is how far the operation of the administrative executive in India conforms today to this new conception.

Many civil servants are nowadays attracted by the role of the social activist, from a mixture of moral and political considerations. In the seventies and eighties, when I was a regular visitor to the National Academy of Administration at Mussoorie, I had many conversations on the subject with probationers and young serving officers. I was struck by the number of them who were disenchanted with the service as they found it, and wanted a more active role for themselves and their service in eradicating poverty and illiteracy, and in fighting oppression and injustice. Some of them were driven by a generous moral impulse, but others I thought were politicians in the making. Whatever the case may have been, I do not believe that it is any more consistent with the responsibilities of the modern official for him to be a social activist than it is for him to be a patron.

I am not certain that the new recruit to the IAS will always agree that the role of the social activist is inconsistent with that of the civil servant. Clearly, those who are at the apex of the administrative executive should not rest content with the routine of clearing files. They have much to contribute to the shaping and not just the implementation of policy, and about this I will have more to say later. At the same time, there are strict limits to the extent to which they can act as shakers and movers of things. The social activist can take independent initiative in political action; the civil servant can do so only within limits that are set by others. The civil servant's relation to the public is defined by the obligations of his office; it is fundamentally different from that of the social activist who is, besides, free to choose an appropriate public, or segment of the public to act upon. The IAS is not a voluntary association whose members are free to determine their own terms and conditions of work. If the civil servant is to stand on his own ground in meeting his political masters, he cannot at the same time adopt the stance of a social activist.

It is well to remember that the IAS is a relatively new implant on a very old society marked by its own pattern and rhythm of life. There are many other institutions and associations that are also relatively new implants, and they too are facing difficult problems in coping with the environment in which they have to operate. These institutions and associations are responsible for a variety of specialized functions in such diverse fields as health, education, research, communication, finance and many others. Their success, and not merely that of the administrative executive, is a precondition for the growth of the kind of civil society that is envisaged in the Constitution (Béteille 1996).

The traditional order in India had its distinctive social morphology as well as its distinctive normative structure. The social morphology and the normative structure were consistent with each other, and their mutual reinforcement gave a degree of stability and continuity to society over a very long period of time. The stability and continuity have now been broken, and society is changing, although not all parts of it are changing at the same pace or even in the same direction. It is a part of the responsibility of the administrative executive, as of all modern institutions, to cope with these changes and at the same time to give them direction.

There has been a sea change in the normative structure of Indian society. This may be seen by contrasting the Constitution of India, which is the charter of modern Indian society, with the Manusmriti which was in some sense the charter of traditional Hindu society. The two most significant departures from the past in our new normative order are, firstly, the stress on equality, and, secondly, the stress on the individual as an autonomous legal and moral agent. Unless we are able to create spaces in our society in which conduct is regulated by these principles, the new normative order will remain only on paper. The administrative executive has a significant part to play in the creation and consolidation of these spaces.

Despite the changes in the normative order of society through the adoption of a new constitution and new laws, many features of the old social morphology still remain prominent. The lack of fit between the new normative order and the social morphology inherited from the past may be seen in virtually every sphere of life. Nor is this all. The values prevalent in contemporary Indian society, or the ends that are considered as socially desirable, are themselves often at variance with each other. There is the commitment to equality that is a part of the modern scheme of things; but the commitment to hierarchy that marked the traditional order is still widely manifest beneath the surface. Recognition of the autonomy of the individual and the respect due to him is now an important value; but it is at odds with the strong sense of obligation to the group of which one is a member by birth. The contradiction is not simply between 'modern' institutions and their 'traditional' environment; it is lodged within each one of those institutions.

Here I would refer very briefly to a point whose significance will become clearer in the subsequent discussion. I have said that the basis of the new constitutional and legal order is equality rather than hierarchy. Hence, just as the traditional institutions of village, caste and joint family were governed by hierarchy, we might expect the modern institutions of which I have just spoken to be governed by equality. Yet, this clearly is not the case in every sense, either in India or anywhere else in the contemporary world. The university, the laboratory and the hospital cannot function without a structure of superordinate and subordinate positions. So much is this the case with the administrative bureaucracy that its 'rigid and inflexible hierarchy' is a favourite target of every citizen's attack. How are we to reconcile this with the strong guarantees of equality inscribed in the constitution?

The inescapable fact is that the idea of equality is itself ambiguous and equivocal, being made up of diverse components that are not always easy to reconcile with each other. There is equality of status and condition, and equality of opportunity. Formal equality of opportunity is not the same thing as substantive, or even 'fair', equality of opportunity. It is no mystery that in an open, competitive system, there can be equality only before the competition and not after it. Some advocates of equality stress equality of opportunity while others stress equality of outcome, or the equal distribution of benefits and burdens. However firm and extensive the guarantees of equality in the constitution may be, every modern institution has to accommodate some degree of inequality in the distribution of income, esteem and authority.

Nevertheless, the place of inequality in the administrative executive is very different from its place in traditional social arrangements. Modern institutions, unlike village, caste and joint family, are open, secular institutions. Recruitment to public hospitals, universities, national laboratories—and, above all, the IAS—is, at least in principle, through open competition. What is decisive in each case is the technical qualification, no matter how broadly conceived, of the candidate, and not his social origin. Moreover, it was the civil service that provided the first model for 'careers open to talent' in early nineteenth century France that was subsequently adopted by other modern institutions throughout the world. The inequalities that are present in their internal arrangements have to do with ability and qualification, and not with birth in a particular family, caste or community.

A modern civil service is not only an open system, it is, like other modern institutions, also a secular system in the sense that it is regulated by rational, man-made rules rather than by religious tradition or authority. It should be stressed that in the systems to which I have referred, there is a requirement of consistency between the principle of recruitment and the pattern of internal relations.

From the sociological point of view, the IAS may be seen as an organ (or a part of an organ) in a large and differentiated society with many different segments and organs interrelated in complex ways. It is an administrative organ of a particular type, based on what has been described as the rational-legal principle. Bureaucratic administration based on the rational-legal principle is not the only type of administration known to history. In fact, it is a relative latecomer, and where the environment is governed by principles of a different kind, it needs to be carefully nurtured. Nowhere does rational-legal administration operate in its pure form, uncontaminated by extraneous elements, and certainly the ICS of a hundred years ago approximated to it in only a very broad way.

It is important to begin by considering bureaucratic administration as a pure type, if only to see on how many points it departs from the social environment in which it has to operate. Here, I shall base myself on the classic representation of bureaucracy as an ideal type in the work of Max Weber (1978: 956–1005) where, I hardly need to emphasize, it is an analytical term and not a term of disparagement as it is with the popular press in almost every country.

The following are the main characteristics of the bureaucratic form of administration based on the rational-legal principle. Firstly, there are clearly demarcated jurisdictional areas within which each official functions. Secondly, there is a hierarchical co-ordination of superordinate and subordinate offices. Thirdly, office work is organized on the basis of written documents or files conforming to impersonal rules. Fourthly, the modern official requires training of an increasingly specialized and even technical nature both prior to entering his career and in the course of it; he is trained for his office, not born to it. Fifthly, it is only in the bureaucratic form of administration that the office becomes a full time occupation, lasting generally for the whole of one's working life. And finally, the general rules of administration are in principle open to continuous review and reformulation, the objective being to make them as fully systematic as possible through conscious and deliberate action.

Critics have argued that Weber idealized bureaucracy, presenting it as a smooth and streamlined apparatus, the most efficient machinery of administration known to history, whereas actually existing bureaucracies, they say, are rigid, inflexible, dilatory, inefficient and corrupt (Merton et al. 1952). The enlightened citizen's assessment of bureaucracy the world over is more a negative than a positive one, but that may be because he rarely thinks of any other system of administration to compare with it. If the enlightened citizen were made to choose between bureaucratic and patrimonial administration, he might in fact choose the former, if only as the lesser evil. Much of the public criticism of bureaucratic administration is misdirected. At least in this country, the failure of bureaucracy is most often its failure to overcome its contamination by patrimonialism.

Central to the bureaucratic form of administration is the administrative office which develops fully only under it: authority rests in the office and not the official. This requires the clearest separation in principle between what is 'official' and what is 'private'. It is from this that 'bureaucracy' draws its primary meaning, which is rule from and through the office. Today, the office is above all where a particular type of functionary works, at his desk, with his files and within a demarcated field of action. To be sure, this is not all that there is to modern administration, but it is what gives to that administration its defining features.

Under patrimonialism and all previously existing forms of administration, there is no clear separation, even in principle, between the 'official' and the 'private', between 'office' and 'household'. In speaking of household here, I use the term in an extended sense to refer to all kinds of ties based on kinship, caste and community. These ties exercise their claims in most societies, and it is only under bureaucratic administration that such claims are strictly separated, in principle, from the claims of office. Under all other forms of administration, it is considered morally right rather than wrong to place one's nephew and one's son-in-law, one's caste fellow or one's co-religionist in office and to advance his career. In the first half of the nineteenth century, the word 'nepotism' was a new word in the English language, adopted to refer to something that was only then beginning to be considered improper in administration.

It will be disingenuous to maintain that the ties of kinship, caste and community establish no moral claims in our society, or that the civil servant, no matter how upright or efficient, can simply overlook those claims in the course of his official work. The claims of kinship, caste and community are stronger and reach further in our society than in many others, and within certain spheres those claims are legitimate as well. But there are other spheres in which they are not legitimate and which must therefore be insulated from them. In a democratic system, it would be unrealistic to expect the politician to remain wholly indifferent to those claims, for democratic politics cannot operate without the mobilization of support. The civil servant should not have to depend on that kind of support at all, and can therefore be expected to remain relatively immune to the pressures of caste and community.

Middle-class Indians tend to be quite free with their criticism of others for using family and other personal ties in the pursuit of their careers even when they use those ties themselves. But the malady needs to be understood before it is attacked. It is by no means the case that personal ties based on family, kinship and community are out of place in every kind of modern profession. A doctor or a lawyer may legitimately engage his son or his nephew in his own clinic or chamber; he is not obliged either legally or morally to select those who will work with him through open general competition. But a modern civil servant does not have the same choice because he does not have his own private practice. Even the elected politician, although he holds a public office, may legitimately claim a little more room in this respect than the appointed official.

In India, as elsewhere, the state has been criticized for recklessly expanding the size of its administrative apparatus. There appears to be fairly wide agreement today that this expansion has to be contained and to some extent even reversed. At the same time, the very persons who complain about the expansion of the government expect it to undertake a wider range of tasks than before. The state is concerned today not only with the maintenance of law and order and the collection of revenue, but also with development and welfare. It can reduce the scale of its administrative tasks somewhat but not to a very large extent. The nature and form of an administrative system cannot be made wholly independent of its scale.

Given the range of tasks that the government has minimally to undertake, it is difficult to visualize any type of administration other than the bureaucratic type described above. In a small and homogeneous island community where the government has only a few tasks to perform, a more traditional type of administration might be technically adequate. But a modern society requires a modern system of administration, which means one based on the rational-legal principle. The chief recommendation for such a system is its technical superiority. As Max Weber (1978: 973) put it: 'The fully developed bureaucratic apparatus compares with other organizations exactly as does the machine with the non-mechanical modes of production'.

Bureaucracy has been likened over and over again to an apparatus or a machine by both its admirers and its detractors. The metaphor must be used with caution for, taken literally, it can be misleading. Looking forward to the future society nearly two hundred years ago, Henri de Saint-Simon had expressed the hope that in it the government of men would be replaced by the administration of things. Then the citizen would not be troubled any more by the law's delay or the insolence of office, but have his problem disposed of efficiently, smoothly and painlessly. No bureaucracy has ever functioned in that way and we know today that none ever can. Asymmetries of status and power are ineradicable features of human arrangements, and a bureaucracy is in the end not an arrangement of shafts and gears but of human beings. Nevertheless, it has a better capacity than any other comparable system to work smoothly and impersonally while handling a much larger range of tasks.

The impersonal nature of bureaucracy itself imposes its own human cost. Citizens are often troubled by the nameless, faceless and soulless character of the bureaucratic system. Instead of dealing with each individual citizen on the human plane, the system merely throws rules at his face. The civil servant is notorious for deploying rules to avoid having to take decisions. But here there is often an exaggeration as well as a misunderstanding. To apply rules impersonally, without fear or favour, is not necessarily to ignore the specific nature of the individual case. Bureaucratic administration acts in accordance with rational-legal principles; that does not mean that the individual bureaucrat does or ever can dispense with the responsibility to take decisions.

Bureaucratic administration has to steer an uneasy course between being entangled in networks of patronage and operating as a dehumanized machine. Max Weber, who praised bureaucracy for its technical efficiency, also spoke against its relentless drive towards the 'parcelling-out of the soul', and the creation of a world 'filled with nothing but those little cogs, little men clinging to little jobs and striving towards bigger ones' (Mayer 1943: 127–8). Since Weber, a succession of sociologists have attacked the dehumanizing effect of bureaucracy; but their gloomy predictions have not been fulfilled, despite the spread of technological rationality, in even the most industrially advanced societies. There seems little immediate danger of the Indian soul being destroyed by rational-legal administration; the greater danger in India is of the relapse into patrimonialism.

Having considered the internal organization of the administrative executive, we may now turn to its social composition. Even those who acknowledge the need for an administrative elite in a democratic polity might like to make sure that it is recruited from the widest social base. Napoleon, who may be regarded as the first great architect of the modern administrative system, gave the slogan of 'careers open to talent' at a time when in most European countries social origin counted for more than individual talent in admission to positions of respect and responsibility. To what extent are careers in the IAS in fact open to talent and not just the advantage of birth?

The principle of recruitment to the IAS by 'open national competition' which draws out the best talent in the country is an important part of the self-image of the service. Several members of the batch of 1958 have recounted their delight—and in some cases their surprise—on learning that they had made it to the enchanted world of the IAS. It is natural for a young person who has succeeded in such an exacting competition to think well of himself. This self-satisfied feeling, understandable in someone who is 23 or 24, unfortunately lingers too often until the age of retirement, and even beyond. It makes members of the IAS targets of envy as well as of ridicule.

A casual examination shows that the social background from which the 12th Metcalfians (the twelfth batch of civil service probationers trained at Metcalf House, Delhi) entered the service was overwhelmingly urban middle class. That shows that the Indian elite is in large measure a self-recruiting one. But beyond that, there is more than one conclusion to be drawn from the very limited material available. The urban middle class as a whole is no doubt better off than the rest of Indian society, but the facts do not indicate that all those who entered the service in 1958 came from privileged families. They were not all educated in the most expensive schools, and their parents were not all at the top of the occupational ladder. Even forty years ago, it was not very uncommon to make one's way into the administrative elite from a lower-middle class home; individual talent and luck played some part in overcoming social and economic disadvantages, provided the disadvantages were not too severe.

There is no country in the world in which the principle of careers open to talent works to the equal advantage of individuals from all strata of society. Entry into superior administrative, managerial and professional occupations is everywhere easier for those belonging to the educated middle classes than it is for most others. This kind of filtration is governed not merely by economic advantage but also by favourable social and cultural endowments. Selectivity in recruitment, leading to the reproduction of inequality, may be found everywhere, though of course not to the same extent. It appears particularly striking in India partly because the educated middle class is a much smaller proportion of the total population here than in industrially advanced societies.

The base of recruitment to superior occupations in the middle and upper middle classes broadens in all societies in the course of modernization of which it may be considered one of the principle attractions. However, this is a slow and gradual process, and it takes place within certain limits. The idea of a society in which individuals freely move upwards and downwards solely according to their merits is a myth without any foundation in sociological understanding. All modern societies display two conflicting tendencies: the first is for individuals to move up and down the occupational ladder within and between generations; and the second is for the system of stratification to reproduce itself. In India, the second tendency is the more marked, although the first is by no means absent.

Although there are limits to upward mobility in all societies, some societies would appear to allow more of it than others. The comparative study of rates of mobility is a difficult and technical subject whose methods and findings cannot, for obvious reasons, be discussed here. We simply do not have the kinds of data that will enable us to make reliable comparisons between our country and others in regard to the chances of entry into the higher civil service of individuals from the different social strata. Even for such countries as Britain, France and the United States, where data on occupational mobility have been systematically collected for decades, sociologists have found it difficult to reach agreed conclusions (Erikson and Goldthorpe 1992).

Going by impressions, one may say that the social base of recruitment to the IAS has broadened somewhat in the fifty years or so of its existence. One significant change is the recruitment of more women into the service than at the time of its inception. The number of women entering the service rose steadily in the first two decades of its existence, and then stabilized around a figure of 12 or 15 per cent. It has not shown any marked tendency to rise further in the last two decades. It will be difficult to attribute this ceiling either to the innate inferiority of women or to any conscious effort on the part of the Union Public Service Commission to discriminate against them. Its roots lie in a much deeper social and cultural inertia against which there is no simple antidote.

Although the educated middle class still sends the largest proportion of entrants into the higher civil service, it is likely that the entrants come from a somewhat wider social background than they did fifty years ago. This is partly because the middle class itself has expanded and become more differentiated in the interval. If we look at gender and class together, we will find that the women recruited to the service through open competition tend to come from a narrower band of classes than the men. This is in conformity with sociological expectation, the grounds for which cannot be discussed here.

The information available on the social origins of higher civil servants is generally sketchy and sometimes unreliable. Where the father's occupation is shown as 'agriculture' or 'farming', it gives only the vaguest indication of his income or social standing, or indeed of what he actually did. Likewise, a person's birth in a village or his early education in a small town may not tell us a very great deal about his actual social origin. In looking back on his own past, a person may exaggerate either the favourable endowments of his family or the dire hardships against which he as an individual had to struggle. Autobiographical accounts of successful Indians do both, and they are not the best material for a systematic study of social mobility.

The social composition of the administrative elite, from top to bottom, is almost certainly more diverse in terms of caste and community than was the case in the wake of independence. The upper castes, comprising a very small minority, were represented in superior administrative and other occupations in far greater numbers than in the population as a whole. This was to be expected in a hierarchical society in which positions of respect and responsibility were open only to members of the highest castes. Things began to change with changes in the legal and educational systems, and restrictions on the entry of members of the lower castes into superior occupations were removed in principle and began to be eased in practice. But the administrative executive is still predominantly upper caste, as it is still predominantly male.

Why do administrative and other elites tend to reproduce themselves in our society and in other democratic societies that have adopted the principle of equality in their legal and constitutional orders? What are the impediments that in all stratified societies prevent the full realization in practice of the principle of careers open to talent? These are large questions that cannot be treated exhaustively here, but some provisional answers may be attempted.

There are several agencies through which inequalities are reproduced in all modern societies. Two of the most important among these are the family and the school which together play a crucial part in the formation and maintenance of the middle class and the internal divisions in it.

In all stratified societies, families have unequal endowments of capital, and the advantages and disadvantages of these endowments are transmitted to successive generations through the processes of everyday domestic life (Bourdieu and Passeron 1979). Here we need to use an extended concept of capital that will include not just material or economic capital but also cultural and social capital. We will not get very far in assessing the chances a person has of competing successfully for entry into the IAS if we take into account only the income or wealth of his family. The latter are certainly important, but education and other socially-acquired abilities and associations are also important. College and school teachers and middle- or lower-level government functionaries might live in straitened circumstances, but they are often able to provide their sons with the education, information and motivation essential for success in the competition for higher administrative positions.

Economic and culture capital go together only up to a point. A family in straitened circumstances whose members have been educated and held white-collar employment for three or four generations is likely to provide better opportunities for entry into the civil service to its children than one that is much more wealthy but without experience of urban middle-class culture. This is particularly true for women. The daughter of a college teacher in a metropolitan city is likely to get off to a better start than the daughter of a much more wealthy trader or landowner in a small town or village. Of course, it is best for the aspirant if his family is well endowed with both economic and cultural capital. But then again, the emotional support provided by the family to the growing child is important and that is not strictly determined by any of the forms of capital referred to above.

In drawing attention to the part played by cultural and social capital, I do not wish to discount the importance of individual ability. That is indispensable for upward social mobility, but its role must not be exaggerated as is regularly done by those who enter the IAS from families with only modest economic and other endowments. Not only ability, but luck also plays an important part in individual mobility in all societies. Children from families with very similar endowments of economic, cultural and social capital may not move upward or downward to the same extent, and even full siblings may fare very differently in the competition for employment. All this simply means that upward and downward mobility do take place, but they take place within socially-determined limits. Mobility is governed by the family's endowment of material, social and cultural capital; by the individual's own ability, effort and motivation; and not least by luck or chance.

Middle-class Indian parents are on the whole supportive of their children. In many cases they are also deeply concerned, sometimes to the point of obsession, about the career prospects of their sons. Language abilities and other socially useful skills are first acquired, consciously as well as unconsciously, within the home. Some homes are plentifully stocked with books and other culture accessories; others hardly at all. Families also differ enormously in their range of social connections, and this too is only partly, and never wholly, a matter of income and wealth. Crucial to planning and preparing for careers in administration, management and the professions is access to information. In this respect, middle-class families in metropolitan cities have a decided advantage over others, but they are not by any means all equally advantaged.

Next to the family, the school plays a significant part in the formation of elites in all contemporary societies. It is the crucial link between family and career. Schools in India, as in all modern societies, are of many different types, and, in general, the more highly stratified the society, the more differentiated its system of schools. The system of schools is related to the system of stratification in a very complex way. It is true to only a certain extent that the modern educational system facilitates individual mobility; it also reinforces the system of stratification by providing different sorts of education to children from the different social strata.

In India, only a small minority of schools provide the kind of education that is indispensable for entry into superior administrative, managerial and professional occupations. These schools are expensive, but the expense is not the only factor that restricts access to them. Parents play a crucial part in the choice of schools, and only parents with certain kinds of social and cultural endowments can reasonably expect to get their sons admitted to the kinds of schools that are the training grounds of elites. Money counts, but other things are also important. Individual talent also counts, but generally only after admission to a reasonably good school has been secured.

Most of the good schools are private schools, and they are both expensive and socially exclusive. Some of them offer scholarships to exceptionally talented pupils from disadvantaged families and these open up avenues of mobility, but such mobility can alter the social composition of the elite to only a small extent and over a long period of time. We observe that, when they do get to school, most children have to put up with poor schools largely because they live in villages or small towns or because their parents are indigent and ill-informed, and we ask ourselves why this should be so. Can the state not intervene and provide high quality education at affordable prices to all children irrespective of their place of residence and the social and economic standing of their parents? The problem is that high quality secondary education is very expensive, and the state can afford to provide it at little or no cost only on a very selective basis. It is difficult to see how the state can intervene to cancel out the advantages of schools with superior economic, social and cultural endowments without seriously damaging the endowments of society as a whole.

The years since independence have witnessed the continuous differentiation of schools. The better schools have improved their facilities but the vast majority of them are poorly equipped. While the poorer schools languish throughout the country, every decade witnesses the opening of a few new schools in the metropolitan cities that are more expensive and more exclusive than any that have existed in the past. Unable to cope with this relentless process of differentiation, educational reformers take refuge in rhetoric. They make speeches and write articles in support of a uniform school system and simultaneously do their best to secure places for their children in the most exclusive schools affordable. The fact remains nevertheless that successful entrants into the IAS have at no time come only from the most expensive, the most exclusive or even the best schools.

The constraints against a fully open administrative or educational system may be better understood if we consider very briefly a different society with a longer historical experience of recruitment through open general competition. The example I have in mind is that of France which was the first modern society to try to give institutional form to the principle of 'careers open to talent'. The French have in the last two hundred years built up one of the most efficient systems of public administration known to history. This system is maintained through the combined operation of France's elite professional schools (the *grandes écoles*) and her elite administrative corps (the *grands corps*). Both the *grandes écoles* and the *grands corps* recruit their members through open general competition. They are both highly selective and highly exclusive, and self-consciously elitist in character; and a recent critic of the system has described them as the 'state nobility' (Bourdieu 1996). This state nobility has played no small part in the twentieth century in enabling France to maintain a measure of stability through the military ravages of two world wars and the political turmoil of the Fourth Republic.

Napoleon had hoped to dismantle the elite based on birth that France had inherited from the *ancien régime*. and to put in its place an elite based on talent and proven ability. He succeeded to only a limited extent. For a long time it was widely believed that the French administrative elite was recruited from all social classes, that individual talent was what really counted, and that the advantage of birth had very little to do with its constitution. That belief has failed to stand up to critical empirical examination. Entry into the elite administrative corps is more or less strictly regulated by the system of technical and professional schools, and entry into the best among these favours pupils from the middle and the upper-middle classes to a substantial extent. No doubt some individuals from socially-disadvantaged families succeed in entering the *grandes écoles*, and, through them, the *grands corps*, but their numbers are relatively small.

In any given society at any given phase in its historical development, there are limits to which technical excellence in administration can be combined with recruitment to an administrative elite that is open not only in principle but also in practice. The French have invested a great deal in developing a reasonably broad-based system of secondary education of reasonably high quality. Our achievements in that regard can hardly be said to inspire confidence. Given our record of the last fifty years, it is unlikely that we will be able to broaden the base of secondary education substantially without lowering its quality to some extent. This will be the most serious obstacle to any effort to radically alter the social composition of the administrative executive and at the same time maintain, let alone improve, its technical quality.

The social composition of the higher civil service alters slowly and up to a point if matters are left to free and open competition. This has been the case in India with both gender and caste, though in somewhat different ways. But matters need not be left entirely to free and open competition. The state can intervene directly to make the higher civil service more socially representative, to make it look more like India. In this country, the idea of distributing what is at the disposal of the state according to quotas appeals to large sections of people, including not only the political but also the administrative elite.

Will an administrative executive made up of equal numbers of men and women, and of members of the different castes and communities selected in proportion to their strength in the population be representative of the people of India? Suppose all these persons came from educated and well-to-do urban middle-class families, would they still be considered representative of the Indian people? In such a complex society as ours, with so many cross-cutting divisions based not only on gender, caste and community but also on income, occupation and education, is it possible to create a civil service that will have a face in every office to represent every section or sub-section of the population?

Caste quotas in administrative positions were introduced during British rule. At that time, the administrative machinery was relatively small, and caste quotas were instituted in some and not in all parts of the country, and moreover in only the subordinate administration. It is doubtful that such quotas were even contemplated for the ICS. In introducing caste quotas in the administration, the colonial government was concerned largely with maintaining a balance between communities; and it was not restrained by any constitutional guarantee of equality of opportunity or any constitutional impediment against discrimination on the basis of caste and community. In the first ten or fifteen years after independence, caste quotas were on the whole viewed as politically divisive, and the courts treated them with some suspicion. But the political pressure for quotas began to increase steadily after 1977, and since then the courts have found many ingenious arguments to permit or even support them. Today, caste quotas have become as important as open national competition in recruitment to all branches of the civil service and at all levels. It is not unlikely that quotas for women will be added to caste quotas in the not-too-distant future.

A civil service recruited on the basis of quotas is different from one recruited through open competition. It will be naive to believe that quotas will alter only the social composition of the service and leave unchanged its self-image, its coherence and its mode of functioning. The political impulse that introduces caste quotas into the civil service will enter inside it and give form and colour to its internal relations and to its relations with the outside world.

As I have indicated, a part of the self-esteem of the IAS officer derives from the fact that he has been selected for his success in an exacting competition. That self-esteem is undermined to some extent when quotas are superimposed on competition for the selection of members. A person who has been selected on the basis of caste is not likely to have the same sense of his own worth as someone who has been selected through open competition; and others are unlikely to think that the two are of the same worth. The IAS also had a certain *esprit de corps* born out of shared experience of the same kind of training and the same kind of career. That *esprit de corps* has been weakened due to a variety of reasons and will be further weakened when professional considerations have to compete with caste considerations in selections, promotions, postings and transfers. It is true that *esprit de corps* sometimes becomes an euphemism for a closed-shop mentality; but recruitment through quotas can hardly be a remedy for that.

The well-being of democracy requires a plurality of institutions, performing a variety of functions. It is a very narrow conception of democracy to expect all its institutions to be constituted in the same way, irrespective of the functions entrusted to them. Here it is important to keep in sight the distinction between the pluralist and the populist conceptions of democracy. Populism is antithetical to a differentiated institutional system, and in particular to all institutions that are or appear to be selective or exclusive; it is loath to admit any justification for their existence on the ground that they are technically required for the functions they have to perform.

In a parliamentary democracy, the administrative executive performs technical and not representational functions; representational functions are performed by the political executive. A civil servant is not expected to and should not seek to promote the interest of the caste or community to which he belongs, as the politician may to some extent legitimately do. To say that there should be more civil servants from particular castes or communities, or else their interests will be over-looked, is to misconceive the nature of a rational-legal system of administration and to confuse it with its opposite, that is, a patrimonial system. Under the former system of administration, once the political executive has decided that certain castes or communities require special attention, it becomes the responsibility of *all* civil servants and not just civil servants from those castes and communities to specially look after their interests. To act on the opposite presumption is to drive a wedge into the civil service against which its members do not have any real protection.

One can certainly argue that a civil service made up of only men or only members of a handful of castes is likely to be less resilient, less sensitive and less rich in its experience than one that has both men and women and from every major caste and community. As I have already indicated, some broadening of the base of recruitment comes about in the ordinary course of modernization through the spread of education, and through changes in the attitudes of people, their aspirations and their inhibitions; and this is always to be welcomed. A hundred years ago, very few respectable upper-caste families would think of sending their daughters to university. Now this has become a commonplace, not so much through direct intervention by the state as through changes in the aspirations and inhibitions of the middle classes. So, more women are joining the IAS as a result of the same currents that lead more of them to enter the universities and to become doctors, lawyers and journalists.

The general course of the broadening of the social base of superior administrative, managerial and professional occupations is governed by the expansion of the middle class as a whole. This comes about through linked changes in the educational and occupational systems. Changes in the educational and occupational systems are slow and not without social and economic costs. State action can contribute something to such changes; it cannot be a substitute for them.

Recruitment through open general competition is a requirement of a rational-legal system of administration which is the model for the Indian civil service. If such recruitment fails to create a service with a sufficiently broad social base, the procedures for recruitment may be adjusted or amended within certain limits. But to disregard the principle of open national competition will be to put at risk the very basis of the administrative system as a politically-neutral and technically-efficient apparatus.

Those who call for a civil service that will be representative of all the classes and communities in society are not always mindful of the technical requirements of modern administration. Those requirements are of the greatest importance, but they tend to be easily overlooked. The average Indian is inclined to believe that the civil servant sits in his office pushing files, and divides his time between throwing his weight on hapless citizens and making deals with unscrupulous politicians. The doctor, the engineer and the scientist believe that administration is something that any intelligent man can do in his spare time and with his left hand.

Among modern social theorists, it was Max Weber who first drew attention to the complex and exacting technical requirements of the bureaucratic form of administration, and Weber was substantially right. This is not to say that the Indian bureaucracy or any other existing bureaucracy meets all or even most of these technical requirements fully in practice. There is in fact evidence to show that they have become progressively diluted in India in the course of the last two decades. But that may have less to do with the inherent weakness of rational-legal administration than with the social and political pressures with which the bureaucracy has had to contend in India. To be sure, such pressures are not all simply imposed from outside; there are some in the bureaucracy who openly welcome them.

The representational functions of the civil service will receive more and more attention as its technical functions are disparaged. When people believe that administration does not require much by way of technical ability or training, they naturally incline to the feeling that the civil service ought to do a little more in the interest of social justice. The same expectations come to be formed of the administrative and the political executives as their functions become conflated. But the long-term interest of the civil service as well as of parliamentary democracy requires that the two functions be kept separate as far as possible.

People do not think of the technical requirements of modern

administration in the same way in which they think of the requirements of work in scientific and judicial institutions, or even in military organizations. In the latter cases, they are prepared to concede that the technical requirements of work provide them some immunity from the demands of representativeness. They believe that the nature of work in a scientific research laboratory is such that it requires recruitment and promotion on the basis of merit. Similarly, they will concede that the judge's work is such that judicial appointments, at least at the higher levels, should be kept free from considerations of caste, community and gender. But they take a different view of civil service appointments, and to the extent that that view gains ground, it reinforces the interpenetration of administration and politics.

The devaluation of technical requirements, the emphasis on representativeness, and the interpenetration of politics and administration move the civil service away from the bureaucratic to the patrimonial model. Patrimonialism has deep roots in Indian society; it is bureaucracy that is relatively new. A rational-legal system of administration can play an important part, not only by carrying forward programmes of development and change but also by acting as an exemplar in a society and polity riddled with narrow parochial concerns. It can play that part only if its members cultivate a clear perception of the constraints under which they have to act in an environment that places many snares and pitfalls in their way. In this endeavour, they are not likely to receive much support or sympathy from their present political masters.

The effective functioning of democracy under our kind of constitution depends on a balance being maintained between the political and the administrative components of the executive. That balance is in the best of circumstances a delicate one, and in India it has become increasingly precarious in the last two decades. The rapid transfer of IAS officers in Uttar Pradesh that has been much in the news provides one of the many striking examples of this.

Politicians have fallen steadily in general esteem in the last two decades. But whereas journalists, lawyers and professors can voice their disesteem more or less openly, this is not easy for the civil servant in view of his written and unwritten code of conduct. The issue of corruption has now come to occupy an increasingly important place in public debate. Politicians freely castigate businessmen and bureaucrats for their corrupt ways. The businessman goes about his business without paying too much heed to what the politician says about him at public meetings; but the bureaucrat can only rage inwardly on hearing the pot call the kettle black. The first virtues of the civil servant are discipline and restraint; they are not necessarily the first virtues of the politician.

Precisely because of the overlap and the interpenetration of political and administrative roles, it is important to keep the distinction between the two clearly in sight. Modern institutions can be properly co-ordinated only if institutional roles are clearly differentiated. The confusion of roles between the politician and the civil servant acts to the detriment of both. This does not mean that a person cannot change roles in the course of his lifetime. It is unusual for the politician to decide in mid-career to adopt the civil service as his career. But civil servants can and do enter politics during their career or at its end. Politics draws its members from all communities, classes and professions, but the converse is not true to the same extent. Moreover, while a lawyer, a doctor or a journalist may remain in his profession while engaging in politics, this is not possible for the civil servant. The civil servant has to leave his service if he is to enter politics openly. He may of course try his hand at politics, including party politics, but not openly. In the past decade, civil servants have increasingly engaged in political or semi-political activity while remaining in service and enjoying its security and its benefits. If this trend continues, it will undermine the credibility of the service as a whole.

Many of the differences between the two components of the executive correspond to the distinction between the appointed official and the elected representative. Naturally, the correspondence is not perfect and, in the case of the politician, it admits of important exceptions. Some very successful politicians have been notorious for avoiding elections. Able and successful lawyers, engineers and economists have from time to time been inducted into the political executive and then been found safe constituencies. But while the principle of election may be relaxed or even waived for the politician, the civil servant is in our system invariably appointed and never elected.

In a constitutional democracy, the politician and the civil servant both exercise authority, although not in the same way. Even in the best of times, each is to some extent jealous of the authority enjoyed by the other. Politicians are inclined to believe that civil servants who have only subordinate authority nevertheless use it negatively, to obstruct the fulfilment of larger social objectives; for the politician, the bureaucrat is, above all, someone who invokes rules in order to show why a certain thing cannot be done. The civil servant in his turn feels that what the politician has is not authority but power which he uses arbitrarily and recklessly in his own interest or in the interest of his party. There is plentiful evidence of both types of misuse and abuse, and the evidence seems to mount with each passing year. The important point here is that the unlawful use of power by the politician and the obstructive use of authority by the official tend to reinforce each other, making governance in the broad sense more and more difficult.

The distinction between power and authority is a difficult though important one in political theory. Put in the simplest terms, power is transformed into authority by being legitimized and by being exercised in and through an institutional arrangement. There is no such thing as illegitimate or non-legitimate authority; authority is by definition legitimate. However, there are different forms and different sources of legitimacy, and those whose authority is based on one form of legitimacy are jealous and suspicious of others who derive their authority from a different source of legitimacy.

Constitutional democracy contains within itself a tension between the authority derived from numbers and the authority derived from impersonal rules. There is no escape from this tension; the art of governance consists in coping with it in its various and changing manifestations. Certainly, this tension cannot be resolved through any simple formula of the hierarchical subordination of the administrative to the political executive, for the question is not simply of greater or lesser degrees of legitimacy, but of different types of it.

The importance of popular support and the legitimacy derived from it in a democracy can hardly be exaggerated. Democracy cannot function in the absence of elected leaders who represent the ideas, interests and sentiments of their constituents. The mobilization of popular support is the first concern of the political leader in a democracy. For this purpose he has to project his qualities of leadership before the public on whose support his authority ultimately rests. Not all political leaders are endowed with an abundance of personal charisma, and such charisma as they have generally evaporates very rapidly. Nevertheless, it has to be recognized that personal charisma is a legitimate component in the authority of the elected representative .

The appointed official does not derive his authority from personal charisma but from a different source. He derives it from his mastery of a body of impersonal rules, his trained capacity to select the particular rules that fit the case in hand, and his ability to apply the rules rationally, responsibly, and without fear or favour. The pursuit of charisma, the cultivation of popular support and the projection of personality, which are all legitimate parts of the politician's life, are not consistent with the office of the civil servant. This view of the appointed official can be easily trivialized by presenting his work as the mechanical application of procedural formulas. But bureaucracy necessarily operates under conditions of greater or lesser uncertainty, and in India the uncertainties are large and growing larger. Hence the civil servant has not only to select and apply existing rules but also to continuously initiate the creation of new rules where the old ones have ceased to be adequate.

I cannot emphasize too strongly the initiative and the creativity required for carrying forward a system of governance based on rational, impersonal rules. The problem is particularly acute in India, because the conscious regulation of affairs by impersonal rules is not in conformity with the basic tendency of our social life. As I have indicated earlier, the civil servant has to act against the grain of the social structure, hence his failures are more conspicuous than his successes.

I have argued elsewhere that our orientation to rules is characterized by two features which may be observed in all public institutions, and not only in those associated with the administrative executive in the strict sense. The first is the drive to create more and more rules of every possible kind and to meet every possible situation. The second is the tendency to wilfully disregard if not violate those very rules in the name of immediacy, urgency and pressing political and moral compulsions. The proliferation of rules and the disregard of rules are two sides of the same coin, and they reinforce each other. Instead of serving as facilities, rules becomes weapons of offence and defence in the hands of our bureaucrats.

Who is to blame for the crisis of governance that has now become so plainly manifest in the country? Is it the system or its environment? The jungle of rules has become so dense that it is impossible to make one's way through it without taking short cuts or cutting corners. The temperature of public life in the country is now such that the important has always to make way for the urgent. Short cuts have to be taken and corners cut, but as soon as this becomes evident, there is a clamour for more rules to ensure that the existing ones are not violated. So the jungle becomes thicker, and the need for cutting corners more pressing.

Neither the cavalier attitude to rules of our politicians nor the obdurate attitude to them of our bureaucrats can fully explain the peculiar orientation to rules characteristic of Indian society as a whole. Iravati Karve, one of the most distinguished anthropologists of the previous generation, drew attention to a peculiar feature of traditional Indian culture that may help us to understand our present predicament a little better. She maintained that the basic pattern of Indian civilization has been shaped by the principle of accretion. 'The historical process is one of continuous accretion. There does not seem to be a stage where a choice was made between alternatives, a choice involving the acceptance of one alternative and a definite, final rejection of the others' (Karve 1968: 7). On the plane of the present discussion, this means that when we add new rules, we do not necessarily discard old ones, so that the rule book becomes crowded with obsolete, anachronistic and inconsistent rules. This makes it possible for the obstructive bureaucrat to trip up the citizen, or even the politician, with one rule or another; and it confirms the feeling in the person tripped up that all rules are obstructive. In India, administration by impersonal rules resists systematization because that demands the continuous elimination of obsolete and anachronistic rules.

It is no doubt necessary to assess the performance of civil servants in their official work, and it may well be that many or even most of them will come off badly in such an assessment. The mood of the workshop in Mussoorie in May 1997 was largely one of self-criticism if not self-recrimination. To the outside word, the IAS generally presents an appearance of self-satisfaction; and, although a certain amount of self-criticism is a sign of health, it may not be such a good thing to swing from the extreme of self-satisfaction to the extreme of self-recrimination. Quite apart from any assessment of the performance of individual officers, or of the IAS as a whole, the fact remains that the civil service in India has to operate in an adverse environment. This, as I have indicated more than once, is true to a greater or lesser extent of all modern institutions, but it is specially true of the higher civil service because of the immediate political pressures it has to contend with over and above the generally permissive attitude towards impersonal rules in the wider society.

A well-known Soviet dissident on observing the chaos and disorder in his country after his return from exile, said that the Russian people had still to learn that democracy hangs by the thin thread of procedure. The same can be said with equal if not greater force about the Indian people. Even educated Indians find it much easier to appreciate the significance of numbers than that of rules in the life of a democratic polity. The civil service has many important tasks to perform in the administration of the country: in revenue administration, in the administration of law and order, in development administration, and in a hundred other specific fields of administration. But it can play a transformative role in society only if it upholds its responsibility to bring about a new orientation to rules, not just the grand ideals of liberty, equality and justice, but the ordinary rules by which the everyday conduct of public affairs has to be regulated.

References

Béteille, André. 1996. *Civil Society and Its Institutions*. Calcutta: United States Educational Foundation in India, see chapter 8, this volume.

Bourdieu, P. 1996. *The State Nobility*. Oxford: Polity Press.

Bourdieu, P. and J.C. Passeron. 1979. *The Inheritors*. Chicago: University of Chicago Press.

Erikson, R. and J.H. Goldthorpe. 1992. *The Constant Flux*. Oxford: Clarendon Press.

Karve, I. 1968. *Hindu Society: An Interpretation*. Poona: Deshmukh Prakashan.

Mayer, J.P. 1943. *Max Weber and German Politics*. London: Faber & Faber.

Merton, R.K. et al. (eds). 1952. *Reader in Bureaucracy*. New York: The Free Press.

Trevelyan, G.O. 1864. *The Competition Wallah*. London: Macmillan.

Weber, Max. 1978. *Economy and Society*. Berkeley: University of California Press.

12

Empowerment*

Background and Context

The idea of empowerment has taken a hold over the minds of increasing numbers of persons in the last few years. It is now widely employed in the press, on television, and in political, academic and even legal circles. There is talk about the empowerment of the poor, of back-ward communities, of women and of various other disadvantaged sections of society. Empowerment is seen by many politicians, publicists, social activists and a growing section of the intelligentsia generally as the only effective answer to oppression, exploitation, injustice and the other maladies with which our society is beset.

The idea of empowerment contains exciting possibilities. It seems somehow to fit our present Indian reality particularly well. But in its current, widespread use, the idea is new and, as with most attractive ideas that are new, it means different things to different persons, and in some cases even to the same person. It bears the risk of being put to too many uses by too many persons to serve the requirement of systematic social analysis. At the same time; when an idea comes to be used so extensively within a society, it is the obligation of the social analyst to submit it to critical scrutiny, to examine its presuppositions and implications, its scope and its limits. What I propose to do here is to make such an examination of the idea of empowerment from the sociological point of view.

The first thing to note is that there is very little guidance available in existing social theory on the idea of empowerment as it is currently

* Originally published in *Economic and Political Weekly*, vol. XXXIV, nos 10–11, 1999 as the text of the seventh Dr D.T. Lakhdawala Memorial Lecture.

used in public discussion in India. A quick check through dictionaries, encyclopaedias and glossaries of popular text-books of sociology shows that the term itself is largely absent. In the absence of well-formulated concepts, sociologists tend to use their common sense to construct such arguments about empowerment as the occasion demands. It is difficult to construct arguments in that way that will be consistent across a range of contexts. I shall avoid the usual practice, and turn instead to cognate concepts such as power, authority and legitimacy that are already established in sociological usage to work towards a clearer understanding of the subject.

By and large, the scholarly discussion of empowerment has been context-driven rather than theory-driven. What is the context that brings the idea of empowerment so insistently to the attention of Indians today? In a nutshell, that context is the contradiction between a hierarchical social order and a democratic political system. To be sure, the contradiction was present and perceived even at the time of independence. But at that time it was hoped and believed that the contradiction would be inevitably eased with the transfer of power from British to Indian hands. This did not happen; and the contradiction has become, if anything, more acute, more extensive and more clearly perceived.

Indian society is a notoriously hierarchical society. It is not that nothing has changed, but the change has not measured up to the expectations aroused at the time of independence. The vehement style of public discussion in India tends to obscure the changes, however limited in scope and extent, that have in fact taken place in the last hundred years.

There are substantial inequalities of income and wealth and, what is more striking, vast numbers of persons continue to subsist below the line of poverty in both rural and urban areas. An extensive programme of land reform sought to address some of these problems in the rural areas, but the limited gains from the programme were largely eaten up by the relentless increase of population. In the urban areas as well, income is very unequally distributed. The problems are difficult if not intractable. The experience of economic growth in most parts of the world has been that, at least in the initial phases of growth, inequalities of income and wealth tend to increase rather than decrease. Intelligent policy interventions can do something to keep economic inequalities from increasing, but not a very great deal.

The most deep rooted forms of inequality, built into the structure of traditional Indian society, are those based on caste and on gender. Though the inequalities of caste and gender both run very deep, they also cut across each other since women as well as men are members of every caste, from the lowest to the highest, and there are men in the lowest of castes just as there are women in the highest. The disabilities due to caste and gender were discussed and justified most elaborately in the traditional literature of the Hindus (Sivaramayya 1984), but similar disabilities are present among other religious groups as well.

The traditional disabilities due to caste and gender were social and not just economic. Deep-rooted ideas of purity and pollution governed the social standing of the different castes and sexes; men and women were deemed to be of unequal moral worth as were the different *varnas*: and the social hierarchy was underpinned by a legal order in which privileges and disabilities were carefully modulated according to caste and gender. The law has now changed; social attitudes have also changed though to a much smaller extent. Despite the changes, women and persons of inferior caste continue to suffer from many disadvantages.

India's antiquated and ponderous social hierarchy is markedly at odds with its present political system. Democracy, according to the classic formula, is government of the people, by the people, for the people. In India today, the people are to the fore in some respects; but in the things that really matter, they seem to have very little control of their own destinies. The experience of Indian democracy in the last fifty years has brought into sharp relief a feature of modern democracies everywhere: the gap between formal political participation and effective political control. Universal adult franchise came as a revolutionary turn in the country's history (Srinivas 1992). But with the passage of time, much of the shine has gone from the electoral process. The ordinary people of India—rich and poor, rural and urban, Brahmins and Harijans, Hindus, Muslims and Christians, men and women—have by now experienced many general elections. They have voted governments into power, and they have voted them out of power. Yet the ordinary person feels that his own life has hardly been enhanced as a result; and this feeling is expressed in a magnified, not to say an exaggerated, form by reporters, columnists, social scientists and other members of the intelligentsia.

Here again, a sense of proportion and balance must be maintained. It would be true to say that what universal adult franchise has achieved has fallen far short of what was expected, but false to say that it has achieved nothing. Representative government works in complex ways.

Leaders who are voted into power even in free and fair elections, once in office, rarely live up to the good faith reposed in them by their electors. One set of leaders is replaced by another, but the new leaders quickly fall into the ways of the old ones. There has undoubtedly been a change in the social composition of the political class in the last fifty years, and that class has almost certainly become more accessible to the persons on whose support its members depend. But that does not mean that there has been a great increase in the powers of ordinary persons.

The Indian Constitution was written at a turning point in the country's history. It is not merely a set of rules relating to governance, but a design for a new kind of society. The older society that had prevailed for centuries and millenia was based on the principle of hierarchy; the new society envisaged in the constitution was to be based on the principle of equality. The equality provisions in the constitution were not confined to political equality at election time, but sought to reach into basic social and economic matters. Similarly, the concept of justice embodied in the constitution was a wide and capacious one.

The Constitution of India took several years to write, and it is one of the lengthiest documents of its kind. But despite the great care taken in its writing, not everything has gone well with it. Some say that the provisions of the constitution did not go far enough, and others that too many provisions were written into it. Some fourscore amendments have already been made to the constitution in its life of less than fifty years, and there are pressures from various quarters to have a comprehensive review of it. All of this has been accompanied by a growing disenchantment with what can be achieved in the cause of equality and social justice through the provisions of the constitution. Fifty years ago people expected a very great deal from the constitution; now increasing numbers of persons seem to expect hardly anything at all from it.

The disenchantment with the Plans has been, if anything, even deeper. This is in part a worldwide phenomenon, greatly reinforced in recent years by the collapse of the Soviet Union. But the trend had set in earlier, and the Planning Commission, once Nehru's favoured child, had lost much of its aura by 1977. Economic planning still has an important part to play, but it is now widely accepted that its aims have to be more modest if it is to be effective. With the passage of time, the realization has grown that a whole social order cannot be transformed, or transformed quickly enough, merely by having regular elections, good laws and good plans. That kind of transformation calls for something else, and it is thus that public attention has come to be focused on empowerment. Party leaders and technical experts have been tried out and they have failed; the people must now get their turn, for empowerment means above all empowerment of the people.

Diverse Meanings of Empowerment

Empowerment is about social transformation; it is about radical social transformation; and it is about the people—ordinary, common people, rather than politicians, experts and other socially or culturally advantaged persons. Above all, it is about power, although the concept of power contained in it is generally left unspecified. Empowerment is both a means to an end and an end in itself. The term adapts itself differently to different situations, and its signification is both variable and fluid.

The idea of empowerment may be invoked in virtually any context: in speaking about human rights, basic needs, economic security, capacity building, skill formation or the conditions of a dignified social existence. It is well known that the constitution has created many rights for all members of society, irrespective of their social or economic standing. It is equally well known that for millions of Indians those rights exist only on paper. Creating rights is one thing, and giving security to them is quite another. The legislators have been prodigal in creating rights but have not paid much heed to the enforceability of those rights. Empowerment is seen as a way of addressing the problem of rights that remain unenforced.

Empowerment is also invoked in the context of economic weakness and insecurity, particularly of marginalized, unorganized and other disadvantaged groups, classes and categories. It is then seen as a condition or an aspect of capacity building. Economic deprivation is widespread in India and is of many different kinds and has many different sources. Some of it goes back to age-old practices and institutions and some of it is the result of the ongoing economic transition. Moreover, problems of economic viability manifest themselves differently at different levels, for example, the community, the household and the individual. A community may be doing moderately badly on the whole but particular households in it may still enjoy a high standard of life; conversely, the women members of even well-to-do households may have no economic security at all.

Where one might have said in the past that women, Adivasis, or even agricultural labourers were disadvantaged, one is more likely to say today that they are unempowered. This change of language betokens a change of orientation from the economic to the political. It is not that the planners and policy-makers of the early years of independence did not know that poverty and deprivation were widely prevalent or even that they were especially concentrated in certain sections of society. But they sought more or less conventional economic remedies for these problems and hoped that they could be made to work without a radical redistribution of power. They were well aware that growth and equity did not always go hand in hand (Tendulkar 1983), but they hoped that they could somehow create a balance between the two.

The focus on empowerment has given a new emphasis to the building of economic and social capabilities among individuals, classes and communities. As one would expect, interventions of various kinds are being considered and recommended. The supply of credit on easy terms, of bullocks to impoverished farmers, of goats and poultry to tribal women—these have all been viewed at one time or another as steps towards their empowerment. Capacity building through craft training, specially for women, whether for full-time or part-time employment, is seen in a similar light. There is finally the drive towards literacy and education where much still remains to be done despite the Directive Principle of State Policy for providing universal elementary education upto the age of fourteen.

Implicit in the idea of empowerment is a certain theory of social change, in particular of change from a hierarchical to an egalitarian type of society (Béteille 1983), or in a slightly different language, from an aristocratic to a democratic type of it (Tocqueville 1956). A hierarchical or aristocratic society is based on the privileges and disabilities of groups whose unequal placement in society is widely acknowledged by its members; a democratic society is based on the recognition of the equal rights of all the individual members of it. The passage from the one type of society to the other has been a common experience in the modern age. But even where the direction of change has been broadly the same, the pace of change and the stages through which it has taken place have differed from one case to another. The radical redistribution of power has not played the same part in it in every case.

One significant path of the transition referred to above has been through the expansion of citizenship. This happened in many western countries, but most characteristically in Britain where it has received much attention from sociologists (Bulmer and Rees 1996). There it has been shown how equality came to be gradually realized as a social value as citizenship became the main component in the status of the individual (Lockwood 1992; see also Parsons 1965). The point, simply, is that equality is not just a question of the redistribution of power, it is also a question of a change of values. It is here that theories of social change tend to diverge, for some theorists believe that social change comes about mainly through the redistribution of power whereas others assign at least as much importance in it to the reconstitution of values.

In a classic essay on the subject, T.H. Marshall (1977) identified three basic elements of citizenship: civil, political and social. The civil element, according to him, was composed of the rights necessary for individual freedom; the political element consisted of the right to participate in politics through representative institutions; and the social element comprised certain basic rights to economic welfare and social security. He argued that in Britain, the eighteenth century saw the emergence of civil rights, the nineteenth of political rights and the twentieth of social rights, although he was well aware that one phase generally ran into the other.

The transition outlined above has been described by many different authors in many different ways. Different components have contributed to it at different times and different places, and they have not all been stressed to the same extent by every author. Even in Britain, where the transition was relatively smooth, political mobilization if not political revolution played some part in the evolution of citizenship. Elsewhere in Europe, it played a more prominent if not a more profound role. But even in France, where the Revolution of 1789 became a landmark and a symbol, many different factors, and not just politics, contributed to the unfolding of citizenship.

There is something in the development sketched out above that has the appearance of paradox. It is undeniable that the expansion of citizenship in the nineteenth century was on the whole a movement towards equality, and that is how it was experienced by many of those who lived through that period. Yet the evidence seems to be clear that the very same period witnessed an increase and not a decrease of inequality in the distribution of income (Kuznets 1955). This indeed was the main burden of the argument of T.H. Marshall (and in a different form of Alfred Marshall before him), that citizenship and social class develop contrapuntally in such a manner that the one places constraints on the uniform advance of the other.

Despite all that has been gained from it, the advance of citizenship has been not only discontinuous but also time-consuming. For instance, in Britain, even after more than two hundred years, one can hardly claim that 'full' or 'substantive' citizenship has been secured for ordinary members of society (Lockwood 1992: 260–2). And that takes away a very great deal from its attraction, particularly in countries that are latecomers to the field and have much ground to cover before citizenship becomes properly acknowledged as a value.

Although the equal rights of individuals as citizens is central to our legal and constitutional structure, the idea of citizenship in the sense described above is relatively new to our society and polity. Within the social order, the individual was, to an unusual degree and over a very extended period of time, subordinated to the group: joint family, caste and village. The building blocks of the social order were these groups rather than individuals conceived as autonomous moral agents. The relationship between the individual and the larger society was mediated by family, caste and community, whereas it is of the essence of the modern idea of citizenship that the relationship between the citizen and the state is mediated in a totally different way (Béteille 1998).

To many persons, and to increasing numbers of them in India, empowerment appears as an attractive alternative to the slow and tortuous path of citizenship for dismantling the old social structure and putting a new one in its place. No matter how we assess its costs and benefits, the main point behind empowerment is that it seeks to change society through a rearrangement of power. What this might entail cannot be considered without a detailed examination of the nature of power to which we turn in the following section.

Concepts of Power

The concept of power has been extensively, if often loosely, used in a variety of fields ranging from electrical engineering to moral philosophy. The term certainly has a wider currency, both in popular speech and in the scholarly literature, than the term 'empowerment' which clearly is a derivative of it.

Before turning to the discussion of power in social theory, I would like to note that there is a certain ambivalence about it in the popular mind that frequently seeps into the scholarly literature. The ambivalence of power has been forcefully brought out in the writings of the French philosopher and historian of ideas Michel Foucault whose work has had great influence in recent years (Foucault 1980). But although they are rich, fertile and ingenious, Foucault's arguments about power remained inconclusive. They are difficult to apply to contexts outside the ones in which they emerged, and, while noting their great originality, I will refrain from trying to use those arguments in the discussion that follows.

The ambivalence with which I am concerned is nicely expressed in Lord Acton's dictum that power tends to corrupt and absolute power corrupts absolutely. There is a pervasive tendency to think of power as something evil or at least as having an evil component, so that one can say at best that it is a necessary evil. If that is admitted to be the case, how can one account for the enthusiasm for empowerment? The fact is that those who believe that power is evil may also believe that it can be redeemed by being placed in the hands of the dispossessed and the disinherited, such as workers, peasants, tribals, untouchables or women.

The sociological conception of power may be best understood by being viewed in opposition to the anarchist and the populist conceptions of it. In the anarchist conception, power itself can be abolished and human life reconstituted in such a way that the exercise of power becomes redundant. In the populist conception, the emphasis is not so much on the abolition of power as on its radical redistribution such that all sections of society and all members of each section participate equally in its exercise. These two closely-related conceptions of power are both animated by strong moral concerns.

Moral concerns are not absent from the sociological approach to power, but they are restrained in the interest of what can be known, from observation and experience, about human societies in different places and at different times. Observation and experience have shown that power is present in all societies and indeed we can speak of it as being constitutive of human societies as we know them. They have shown, further, that in general, power tends to be unequally distributed: the equal distribution of power, where it is found, represents the limiting and not the typical case, and it is unstable. These two propositions underlie all sociological conceptions of power, no matter how different they may be in other respects.

The sociological discussion of power is now a hundred years old. Two pioneers whose ideas have greatly influenced the subject were Vilfredo Pareto and Max Weber who, it may be noted, both began their academic careers as professors of political economy. I do not need to speak here about Pareto's work on income distribution which is well known among economists. But it is worth pointing out that he wrote a trenchant critique of socialist systems (Pareto 1926) in which he argued that the belief that the abolition of property would lead to equality was a delusion since the real basis of inequality was not property but power. This view is echoed by J.R. Hicks (1942: 190) in his brief discussion of income distribution in Britain which concludes with the following observation: 'Inequality of income is the form taken in our society of a more fundamental inequality—the inequality of power.' (It may be noted in parentheses that while sociologists in general acknowledge the importance of the inequality of power, they do not all believe that it is the ultimate source of every form of inequality.)

More than any other scholar, it is Max Weber who has had the largest influence on the sociological study of power to which he assigned a wide significance in every major social domain. He wrote, 'Now: "classes", "status group" and "parties" are phenomena of the distribution of power within a community' (Weber 1978: 927).

Weber's oft-quoted definition of power is as follows: 'In general, we understand by "power" the chance of a man or a number of men to realize their own will in a social action even against the resistance of others who are participating in the action' (Weber 1978: 926). This is a very capacious conception which includes coercion, domination and manipulation (Shils 1975: 239–48). The point I wish to stress is that in this conception, a relationship of power is by its nature an asymmetrical relationship since power is something that one set of persons has over others. It may of course be that, while A has power over B in one domain, B has power over A in another, so that they can be said on balance to have equal power; but, again, such a situation would be unusual rather than typical.

The conception of power referred to above—power as that which some have over others; power as coercion, domination and manipulation—corresponds to what may be called the zero-sum approach to power. Some have power to the extent that others are without it; the more power some have, the less others have of it. The power of one party can be enhanced only by reducing the power of some other party. In other words, empowerment and disempowerment go hand in hand: the empowerment of some sections of society has to be accompanied by the disempowerment of other sections of it.

It may be said without too much exaggeration that radical and revolutionary theories of politics are as much about disempowerment as they are about empowerment. This is certainly true of the Leninist and Maoist theories which have had great influence in large parts of the world. According to them, the rise to power of the workers and peasants would be accompanied by the fall from power of the capitalist and landed classes. The theory of the class struggle has lost some of its appeal, but it has left a certain residue in the vocabulary of radical politics in many countries. Some of the radical drive of the older variety of class politics has been taken over by the politics of backwardness, many of whose proponents appear to regard the disempowerment of the upper castes or the *savarnas* as a necessary condition for the empowerment of the Scheduled Tribes, the Scheduled Castes and the Other Backward Classes.

Not all students of the subject subscribe to the zero-sum conception of power. An alternative conception and approach has been proposed by the sociologist Talcott Parsons (1963). He argued that power may be viewed not simply as what some have over others, but as a resource of the community as a whole which it may use more or less effectively in the attainment of its goals. If we take a long-term view of human endeavour and achievement, then it may appear that societies have in fact expanded their capacity to act effectively in the pursuit of larger objectives. Power, in this conception, is compared to wealth, and just as the wealth of a nation may be augmented over time, so also may be its power. It is certainly conceivable that every increase in the power of some may not require a corresponding diminution in the power of others. But however persuasive the analogy between the two may be, it has very serious limitations since power cannot be measured in the same way as wealth.

There are two further points to be made here. Even if we admit that the power of a community as a whole need not remain at the same level but may increase over time, it does not follow that the increase can be brought about according to the will and pleasure of individuals under any condition whatever. There are definite social conditions that have to be met for the increase to be possible and effective. Parsons himself would assign great importance to the simultaneous expansion of the rights of citizenship and the capacities of institutions.

The second point to be noted is that a positive-sum approach to power does not in any way entail the belief that the distribution of power can or should be made equal. Here again the analogy with wealth is useful. Changes in the wealth of a nation and in its pattern of distribution are two different things. There is no ground for believing that the equal distribution of wealth can be ensured by increasing—or decreasing—its wealth as a whole. Even if it is possible to increase a nation's capacity to attain its own goals and to say that there has been an overall increase in its power in that sense, it does not follow that that power will come to be more equally distributed.

Power and Authority

I would like to return briefly to the ambivalence surrounding the idea of power. As will be evident from the preceding discussion, power is viewed as a source of corruption and evil; but it is also viewed as a prime mover in a nation's progress and advancement. This double nature of power is perhaps most acutely felt in modern democratic societies where government and opposition speak in radically different voices but are seen, when the turn comes for exercising power, to be acting in remarkably similar ways. It is this that gives to the idea of empowerment its peculiar fascination. For the hope remains that power, which is a source of so much evil, can be made into a source of everything that is good by being transferred from the wrong to the right hands, from the capitalists to the workers, from the landlords to the peasants, from the upper to the lower castes, and, now, from men to women.

As we have noted already, power may be exercised in a variety of forms, such as coercion, domination and manipulation. Here I shall be concerned not so much with the contrast between the evil and the good aspects of power as with that between untamed power and power that has been tamed or institutionalized. Central to the entire subject of political sociology is the distinction, that we owe principally to Max Weber, between power and authority, or between power and legitimate domination. Important though the distinction is, it has proved to be one of the most difficult distinctions to apply consistently in political analysis. But once we admit the value of the distinction, we cannot escape the question as to what the project of empowerment will entail not just for the distribution of power as such but, more specifically, for structures of authority in the major institutions of society.

At the heart of Weber's distinction lies the idea of legitimacy. The difficulty here is that while Weber has discussed in some detail the principal types of legitimacy and even the principal sources of it, there is no clear or consistent definition in his writing of legitimacy itself. 'Traditional', 'rational-legal' and 'charismatic' domination are ideal types of domination; they are not average types; they refer to differences in kinds of legitimacy, not degrees of it . It is difficult in the nature of the case to provide a test for determining whether a given system of domination is or is not legitimate, or to what degree it is legitimate. The most that we seem to be able to say is that a system is legitimate because it is accepted as legitimate; as to whether it should or even will continue to enjoy its legltimacy, nothing very much can really be said.

Coercion and manipulation as forms of power are no doubt important features of the real world. But no political order can be sustained for long unless it is acknowledged, more or less widely and more or less actively, as being right, proper and desirable. Broadly speaking, this is as true of monarchies and aristocracies as it is of republics and democracies. Political regimes have come up from time to time that have sought to maintain themselves mainly through coercion and manipulation, but they have not been stable. The concept of legitimacy draws attention to the fact that the stability of a regime requires that the exercise of power be sustained by the values commonly held by the members of society. The stability of a regime is affected not only by conflicts of interests, but also by conflicts of values.

It will be generally agreed that all political regimes enjoy some legitimacy. But there is much variation in the degrees and types of legitimacy. For those viewing a political regime from within, the first question is of the degree of legitimacy it enjoys. As we have seen, every system enjoys some degree of legitimacy, because otherwise it would not last; and it is hard to imagine a system that enjoys full and complete legitimacy, because such a system would never change. Beyond this, it is very difficult to make exact comparisons between systems in terms of their degrees of legitimacy. Nevertheless, the discussion of the ideal types of legitimate domination has been very fruitful since it has brought out the connections between the organization of authority and the system of values by which each type of organization is characteristically sustained.

As we have seen, domination as a form of power has to be distinguished from both coercion and manipulation. Weber saw quite clearly that the forms of domination are themselves almost infinitely variable. He dwelt especially on two of them, and on their contrasting natures. They are, in his own words, 'domination by virtue of a constellation of interests (in particular: by virtue of a position of monopoly), and domination by virtue of authority, i.e. power to command and duty to obey' (Weber 1978: 943). We may, for short, refer to the first as 'economic domination' and to the second as 'legitimate authority'.

Economic dominance has a general and pervasive significance in society. It is not illegitimate in the sense that coercion mostly is from the legal point of view and manipulation from the moral point of view; at the same time, it does not enjoy quite the same kind of legitimacy as the exercise of institutional authority does. It is undeniable that the manufacturer, the moneylender and the landowner are generally able to impose their will on the job-seeker, the credit-seeker and the land-seeker. Their power is different from that of the gangster or the schemer; nevertheless, it is not quite the same as that of the official, elected or appointed according to established procedures.

A great deal of the argument for empowerment is addressed to the issue of economic domination that is neither patently illegitimate (like brute force) nor clearly legitimate (like the authority of the public official). Shifts in the balance of economic power between classes, between communities, and between men and women have been taking place throughout the world in the last hundred years. These shifts operate in many different ways, both visible and invisible, but they rarely if ever lead to the empowerment or disempowerment of any major class or section of society as a whole.

The simple definition of authority as power backed—or restrained—by legitimacy is in need of some elaboration. What is at issue here is not simply legitimacy but also a regular and continuous chain of command and obedience. The two aspects are analytically distinct, but they are functionally related. Where power flows openly and continuously along pre-existing channels, its legitimacy comes to be generally acknowledged; and it is unlikely to be acknowledged as legitimate if its flow is sporadic, irregular and concealed. Economic power acts in a different way from legitimate authority. No matter how much power the moneylender has over credit-seekers, his power is not sustained by a continuous chain of command and obedience.

The exercise of legitimate authority, as against many other forms of power not all of which are illegitimate, takes place in conformity with acknowledged rules. The legitimacy of authority is in large part the legitimacy of the rules in conformity with which it has to be exercised. These rules provide at best a broad framework within which the exercise of authority must be confined. They cannot predetermine the correct course of action for a given authority in anticipation of every possible situation. Were that to be the case, the authority concerned would act simply as an automaton without any power to decide between alternative courses of action.

The capacity to decide between alternative courses of action is vested in some social positions and not in others, or more in some than in other positions. We may speak of the power associated with such positions, or, when they operate within an acknowledged framework of rules, of the authority vested in them. What I wish to stress here is that although the exercise of authority is in many ways different from the exercise of other forms of power, it is nevertheless at bottom a form of power. It is for this reason that we cannot speak of empowerment without taking into account the structures of authority in a society.

If the exercise of authority is associated with continuous chains of command and obedience, it is seen most clearly in the various types of associations that are a feature of every type of society except, perhaps, the most primitive bands of food gatherers. Here I use the term 'association' in a very broad sense to include every kind of institution and organization with a corporate identity that is recognized by both members and non-members. Examples of these would be schools, colleges, universities, hospitals, the Reserve Bank of India, the National Physical Laboratory, the Times of India and many others. Each is a field for the exercise of authority which is distributed in a more or less determinate way among its members according to the positions they occupy in it.

A school as an institution has a certain corporate identity and a certain division of labour. Its activities are co-ordinated in various ways among which the exercise of authority by some over others is a significant one. When the institution functions effectively, the authority does not have to be exercised with a heavy hand. But no institution in the real world functions smoothly enough for it to be able to dispense with the exercise of authority by some over others; not even communes and *ashrams* are exceptions to this rule. Most persons would acknowledge that masters have to be given some authority over pupils, and the headmaster over the other masters if a school is to attain its goals. But even this may be challenged, as was done on a large scale during the Great Cultural Revolution in China and sporadically during the Naxalite movement in India.

A bank is a very different kind of institution from a school. Its internal division of labour is a division of labour among adults. It is a part of this division of labour that authority is unequally distributed so that some can take decisions that will be binding on the others. A bank would hardly be able to serve its customers if nobody had the authority to take such decisions, or if that authority were randomly distributed among its employees. I have been the victim of a local branch of a nationalized bank where such is sometimes the situation. But I doubt that even the most radical proponents of power sharing will ordinarily recommend that the State Bank of India be run on anarchistic principles.

I can multiply examples from many different domains, but that will not be necessary. I have said enough to show that a certain amount of imperative co-ordination, that is, co-ordination through the exercise of legitimate authority is essential to the proper functioning of virtually every kind of institution, organization and association. The generic term proposed for these is 'imperatively co-ordinated association' which is a somewhat clumsy English translation of the term 'Herrschaftsverband' used by Max Weber (Dahrendorf 1959: 167). Their significance has been viewed differently by different persons. Some have regarded them as obstacles to the empowerment of the people, whereas others would maintain that it is through their differentiation and expansion that the reservoir of power at the disposal of the nation as a whole and its individual citizens is augmented.

Redistribution of Power and Social Rearrangement

The distribution of power is not a separate or detachable part of society but permeates every type of arrangement in it. Any major alteration in the distribution of power is bound to have both direct and indirect, foreseeable and unforeseeable, consequences running through society as a whole.

Society may be likened to a mosaic of many different components. Even that would be too simple an analogy, for the components differ widely in form and dimension; they are interpenetrating rather than mutually exclusive; and they continually change their aspect. A large and complex society such as ours cannot be thought to be made up simply of individuals (or citizens) at one extreme and the nation (or the state) at the other. When we think of the redistribution of power, of empowerment and disempowerment, we cannot think only of India and 950 million Indians. We must think also of everything that stands in between—the varieties of communities, classes and categories; of associations, organizations and institutions; and of the many networks of relations that link the individual members of society to each other and to society as a whole. Because changes in the distribution of power affect all of these in one way or another.

Our society is divided, first of all, into classes and communities, and their economic and political significance is widely recognized. An Indian is not simply an Indian; he is a peasant, a worker, a manufacturer a trader or a moneylender. As such, he is linked to others of his own class and of other classes through a variety of ties. These ties are of great significance not only to his membership of his own class but also to his identity as an Indian. By far the most persuasive theories of empowerment and disempowerment in the last hundred years have taken their point of departure in the division of society into classes. Changes in the balance of power between classes have taken place throughout those years, but those changes have been very different from what had been anticipated by those who maintained that a revolutionary transformation of society would be the inevitable outcome of the class struggle. Class divisions are important; but other divisions are sometimes even more important.

Distinct from class are identities of community based on language, religion, sect, caste and tribe. Language is not just a vehicle of thought and speech, it is also a basis of social identity. It unites those who are of the same tongue and at the same time divides those who are of different tongues. The same is the case with religion; socially and politically, it unites as well as divides members of the same nation. Then, of course, there is caste which was the basis of the social hierarchy in the past. While it has lost many of its religious functions, it has acquired new political functions; it is very much in the forefront of the discourse on empowerment today.

Where the politics of identity is concerned, language, religion, sect and tribe act in ways similar to that of caste. Indeed, the same term *jat* or *jati* is used for all of them in many parts of the country in the context of social and political identity (Béteille 1996a). Today, the politics of backwardness has spread from castes to communities of other kinds. It is not simply the backward castes—the Yadavas, the Kurmis, the Kolis and the many others—who want more power for themselves, but also the religious and linguistic minorities. Each community looks at itself and finds that it is disadvantaged in some way, and its leaders stake a claim for more power on its behalf; in this way, its social identity is reinforced and at the same time its bargaining power is enhanced.

Different from the identities of class and community are those based on gender. The division between men and women is the most general if not the most fundamental of all social divisions, and it is found in all societies from the simplest to the most complex, from the most backward to the most advanced. While the divisions of class and community cut across each other to a greater or lesser extent, those of gender necessarily cut across the divisions of both caste and class since men as well as women are to be found in every class and every community. While it may be said, with some degree of plausibility, that there is in fact a great deal of overlap at the bottom of the ladder between the economically disadvantaged classes and the socially backward castes, it cannot be said at all that there is a similar overlap between women as the more disadvantaged sex and either the lowest classes or the lowest castes.

Class, community and gender are important components of the social mosaic; but they are not its only components. There are, in addition, a multitude of institutions performing a variety of specialized functions in administration, finance, education, research, communication, and so on. These institutions—the secretariat, the bank, the school, the laboratory and the newspaper—also serve to link individuals to each other and to the wider society. They have a very different place in society from the place occupied by caste, community and gender; they function in a different way.

Institutions performing specialized functions have grown enormously in our country in the last hundred years. Not all of them are working well or are in a state of good health. Many of them are manifestly corrupt, inefficient and inflexible. There is intermittent talk that these institutions are foreign implants on Indian soil, that they are 'elitist' in character, that they are doomed to be ineffective, and that they should be replaced by alternatives more in tune with the traditions and the aspirations of the Indian people. But such talk is really without issue. The growth of functionally specialized institutions and their differentiation is an inescapable part of the modernization process, and we cannot opt out of the modern world any more than we can jump out of our own skins.

While I am inclined to stress the increasing importance in our society of open and secular institutions (Béteille 1996b), the contemporary discussion of empowerment tends to overlook the requirements of these institutions and, sometimes, their very existence. The object of attention in such discussion is either the people as a whole—the 'people' as against the 'elite' or the 'establishment'—or particular classes, communities and sections of society considered as unempowered, such as peasants, workers, backward castes, religious minorities and women. The question is never addressed in any detail as to whether, and to what extent, the empowerment of peasants, workers, backward castes, religious minorities and women will affect the functioning of the institutions on which the well-being of society as a whole depends.

The most radical theories of empowerment are those that call for the empowerment of the people as a whole. These are populist theories and they are mistrustful of institutions as such, because they see them as obstacles to the aspirations of ordinary people to secure control over their own lives. They ignore or reject the distinction that social theorists have been at pains to make between naked power and legitimate authority. They believe that the well-being of institutions is best secured by having full and equal participation by all in the conduct of their affairs. For the historically-minded, the model of such institutions is the Paris Commune of 1871, once greatly admired by Marx.

Beyond this, a great deal of the argument for empowerment relates to particular components of the social whole. But the principal, if not the sole candidates for empowerment are classes, communities and sections of society rather than its major institutions. After all, one might call for more powers to be granted not simply to peasants, workers, backward castes or women, but also to universities, research laboratories, banks and other autonomous or semi-autonomous institutions. But that is not done or done very rarely in the name of empowerment.

It is of course tacitly acknowledged that the empowerment of disadvantaged classes, communities and sections will affect at least indirectly the major institutions of society. But what the advocates of empowerment seek to alter here is above all the social composition of these institutions and not necessarily their mode of functioning; and their attention rests mainly on those institutions that are believed to be the major repositories of power in society.

Empowerment and Distributive Shares

As one would expect, many of the proposals for empowerment are very broad and general, but others are quite specific and concrete. Among the latter are those that seek to bring about empowerment through a radical change in the social composition of the strategic institutions of society, in particular the various organs of the state. This approach to empowerment has in the last few years evoked much public discussion in India, and, in this concluding section, I will consider briefly its scope and limits, and its implications for the distribution of power and authority, the functioning of institutions and the general well-being of society.

In all traditional hierarchical societies, access to positions of authority in the public domain were restricted largely to men, and among men, to those born into particular families, castes or estates. Appointments to public office went more according to birth than according to the principle of careers open to talent. Men of 'low' birth with exceptional ability might of course rise to positions of authority, but the opportunities available to them were limited; particularly in India. Democracy ushered in a new principle that made public office open to all irrespective of birth. With this the social composition of public institutions began to change in Europe and America, but very slowly at first. In Europe, even now women occupy far fewer positions of authority than men, and in the United States, Blacks and Hispanics fewer than Whites. Achievement replaced ascription as the basic principle, but practice has lagged far behind principle.

When India became independent fifty years ago and adopted a republican constitution, the presence of men belonging to the higher Hindu castes was even more conspicuous in all strategic public institutions. There have been some changes in the last fifty years, but many believe that those changes have not gone far enough. They feel that there should be both men and women, and men and women from all castes and communities in those institutions for democracy to be real and effective.

President Clinton had said on first assuming office that he wanted to have a cabinet that would look like America. That was not meant to be taken literally, but it did make a point. Many would like to see greater social diversity in the membership of our key public institutions than is at present found. But this diversity can be more easily accommodated in some public institutions than in others. As we have seen, the population of India is divided into a number of social classes, differing widely in income, occupation and education. These divisions are by no means unimportant; but members from all the different classes can be accommodated more easily, let us say, in the Lok Sabha than in the Supreme Court or even in the higher civil service.

It does appear odious in a democracy when the organs of public authority are all in the hands of men from a particular social background. A cabinet, a Supreme Court and a higher civil service which has women as well as men, and men and women from all castes and communities is likely to be more open and more sensitive in its approach to the larger problems of society than one whose members are all of the same background. But beyond that it is not easy to say very much. For one can hardly say that a mere change in the social composition of an organ of authority will bring about a definite change either in the concentration of authority or in its mode of exercise. The experience of the Soviet Union does not show that when more peasants and workers secured positions in the organs of authority, those organs exercised their authority with a lighter touch. What in fact resulted was greater concentration rather than greater dispersal of authority.

Most persons now realize that in our kind of system it is not possible to give equal representation in public institutions to the various classes in society. But what cannot be done for class can in fact be done for caste. It is said, somewhat misleadingly in my view, that caste is the form taken in Indian society by class. Be that as it may, caste has this advantage over class that while it is not possible to find persons who have the minimum qualifications for the office of judge or civil servant in the class of unskilled manual workers or of agricultural labourers, it should be possible, at least in principle, to find such persons among even the lowest of castes. The rest can be done by a comprehensive system of quotas. In this way, the burden of empowerment comes to be placed on the system of quotas; it is a very heavy burden for such a system to bear.

Whatever may be the benefits to be gained from a comprehensive system of quotas, it cannot be argued that such a system will have no social costs whatsoever. The Constituent Assembly in fact took an ambivalent attitude towards numerical quotas, admitting the need for them, but only in very special cases and for a limited period of time. After all, it had adopted strong provisions for equal opportunities for all, and creating additional provisions for special opportunities for some was bound to put strains on the former. Dr Ambedkar himself, while advocating special provisions for the specially disadvantaged, had argued that those provisions should not be made so extensive as to eat up the general provision of equality of opportunity for all.

It was hoped at the time of independence that the special provisions would not be needed for very long and that they would gradually be pared down as the country advanced economically and politically. What has happened is the opposite. There has been some economic and political advance no doubt; but the pressure for more comprehensive quotas in the interest of equality and social justice has grown relentlessly. An initial move in the fifties to have quotas in employment for the Other Backward Classes in addition to those for the Scheduled Castes and Scheduled Tribes was aborted; but what was aborted in the fifties came to be adopted in the nineties. The Committee on the Status of Women had in the seventies recommended against the adoption of quotas for women in Parliament and in the state assemblies; but there is now the Women's Reservation Bill waiting to be made into law.

The distribution of benefits and burdens according to community, caste and gender is fundamentally at odds with the idea of citizenship on which the constitution rests. The rights of citizenship are rights vested in individuals irrespective of race, caste, creed, sex or place of birth. It is one thing to acknowledge that benefits and burdens are in fact distributed unequally among castes and communities and between men and women. It is quite another to give legal and moral support to policies that assign precedence in the name of social justice to community, caste and gender over the individual as citizen. Special provisions may no doubt be made for the benefit of severely stigmatized or marginalized groups; but they should be restricted and not pervasive, and their costs to individuals as citizens should not be ignored.

I have earlier referred to the part played by the enlargement of the rights and capacities of citizenship in the transformation of society in the west. Many have argued that it was citizenship that acted as the main force for equality by moderating the inequalities of class (and of gender). When India adopted a new constitution soon after independence, many had hoped that here too citizenship would be the engine of progress. But they now seem to be shifting their attention from citizenship to quotas based on community, caste and gender as the main force for social transformation. These are two different paths to the future, and it is doubtful that we can continue for long to move along both these paths at the same time.

Empowerment through the expansion of the civic, political and social rights of citizenship is a laborious and unexciting process; it is, in Max Weber's famous phrase, 'a slow boring of hard boards'. Empowerment through the class struggle was a different story altogether; but that story has now been played out and it offers hardly any new prospect. There is no doubt the prospect of empowerment through caste war; but that is something that will appeal only to those who have put their minds to sleep. So in the end, the Indian way of securing empowerment for the unempowered seems to be by the safe way of providing, as extensively as possible, quotas on the basis of community, caste and gender.

If what I have said above holds true, quotas, no matter how extensive, can at best touch only the upper fringes of the redistribution of power in a society as large and complex as ours. The belief that they can by themselves bring about a radical or even a perceptible redistribution of power is no more than wishful thinking. Such wishful thinking is not without its cost. The cost will be to the Constitution of India which assigns rights and capacities to citizens as individuals, and not to castes and communities or to men and women separately.

References

Béteille, A. 1983. *The Idea of Natural Inequality and Other Essays*. Delhi: Oxford University Press.

—— 1996a. '*Varna* and *Jati*', *Sociological Bulletin*, vol. 45, no. 1.

—— 1996b. *Civil Society and Its Institutions*. Calcutta: United States Educational Foundation in India, see chapter 8, this volume.

—— 1998. 'The Conflict of Norms and Values in Contemporary Indian Society' in P.L. Berger (ed.), *The Limits of Social Cohesion*. Boulder: Westview Press, see chapter 10, this volume.

Bulmer, M. and A.M. Rees (eds). 1996. *Citizenship Today*. London: UCL Press.

Dahrendorf, R. 1959. *Class and Class Conflict in Industrial Society*. London: Routledge and Kegan Paul.

Foucault, M. 1980. *Power/Knowledge*. Brighton: Harvester Press.

Hicks, J.R. 1942. *The Social Framework*. Oxford: Clarendon Press.

Kuznets, S. 1955. 'Economic Growth and Income Inequality', *American Economic Review*, vol. 45, no. 1.

Lockwood, D. 1992. *Solidarity and Schism*. Oxford: Clarendon Press.

Marshall, T.H. 1977. *Class, Citizenship and Social Development*. Chicago: University of Chicago Press.

Pareto, V. 1926. *Les systēmes socialistes*. Paris: Marcel Giard, 2 vols.

Parsons, T. 1963. 'On the Concept of Political Power', *Proceedings of the American Philosophical Society*, vol. 107, no. 3.

—— 1965. 'Full Citizenship for the Negro American?', *Daedalus*, vol. 94, no. 4.

Shils, E. 1975. *Centre and Periphery*. Chicago: University of Chicago Press.

Sivaramayya, B. 1984. *Inequality and the Law*. Lucknow: Eastern Book Company.

Srinivas, M.N. 1992. *On Living in a Revolution and Other Essays*. Delhi: Oxford University press.

Tendulkar, S.D. 1983, 'Economic Inequality in an Indian Perspective' in André Béteille (ed.), *Equality and Inequality*. Delhi: Oxford University Press.

Tocqueville, A. de. 1956. *Democracy in America*. New York: Alfred Knopf, 2 vols.

Weber, M. 1978. *Economy and Society*. Berkeley: University of California Press, 2 vols.

Name Index

Subject Index